sanctuary
everywhere

Barbara Andrea Sostaita

sanctuary everywhere

THE FUGITIVE SACRED

IN THE SONORAN DESERT

DUKE UNIVERSITY PRESS · DURHAM AND LONDON · 2024

Printed in the United States of America on acid-free paper ∞
Project Editor: Bird Williams
Designed by Matt Tauch
Typeset in Garamond Premier Pro
by Westchester Publishing Services

Library of Congress Cataloging-in-Publication Data
Names: Sostaita, Barbara Andrea, [date] author.
Title: Sanctuary everywhere : the fugitive sacred in the Sonoran Desert /
Barbara Andrea Sostaita.
Description: Durham : Duke University Press, 2024. | Includes bibliographical
references and index.
Identifiers: LCCN 2023050740 (print)
LCCN 2023050741 (ebook)
ISBN 9781478030607 (paperback)
ISBN 9781478026365 (hardcover)
ISBN 9781478059592 (ebook)
Subjects: LCSH: Refuge (Humanitarian assistance)—United States. | Sanctuary
movement—United States. | Asylum, Right of—United States. | Border security—
Social aspects—Mexican-American Border Region. | Immigration enforcement—
United States. | Noncitizens—Government policy—United States. | Mexican-American
Border Region—Emigration and immigration—Social aspects. | BISAC: SOCIAL SCIENCE /
Emigration & Immigration | SOCIAL SCIENCE / Ethnic Studies / American / General
Classification: LCC JV6475 .S59 2024 (print)
LCC JV6475 (ebook)
DDC 323.6/31—dc23/eng/20240404
LC record available at https://lccn.loc.gov/2023050740
LC ebook record available at https://lccn.loc.gov/2023050741

Cover art: Felipe Baeza, *Fragments, refusing totality and wholeness*,
2021. Ink, embroidery, acrylic, graphite, varnish, and cut paper
on panel, 16×12 inches. © Felipe Baeza. Courtesy Maureen Paley,
London; Kurimanzutto, Mexico City/New York.

Publication of this book is supported by Duke University Press's
Scholars of Color First Book Fund.

They weren't scared, or dispossessed, or fragile. They were possible.

—JUSTIN TORRES, *We the Animals*

Para papi, quien me enseñó a contar historias,

y para mami, porque el cariño

entre nosotras es plenamente sagrado

Contents

Acknowledgments

Stories are what remain of my home country. Like Lot in the Hebrew Bible, my parents focused squarely on our future when we left Argentina. They did not look back and have not gone back in twenty-five years. But they did pass down stories—of military dictatorships and the return of democracy, music legends and folklorists who teach that *todo cambia*, soccer stadiums and sports rivalries, my grandmother's *canelones* and grandfather's routes as a milkman. Convinced that I could not know myself unless I knew my past, my parents gifted me their stories. And now I know myself largely as a storyteller. This book is thanks to them: Irene Tarico and Daniel Sostaita, who left home in search of the otherwise, who chased possibility, and whose memories are my inheritance.

When I began this project, I was living with my sister, Daniela. She made our small apartment a place of joy and laughter. Without her support, this book may have never been completed. Daniela, *I carry your heart with me (I carry it in my heart)*. When I think of the sacred, my mind goes to you and Victoria, my little sisters. Together, we made up other worlds to escape the trauma of our migrant childhoods. With nothing but our imaginations, we created entire universes.

My husband, Alex Morelli, read countless versions of this manuscript, joined me on almost every fieldwork trip, and took the photographs that accompany this book. *Mi amor*, your commitment to your craft never fails to inspire me. You are my favorite collaborator. You once told me that even though a saguaro can produce fifty million seeds in a lifetime, only one percent germinate. The ones that survive do so because of plants like palo verdes and triangle bursages that nurture and protect seedlings. Our love is like these cacti—rare, interdependent, nothing short of a miracle.

Thank you to Sandra Korn, Courtney Berger, Laura Jaramillo, Bird Williams, and the entire team at Duke University Press for their care and editorial support (including the copyeditor and reviewers whose generous and critical observations transformed this text). I am incredibly grateful to Felipe Baeza for allowing me to use his artwork on the cover of this book. Thank you to the people in Sonora and Arizona who invited me into their homes, shelters, and routes: Maxie Adler, Águilas del Desierto, Nicole Antebi, Carolina Aranibar-Fernández, Alicia Baucom, Susan Briante, Nellie Jo David, John Fife, Alison Harrington, Elisa and Joel Hauptman, Greg Hess, Valarie Lee James, Laiken Jordahl, Bob Kee, Gail Kourke, Peter Lucero, Margaret Mishra, Kathi Noaker, Alyssa Quintanilla, Robin Reineke, Dora Luz Rodriguez, Mary Stephens, Scott Warren, David Whitmer, and Mike Wilson. Thank you especially to Álvaro Enciso for allowing me to play a role in your desert theater every week. Thank you to Panchito Olachea for letting me ride shotgun in your sanctuary on wheels. Thank you to Eva and Alberto Contreras for trusting me with your documents and stories. And thank you to Juana Luz Tobar Ortega, who guided me toward escape routes. There are others I met in Sonora—in migrant shelters, on street corners, while visiting Eloy and La Palma. I shared meals with many of them. I only spoke briefly to some and exchanged phone numbers with others. Their insights and aspirations made all the difference.

○

This kind of project is possible because I teach in a Latin American and Latinx Studies department, a field of study that encourages *autohistoria-teoría*, that dwells in *nepantla*. Thank you to my colleagues at the University of Illinois Chicago, especially to Ralph Cintrón who read multiple chapters of this book and encouraged me to lean into the fragment and embrace paradox. Thank you to friends who accompanied me during the years I worked on this text: Soledad Álvarez Velasco, Meredith Barnes, Roxana Bendezú, Samah Choudhury, Omar Dairanieh, Nicole Eitzen Delgado, Anna Gazmarian, Juliane Hammer, Micah Hughes, Hina Muneeruddin, Annie O'Brien, Ivón Padilla-Rodriguez, and Kaitlin Williams. Thank you to Alejandro Escalante, who has had my back since we attended our PhD orientation together, who read an earlier version of this text in its entirety at the dissertation stage, and who has since offered invaluable feedback. And, it is no exaggeration to say that my life changed the day I met Israel Domínguez. Iz, your friendship is magic and I love you unconditionally. You have taught me to be gentler with myself and with others, to embrace contradiction, that our imaginations can birth new worlds. "Tell me about despair," friend, "and I will tell you mine."

I'm grateful to the Theories of Land Working Group led by Dana Lloyd and Evan Berry for their notes on my writing about the Sonoran Desert, to Vincent Lloyd and the Political Theology Network for multiple opportunities to workshop these chapters, and to Sally Promey and the Center for the Study of Material and Visual Cultures of Religion for supporting my fieldwork from the beginning. Ann Braude's comments on my fourth chapter were nothing short of poetry. Lloyd Barba's reading of the introduction was an act of care. The influence of my dissertation committee—Brandon Bayne, China Medel, Angela Stuesse, and Ariana Vigil—is on every page, especially that of my advisor Todd Ramón Ochoa. Because of Todd, I am a more thoughtful scholar. I have moved away from an obsession with origins and toward a focus on flight. I learned the difference between death and the dead. I now know that all writing is rewriting.

This book received support from the Graduate School at the University of North Carolina at Chapel Hill, the Institute for the Study of the Americas at the University of North Carolina at Chapel Hill, the Carolina Women's Center, the Institute for Citizens and Scholars, the American Association of University Women, the Center for Visual and Material Studies of Religion at Yale University, and the Mahindra Humanities Center at Harvard University.

Lastly, I want to acknowledge the work of the dead in writing this book—the migrant dead, who draw me back into their world year after year, and the work of my ancestors. I write these acknowledgments from my *abuela* Tina's deathbed. Her life was scarred by being an orphan and haunted by loss; perhaps unknowingly or unintentionally, she passed down to me an inescapable sense of being a stranger. My *abuelo* Celso, who died when my mom was still an infant but whom my aunts remember for the sweet lullabies he would play with his accordion every night. My *abuelo* José, whom I also never met, but who carried his union card wherever he went, who took my dad to workers' meetings and Peronista caucuses. I like to think he inspired my dad to become a minister—a profession or calling that, eventually, would lead me to Sonora. My beloved *tía* and *madrina* Adriana, who cared for me as a toddler and taught me to appreciate beauty, movement, and pleasure. My *abuela* Pilar, whose house is the backdrop for the few memories I have left of Argentina, whose tender smile I will never forget, who was made to migrate to Buenos Aires to look for work when her husband's death made her a widow with three girls under the age of ten. Her migration set into motion my mom's eventual move to the capital city, her first encounter with my dad, my birth, our departure to the United States. Migration is my heritage. My ancestors' movements have made any idea of homeland an impossibility. For this, I thank them.

Introduction

The Fugitive Sacred

What she knows is not a solution, but a route.

—ALEXIS PAULINE GUMBS

The first thing I notice about Juana is her thick, curly hair, graying at the temples and parted down the middle. The second is the black ankle monitor squeezing her right leg. As she leads me down a narrow hallway inside the church she has called home since 2017, Juana's cotton skirt flutters back and forth over her compact frame. The skirt falls slightly above the ankle monitor, occasionally brushing the hard plastic box.

I arrive carrying Styrofoam containers from a local Colombian restaurant. During our first and only phone call, Juana joked about the food served at St. Barnabas—an Episcopalian church whose members are almost all white and elderly. And so, having read between the lines, I greet her with two *bandejas paisas*, sampler plates loaded with white rice, red beans, grilled beef, sweet plantains, and *arepas*. There's enough to feed the two of us, plus Juana's granddaughters who are visiting for the weekend.

The church hall is undergoing renovations. While some volunteers unravel new green drapes and hang them from curtain rods, others are busy applying a fresh coat of paint to the white walls. I notice rollaway beds leaning against a corner, awaiting the arrival of the rest of Juana's family. Everything here appears to be suspended in a state of transition. While Juana gathers silverware from the kitchenette, I peer out the window and see two police cars idling in the parking lot. Juana seems unaffected when I point them out, explaining that they have been coming more frequently ever since someone showed up in the middle of the night to harass her. A volunteer sees me eyeing the patrol cars and hints at possible danger,

"Not everyone agrees with us offering sanctuary." I ask Juana if she ever interacts with the police, but she says they mostly keep their distance. She used to wave to them on her walks to take trash to the dumpsters. But after the incident, a church elder cautioned her against leaving the property even that briefly. Now she stays indoors, her view always the same: the cinder-block walls of her makeshift bedroom, the framed Bible verses and linoleum floors of the church hall, the wooden pulpit and altar at the front of the sanctuary. Her trailer park's lively sounds have become muffled and distant, replaced by the occasional speeding ambulance in the distance or desperate bark of a dog who wandered from its home. Juana creates small tasks for herself throughout the day, staying busy to survive. "When I slow down," she confesses, "I remember my situation. And I get depressed. So I have to keep moving."

As much as I try to keep the conversation lighthearted, the topic of her deportation order is inevitable. And, at this point, Juana has spoken to so many journalists and researchers that she has developed a script for first encounters. Juana tells me that she had barely turned twenty when she escaped violence in Guatemala and sought asylum in the United States. A few years later, with her case still pending, Juana returned to her home country to care for her daughter who was battling a life-threatening illness. "It's what any mother would do," she insists, "but it was that decision that led me to this place." Juana used a fraudulent visa to reenter the United States in 1999 and, over a decade later, in 2011, it was for that reason that she was detained at the garment factory where she worked. Because of Barack Obama's Felons, Not Family policy, which ostensibly prioritized deporting migrants with criminal records and avoided separating families, Juana was released under the condition that she appear for mandatory check-ins with Immigration and Customs Enforcement (ICE).[1] Two-and-a-half years before our first meeting, only months after Donald Trump assumed office, Juana was given an order of deportation during one of these check-ins, a practice that some activists call silent raids.

Juana does not elaborate on that moment, nor does she share how she felt when the officer gave her thirty days to say goodbye to the life she created in this country. She instead jumps ahead to how her family mobilized in response to the deportation order. According to her, they sprang into action immediately. Her eldest daughter learned about the tradition of seeking sanctuary in churches after making countless phone calls to lawyers and nonprofit organizations. Someone from the American Friends Service Committee told her about the tradition of harboring migrants in places of worship. They promised her that ICE respects sacred space and that Juana would be safe as long as she remained inside the building. While the family are active members of a Latinx church near their home in Asheboro, North Carolina, Juana could not seek sanctuary there because many congregants are also undocumented or members of mixed-status families. They worried ICE would not honor the bounds of a migrant church in the same way, that its sensitive locations policy would not apply to a congregation of undocumented aliens.[2] Juana moved into St. Barnabas on the last day of May, the

1.1
Peering into Juana's garden, a sanctuary from her sanctuary.

1.2
View of the door that leads out of Juana's sanctuary.

day her flight was scheduled to depart to Guatemala. The church became her home and her prison—simultaneously promising refuge and capture, protection and immobility. Her daughter once described sanctuary as a form of family separation.

At times, Juana and I run out of things to say to each other. Our eyes meet and we smile timidly, embracing the pauses. I notice an assortment of handmade clay bowls sitting at the end of the folding table. Juana tells me that she has taken up pottery while living at St. Barnabas and that she also started a sewing business using machines donated by church members. She crafts bags for yoga mats and pillow covers, and she alters church members' clothing. Within a space of confinement, she finds ways to play and create beauty. Juana tells me that being alone makes her feel closer to God, that she has never prayed as often or as eagerly as she does now.

o

I open this book not in the Sonoran Desert, but in Greensboro, North Carolina—a short drive from the town where I grew up after migrating to the United States and where Juana Luz Tobar Ortega lived in sanctuary from 2017 to 2021. From the church hall where I got to know Juana, I was confronted with the paradoxes of sanctuary—a tradition that Jennifer Bagelman describes as a "prison-like form of protection."[3] Writing about Glasgow, Scotland, Bagelman challenges not only church sanctuary but also cities of sanctuary, both of which position themselves as "idealized site(s)" that "extend universal hospitality," but nevertheless reproduce asymmetrical power relations and suspend migrants in a temporality of waiting.[4] These types of sanctuary "situate the seeker as one who must prove his/her worthiness, rely on the charity of others, and wait."[5] Juana certainly lived in a state of waiting—for family to visit over the weekends, for the next volunteer to arrive for their shift, for a client to request alterations, for a zucchini to bloom, for God to answer her prayers, for a stay of deportation. And while church sanctuary did in fact limit ICE's reach, at the same time it limited Juana's mobility—not so much an escape from as a rearrangement of surveillance and policing.

In the wake of the 2016 US presidential election, the number of churches calling themselves sanctuaries nearly doubled.[6] Restaurants, universities, hospitals, and cities around the country also declared themselves sanctuaries for undocumented migrants in unprecedented numbers (as the Trump administration threatened to withhold federal funding from sanctuary jurisdictions). Pueblo Sin Fronteras, the transborder collective known for organizing migrant caravans, called on Mexico to refuse border militarization and instead declare itself a "sanctuary country." But sanctuary stretched beyond defending migrants. Public libraries announced "book sanctuaries" for banned literature; Black Lives Matter activists created a sanctuary fund for street medics, and organizers in Minneapolis, Minnesota, occupied an abandoned hotel and transformed it into a sanctuary for people experiencing homelessness—calling it an "experiment" or "radical moment of possibility."[7]

The American Friends Service Committee launched a campaign titled "sanctuary everywhere" in 2017, insisting that sanctuary could mean harboring someone in a place of worship, but it might also point to mobile practices of care and mutuality. This book takes its title from this longing to become refuge, from this opacity that facilitates fugitivity. To be everywhere means sanctuary cannot be captured, caged, or pinned down. By the time you think you have caught it, sanctuary has already moved on and fled elsewhere. Though at first I was drawn to places that call themselves sanctuaries—churches, restaurants, hospitals, campuses—in this book I honor moments when migrants and other artists or activists create sanctuary in flight. I trace how sanctuary emerges not when migrants arrive at a singular place of refuge, but as they and their collaborators traverse the Sonoran Desert's sinuous routes. And, while inspired by sanctuary movements that pursue legislative change and political transformation (and indeed, they are a sort of prelude to this text), I study the ways sanctuary plots against the profane and forces open gaps in the everyday.

Sanctuary Everywhere follows the fugitive sacred in the Sonoran Desert. This book turns to four scenes: moments when land disobeys or disregards the policy named Prevention through Deterrence (PTD); incarcerated migrants practice an illicit or contraband touch inside detention centers; a deported nurse heals migrants in Nogales, Sonora; and the migrant dead haunt the living and refuse closure from humanitarians. In these opening pages, I introduce theories of the sacred—as set apart, ambiguous, and, ultimately, fugitive—and detail some possible histories of sanctuary. I then present reflections on methodology and terminology before offering overviews of each chapter. That said, this manuscript is meandering. I invite readers to embrace its unpredictable routes, which echo rivers that change course and streams with unruly migrations. The dots in this book are points on a map and the route is circuitous. Like the red dots that haunt maps of the Sonoran Desert by indicating where a migrant has died, they suggest a pause, an invitation to move your body, to drink water before continuing to the next section, to memorialize deaths not remembered or recorded.

○

Sanctuary traditionally refers to the innermost part of a church or temple, enclosed by a lattice or railing. Teeming with sacred potential, sanctuaries were historically protected and hidden, inaccessible or obscured from view. The term is an anglicized form of the Late Latin *santuarium* and Latin *sanctus*, a perfect passive participle from the verb *sancio*—meaning "to dedicate [to the gods]."[8] *Sanctus* connotes "holy" and "sacred" interchangeably, as does *sacer*, an adjective that comes from the same root. According to Émile Benveniste, the latter is unique in that it emphasizes the ambiguity of the sacred, as both alluring and dangerous to touch. He claims that this "double value," however, is not reflected in *sanctus*.[9] *Sanctus* denotes a place, person, or object that has been made sacred; *sacer*, on the other hand, refers to something that is inherently or intrinsically sacred. This is perhaps why sanctuary is more often related to *sanctus*, given that it is made and consecrated through sacred activity—what Elizabeth Pérez might name micropractices or Elaine Peña might describe as devotional labor.[10]

Both *sanctus* and *sacer* suggest that the sacred is set apart from or incompatible with the everyday or the profane. Contact with the sacred is dangerous, life-threatening even. Roger Caillois references Alfred Ernout and Antoine Meillet's definition of the sacred as "the one or that which cannot be touched without defilement."[11] Caillois explains that when someone committed a crime against religion or the state in ancient Rome, the assembled populace would cast them out, declaring them *sacer*—dangerous and untouchable, or negative sacred. This is precisely the "double value" of the sacred; *sacer* provokes both admiration and repulsion, wonder and fear. "It constitutes supreme temptation and the greatest of dangers. Dreadful, it commands caution, and desirable, it invites rashness."[12] *Sacer* is tied up with exile and the exiled, with those who are cast out of the profane because they have transgressed a boundary and thus pose a threat to the order of things.

Émile Durkheim similarly describes the sacred as the subject of a taboo or prohibition.[13] He insists that the sacred is not the same as what is good, majestic, or divine; it is not to be confused with the "holy." Rather, "the sacred thing is, par excellence, that which the profane must not and cannot touch with impunity."[14] There are moments when humans cross the threshold between the sacred and profane: instances when performance ruptures (and, in doing so, reinforces) boundaries between worlds. In these cases, there are procedures for encountering the sacred: cleansing rites, eating restrictions, sexual prohibitions, dress codes. And there are likewise procedures for leaving the sacred after one has been ritually defiled. Human beings must, therefore, approach sacred beings and spaces with an abundance of caution; they are dangerous, disruptive to the everyday.

Others have similarly made distinctions between the sacred and profane, including Rudolph Otto and Mircea Eliade who both write in the wake of the death of God and the Enlightenment and who are both concerned that an obsession with reason has stripped religion of its wonder and enchantment. Otto is interested in the "numinous," moments when humans are unmade and overpowered by the divine.[15] Though he focuses more on the holy than sacred, Otto's notion of *mysterium tremendum*—how the divine exceeds and overwhelms human reason—is helpful when considering the ways sanctuary disturbs the everyday.[16] For Otto, sacred forces are intoxicating, enchanting, haunting. They are too much—ineffable, unspeakable, incomprehensible. This too-muchness exceeds and escapes the rational human subject. Eliade draws inspiration from Otto to elaborate on hierophanies, or divine manifestations, which he proposes are "of a wholly different order, a reality that does not belong to our world." Yet, whereas Durkheim studies how the sacred is created and nurtured through human activity (*sanctus*), Eliade imagines a transcendent reality (*sacer*), a superhuman or supernatural experience where the sacred "shows itself to us."[17] I embrace these generative ways of thinking about the sacred—as the devotional labor of *sanctus* and as the unruly "double value" of *sacer*, as those forces that overwhelm the profane and so they are made subject to taboos.

Taboos are in place to protect the sacred from the profane and vice versa, to ensure the profane is not contaminated by the ambiguous and disturbing movements of the sacred. Juana, in defying her deportation order, also became separate or prohibited from the everyday. Instead of boarding her flight to Guatemala, she packed a suitcase and held a press conference before crossing the threshold of the church. Having violated the taboo, she was then denied the routine—unable to work, visit the grocery store, schedule a doctor's appointment, or even take her trash outside. As Caillois observes, when transgressing the profane to access the sacred, "all that is part of the ordinary process of human living must be rejected. . . . One who wishes to sacrifice, to enter the temple or to communicate with [their]

God, must first interrupt [their] daily routine. [They are] enjoined to silence, vigils, retreats, inactivity, and continence."[18] Immediately after entering the church to see Juana, visitors were greeted by a binder detailing her background and listing emergency procedures in case of harassment or immigration enforcement. In addition to formalizing Juana's presence in the church, these pages offered instructions for approaching the sacred, ensuring visitors could return to the profane without defilement.

After all, sacred forces must be kept at a distance. As Durkheim writes, they are separated from the everyday and ordinary because of their "extraordinary contagiousness" or because they "radiate and diffuse," because they threaten society's illusion of stability and stasis.[19] And, indeed, Juana's migratory crossings disregarded sovereign borders. Her refusal to obey deportation orders exceeded the authority of the state. Because Juana transgressed these prohibitions, she needed to either be eliminated (through detention and deportation) or cleansed (assimilated and incorporated into the state). For Juana to be granted a stay of deportation, the profane world had to be convinced that she no longer presented a threat. So, when drafting petitions and holding press conferences to defend Juana, her family and supporters emphasized her rootedness—Juana's desire to stay put, to return to her home and her houseplants, to see her US-citizen children and grandchildren grow up, to settle back into old habits and routines.

But sacred beings and spaces are necessarily unsettled and unstable. Citing the sacredness of the totem and the initiation rites of a neophyte, Durkheim warns that "religious forces are so imagined as to appear always on the point of escaping the places they occupy and invading all that passes within their reach."[20] In turn, they provoke a "collective effervescence" or an unruly collectivity that is uninterested with the demands of the mundane. Mary Douglas writes in detail about those forces that refuse to stay put, that disrespect society's boundaries and conventions. Her work is interested in the impure or disruptive sacred; Douglas engages with *sacer's* potential to both consecrate and desecrate. For her, the impure sacred "offends against order"—not dangerous merely by virtue of its existence but because it is not in the place it has been assigned.[21] Taboos, then, "have as their main function to impose system on an inherently untidy experience."[22] Unauthorized migrants, including Juana, engage the sacred through unsanctioned acts of transgression, by violating taboos that are in place to maintain continuity and cohesion. In doing so, they become ritually defiled and therefore must be contained.

Unauthorized migrants threaten systems of order and management. They abandon their nations, many tossing their government-issued documents before crossing. They move clandestinely through militarized and heavily policed deserts and bodies of water. Migrants refuse to stay in the place they have been assigned by systems of governance that draw up nations and manufacture boundaries. Taboos, as Daniella Gandolfo proposes in her reading of Georges Bataille, exist to police these acts of refusal and transgressions which "proper humanity struggles to ward off and exclude from social life but is never able to completely do away with."[23] Migrants like Juana become sacred (that is, dangerous) in their acts of transgression, and their movements can never be completely done away with.

Sacred forces migrate and blur boundaries, escaping what Bataille calls "the order of things."[24] Like Durkheim and Douglas, Bataille differentiates the profane "world of taboos" from a sacred world that "depends on limited acts of transgression."[25] For Bataille, too, sacred forces simultaneously provoke disgust and fascination, horror and respect. He describes the sacred as incompatible with the profane world of law and control, what Gandolfo in her reading of Bataille calls "everything that is inassimilable to the bourgeois order of capital and production."[26] Though human society surrounds sacred beings and spaces with taboos, Bataille suggests that what is sacred cannot be entirely contained (even as it is prohibited and criminalized). For him, the relationship between taboo and transgression (or between the profane and sacred) is less binary and more dialectical; "often the transgression is permitted, often it is even prescribed."[27] Each world reveals how the other is insufficient and incomplete. Each needs the other.

More recently, scholars have challenged categories of the sacred and profane, insisting that the sacred is part of the everyday, inseparable from the quotidian. Mujerista theologians like Ada María Isasi-Díaz insist that the sacred can be found in the everyday lives of women, in *lo cotidiano*.[28] And yet, for many of the people I met in the Sonoran Desert, spaces of everyday life—workplaces, neighborhoods, supermarkets, and schools— are not only inaccessible but impossible. For others, the everyday is simply uninteresting. While in transit, people are constantly being moved and on the move—overstaying their welcome at migrant shelters, packing their belongings and looking for temporary housing elsewhere; venturing into the desert with a group of strangers carrying only a backpack and a gallon of water; praying for the day they are released from detention, only to be deported and forced to attempt the crossing once again. There is repetition, but rarely is there routine. Migrants by definition flee the everyday, pursuing change and transformation. They are unsatisfied with the quotidian. Their movements express a longing for an otherwise.

I read the profane as the routine and quotidian, that which *imagines itself as* or *aspires to be* settled, stable, rooted. Unlike scholars like Caillois, however, I cannot describe the everyday as a time or space of "dull continuity . . . daily repetition of the same material preoccupations" or as the "tranquil labor of the debilitating phases of existence."[29] Many unauthorized migrants are running from precarious profanes; my own family left Argentina in the months leading up to an economic crisis caused by neoliberal austerity that drove people to *cacerolazos* (protests defined by the banging of pots and pans)—where they defaced and destroyed banks and foreign-owned companies—and which culminated in having five different presidents in the span of two weeks. Before we ultimately left, my parents uprooted us from one apartment to another, unable to stay in any one for longer than a few months. There was no tranquility or dull continuity, only the desperation of people refused stability. And so, instead, I understand the profane as those beings and spaces that are invested in order and fixity, in sovereignty, borders, citizenship, nation-states. The profane polices our imaginations the same way it polices prohibitive boundaries and limits our capacity to envision otherwise worlds.[30]

Because of their restless mobilities, unauthorized migrants—and certainly border crossers—are kept from participating in the routine, from laying claim to the everyday.[31] The state excludes them from the world of papers and status through policy and policing. Deportability, or the constant threat or possibility of deportation, makes the routine or everyday even more inaccessible. Undocumented migrants are aware that, at any time, the everyday could be pulled out from under them. An ICE officer could barge into their home in the middle of the night. Police officers could be blocking a two-lane street on their way home from work, checking for valid driver's licenses. They could be swept up during a workplace raid. Locked out of the profane, migrants describe undocumented status as living in the shadows, a fugitive and underground space. The state even describes migrants as aliens, not of this world, unknowable to and incompatible with the everyday. Like Gloria Anzaldúa, who grew up in the South Texas borderlands, I find inspiration in the lives of "aliens," those who are too queer or abnormal to make home in the profane. In her short essay "La Prieta," Anzaldúa writes about not belonging anywhere—not in Mexico, not in the United States: "both cultures deny me a place in their universe."[32] She writes about taking refuge in *el mundo zurdo*, among those who do not fit and, because they do not fit, pose a threat.

Throughout *Sanctuary Everywhere*, I use "sacred" and "profane" instead of religion, agreeing with Todd Ramón Ochoa that "religion is . . . overladen with European assumptions of form, doctrine, and homogeneity, in short, with a static sense of belief and practice." I am drawn to the "sacred" for similar reasons that Ochoa turns to the word "inspiration," because it is "a more mobile term."[33] I am in conversation with theorists who trace the ways in which sacred forces move, including Caillois, who juxtaposes profane things, which are (or aspire to be) fixed in place, and sacred forces, which are "good or bad not by nature but by the *direction* [they] take or are given."[34] The sacred moves, rebelling against stasis and sovereignty. Consider as an example novelist Justin Torres' eulogy to Latin night at the queer club following the 2016 mass shooting at Pulse Nightclub in Orlando, Florida. While other writers mourned the loss of their "sanctuary," Torres extoled "the sacredness" of the queer club.[35] "Outside, the world can be murderous to you and your kind. Lord knows. But inside, it is loud and sexy and on. . . . If you're lucky, no one is wearing much clothing, and the dance floor is full. If you're lucky, they're playing reggaeton, salsa, and you can *move*."[36] Torres describes the world outside the nightclub as constricting, immobilizing. But Latin night at the queer club promises movement, intimacy, release; it is set apart by taboos and teeming with transgression. Latin night is unfit for the profane. Torres writes about how separate the queer club is from the outside, how the sacred makes it possible to lose the self, to loosen, to act loose. "The only imperative," he proposes, "is to be transformed, transfigured in the disco light."

○

The first time I hear someone speak of the Sonoran Desert, I instead hear the word "sonorous" and wonder if the two are related. Sonorous as in fullness, as in a sound that is cavernous and resonant, imposingly deep. Sonorous as the opposite of what deserts represent in the American imagination: empty and arid wastelands, willing and waiting to be tamed. Sonorous as the "inventory of echoes" Valeria Luiselli writes about, "not a collection of sounds that have been lost—such a thing would in fact be impossible—but rather one of sounds that were present in the time of recording and that, when we listen to them, remind us of the ones that are lost."[37] Sonorous as in hemispheric histories that are profound and ongoing: histories of settler colonialism, mass incarceration and Indigenous elimination, borders and their technologies of surveillance. Sonorous as the "fugitive landscape" of the Sonoran Desert—which Samuel Truett insists has "continually slipped out of [the] control" of corporations, states, and settler entrepreneurs seeking to tame and instrumentalize its sacred energies.[38]

Though many contemporary scholars describe the Sonoran Desert as an accomplice in border enforcement, I agree with Truett that land is a witness to and partner in ongoing histories of fugitivity: from Chinese migrants who crossed the desert covertly during the era of Asian exclusion to enslaved Africans who fled to Mexico to evade capture and Indigenous communities who found shelter and plotted escape routes in the mountains. Borders are contested lands, where humans and more-than-human beings crisscross, navigate, and transgress boundaries. The sacred and profane meet here—the world of order, law, and regulation comes into contact and conflict with what Dimitris Papadopoulos, Niamh Stephenson, and Vassilis Tsianos call the "uncontrollable, escaping potentialities of people."[39]

Fugitivity comes from the Latin *fugitivus*, or fleeing, which is a past-participle adjective from the stem *fugere*—which can mean to take flight or run away; leave a country and go into exile; hide, vanish, or disappear; escape someone's notice; or render yourself unknowable and unreadable. From the Old French *fugitif*, the noun *fugitive* refers to a runaway, deserter, or outlaw. By definition, fugitives are at odds with law and oppose order. They make themselves indiscernible to the profane or everyday, render themselves apart from the world of visibility and normalcy. Writing about Black, feminist, and queer US activists in the 1970s, Stephen Dillon suggests that fugitive ways of knowing and moving through the world produce an "estrangement" from the routine and the ordinary. He theorizes fugitive spaces as teeming with "alternative forms of knowledge, living, and seeing that escaped the normativities central to the functioning of the everyday."[40] Because they move through peripheries and underground spaces, fugitives can see what regularly goes unnoticed; they unmask the violences of the present. And, so, the profane criminalizes and polices fugitive movements, implementing prohibitions to control or slow them down. At times, as Papadopoulos, Stephenson, and Tsianos argue, the profane appropriates or absorbs fugitive movements—incorporating select migrants into the citizenry, granting rights and representation.[41] Nevertheless, sacred forces escape. Take, for instance, this line from a poem by Javier Zamora— "Every election, a candidate promises: papers, papers, & more. They gift us Advance Parole. We want flight."[42]

Fugitives are on the move. They are, as Jack Halberstam observes in his reading of Fred Moten and Stefano Harney, "separate from settling," affirming that "there are spaces and modalities that exist separate from the logical, logistical, the housed and the positioned."[43] Their restless movements create other social worlds and political possibilities, ones that collude with more-than-human beings. Felipe Baeza, a migrant artist whose practice embraces printmaking, collage, embroidery, and sculpture, envisions "fugitive figures" that are simultaneously animal, human, and plant. In an interview with Zoë Hopkins, Baeza speaks about fugitivity as a commitment to "always escaping, always fleeing, always evading. . . . [I]t's a condition that deviates from laws and norms." For him, too, fugitivity necessarily involves defying the taboo, crossing the prohibition. According to the artist, fugitives surrender their individuality in favor of being in relation with others, humans and more than human: "They are legible on their own terms, not in the ways that any law demands." And they are hard to pin down, uninterested in fitting into one category or modality. By escaping fixed identities and categories, the fugitive beings in Baeza's artworks are able to nurture relations of immanence. Their nude torsos emerge from the earth, weeds growing out of their mouths. In place of legs, they stand on thorny vines. Red branches sprout from the crowns of their heads. Their human legs merge with the body of an octopus, its tentacles outstretched. For Baeza, these fugitive bodies inhabit interstitial spaces, more interested in the incomplete process of becoming than settling into a fixed being. He insists, "The room for liminality and possibility is what allows a subject to live a life worth living."[46]

Baeza's (and my own) thoughts on fugitivity are indebted to Black studies and to scholars like Moten and Harney, who describe fugitivity as a riotous intimacy or excess touch that is the "terrible gift" of the hold. Tiffany Lethabo King also theorizes Blackness as perpetually outside the borders of the human, confounding the rational, stable Man imagined by liberal humanism. The third chapter of Lethabo King's *The Black Shoals* studies the protagonists of Julie Dash's *Daughters of the Dust* and their indigo-stained skin. For the author, the blue hands of the Peazant family, formerly enslaved people who worked on indigo plantations, undo ontological boundaries that separate plant, land, and human. "Under slavery and conquest," she writes, "the Black body becomes the ultimate symbol of accumulation, malleability, and flux existing outside human coordinates of space and time. . . . Blackness is the raw dimensionality (symbol, matter, kinetic energy) used to make space."[47] Indigo-stained flesh marks "porous sites of instability and transition between states."[48] Fugitives are endlessly in the middle, in movement. To return to Moten, they refuse what has been refused—in this case, Enlightenment categories of the human that are stable, bounded, separate from "nature." What they imagine and create at the borders of the human open up unimaginable possibilities.

Fugitivity—being on the run from the law, at odds with the law—guarantees neither safety nor comfort. It is not paradise, and it is not permanent. But it does offer possibilities for transgressing often unlivable everydays. Many border crossers are fleeing everydays marked by ecological destruction, extractive economies, austerity politics, and capitalist abandonment. Denied the stability of home, they chase futures elsewhere. Not merely at the mercy of push-and-pull factors, however, they pursue transformation and remake life. Their creative movements challenge the power of nation-states to regulate mobility. In *Intergalactic Travels: Poems from a Fugitive Alien*, Alán Pelaez Lopez uses photographs, collages, email and text exchanges, and immigration forms to celebrate the ways fugitive aliens "craft unimaginable lives" that evade capture.[49] A Black and Indigenous migrant who was formerly undocumented, Pelaez Lopez describes fugitive living as losing contact with their family, running from intimacy out of a fear of deportation, experiencing intense anxiety with every knock on the door, "years and years of perpetual non-existence."[50] Pelaez Lopez searches for a "new type of fugitivity," one that (like Baeza and Lethabo King) leads them to more-than-human, "intergalactic" relations.[51] Toward the end of the collection, in a handwritten entry, they describe the first poem they wrote in the third grade, about becoming a sea horse so they could give birth. Pelaez Lopez dedicates this poem to their mom who, though alarmed that her "son" wanted to give birth, surely felt relieved they still had the capacity to dream. Fugitives become sea horse, become indigo, elude legibility. Fugitivity dwells in these moments of escape and transformation, resisting the romance of arrival. Here is where this practice meets the sacred—dangerous, unsettling, uncomfortable, and often unsafe. The fugitive sacred is too much for the profane world and, so, is subject to taboos and prohibitions. Set apart.

o

The date is March 24, 1982, two years to the day that Salvadoran Archbishop Óscar Romero was assassinated by death squad mercenaries as he consecrated the Eucharist. Romero was outspoken in his condemnation of the country's military dictatorship; only weeks prior, he had written a letter to Jimmy Carter urging the president to stop funding El Salvador's junta. John Fife, described by some as more cowboy than clergyman, honors Romero as he addresses the media from a folding table outside Southside Presbyterian Church in Tucson, Arizona. He is joined by his collaborator Jim Corbett, activist attorney Margo Cowan, and other ecumenical religious leaders. To his right sits a Salvadoran refugee who uses the pseudonym "Alfredo." Wearing a cowboy hat and bandana covering the lower half of his face, "Alfredo" offers a *testimonio* of the necropolitical conditions facing Salvadorans, insisting that staying in his country would have been a death sentence.[52]

Though they have been coordinating the clandestine movements of Central Americans since the summer of 1981, on this day the group goes public by calling on the tradition of sanctuary. Before Alfredo delivers his *testimonio,* Fife reads a letter addressed to the US Attorney General—making it clear that Southside will actively defy laws criminalizing the harboring of aliens. He denounces Ronald Reagan's "immoral, as well as illegal" policies toward Central Americans—referring to the US government's support of military juntas in Guatemala and El Salvador.[53] As part of his Cold War strategy, Reagan provided weapons, funding, and training to death squads and contributed to an exodus of hundreds of thousands of people from the region. Salvadorans and Guatemalans who reached US borders were then denied asylum due to the administration's support of right-wing dictatorships. Fife's tone is firm and unyielding as he announces Southside's plans to welcome a migrant into the "care and protection" of the church. He reiterates: "We will not cease to extend the sanctuary of the church to undocumented people from Central America. Obedience to God requires this of us."[54] Cloth banners hang from the church's adobe exterior walls. In handwritten capital letters, they announce: *Este es el santuario de Dios para los oprimidos de Centro América* ("This is a sanctuary for the oppressed of Central America") and *La Migra no Profana el Santuario* ("Immigration: Do not profane the sanctuary of God").

Sanctuary activists in the 1980s drew inspiration from the Underground Railroad and resistance to the Fugitive Slave Acts. Volunteers offered their homes as waystations and helped transport refugees across international borders and within the interior of the United States. Churches and other communities across Mexico offered food and shelter along the way, from Tapachula on the southern border with Guatemala through Mexico City and border cities like Nogales. As Leo Guardado notes, this underground network was especially important considering Mexico's collaboration with the Reagan administration to prevent Central Americans from reaching the US border to seek asylum.[55]

Sanctuary practices were mobile and insurgent, sacred routes for people on the run from enforcement. Across the Américas, fugitives have long engaged in such sacred acts of transgression. Cedric J. Robinson outlines a history of *palenques*, *mocambos*, and *quilombos* that "found sometimes tenuous, sometimes permanent existences" across the hemisphere.[56] These maroons fled to marshes, swamps, hills, and mountains to escape plantations and chattel slavery. In doing so, to invoke Neil Roberts, they articulated freedom not as a destination but as a practice of flight.[57] Derecka Purnell notes that the word *maroons* comes from the Spanish *cimarrones*, meaning wild or feral.[58] She cites Sylviane Diouf, who observes the more-than-human intimacies nurtured through marronage: "their secrecy forced them into a set of interdependent relationships with other maroons, animals, and the earth."[59] Maroons entered into immanent relations with other beings, including land. Their fugitive practices were sacred acts—betrayals of the routine, ongoing acts of transgression.[60]

By turning to marronage and the underground, I follow Aimee Villareal who calls for "a situated historiography of sanctuary in the Américas, one that acknowledges its coloniality as an instrument of pastoral power and centers Indigenous regions of refuge and negotiations with settler colonialism." Villareal describes Indigenous "sanctuaryscapes" as an insurgent response to colonization, "a dynamic autochthonous tradition and Indigenous survival strategy cultivated (and continuously remade) in regions of refuge and rebellion." She presents two examples—Pueblo cities of refuge and Apache autonomous enclaves—to trace how Indigenous sanctuaryscapes evaded the "coercive protection and care of the mission."[61] Meanwhile, the Catholic Church's sanctuary practices were based on ideas of sin and redemption and exclusive to those willing to be baptized. Clergy alone could hear confessions, determine a person's credibility, and grant sanctuary. Unlike conditional Catholic practices of sanctuary, Indigenous sanctuaryscapes facilitated escape routes. They embraced those on the run from colonial officials and favored fugitivity over conditional hospitality.

Sanctuary practices in the ancient world similarly conspired with the outlaw. As Linda Rabben outlines, Diana's sanctuary at Ephesus was famous throughout ancient Greece as a place of asylum for fugitives, slaves, debtors, social outcasts, and criminals. Temples, groves, and other sacred sites were set apart by boundary markers and delineated as inviolable.[62] And, like the 1980s movement—whose tactics involved economic boycotts, cross-country caravans, and political advocacy—ancient sanctuary was not always, or even mostly, imagined as a place. Among Hebrews, for example, there existed both altar and communitarian sanctuaries. Hillary Cunningham explains that the former were usually located in religious shrines and "asylums by virtue of their status as *holy places*," while the latter was based on communal practices that sheltered fugitives.[63] In communitarian sanctuaries, fugitives could claim refuge by petitioning the city's council of elders.[64] Sanctuaries were not only set apart or consecrated sites but also tied to a religious specialist and community. Cunningham notes that early Christians and medieval churches embraced these ancient traditions of sanctuary, affirming both places and people as sacred.

According to John Fife, "Sanctuary was a mobile strategy from the beginning." When I interview him, Fife mentions that he and his collaborator Jim Corbett—nicknamed the "Quaker coyote" by American media—partnered with churches across Mexico to develop an underground railroad into the United States and Canada. Fife shares that sanctuary did not begin when people reached the border; rather, it emerged as people received and offered care in transit. And, as I later notice in archives, workers unions, *comunidades de base*, and coalitions of mothers in Central America had organized to provide material support and facilitate escape routes. During our conversation, Fife recalls one of his visits to El Salvador. "I learned that Catholic and Lutheran churches were filled with refugees and internally displaced families. They had practiced sanctuary for years, long before we did." Even in Tucson, queer and feminist organizers practiced sanctuary before Southside publicly declared itself a space of refuge. As Karma Chávez explains, when Salvadorans began to arrive "with bullets lodged in their bodies" at the Manzo Area Council, a human rights and community aid program, advocates organized to offer legal services at El Centro, a detention facility in southern Arizona. Manzo's director, Margo Cowan, and her partner, Guadalupe Castillo, represented thousands of migrants detained and at risk of deportation. Chávez writes, "Though they lacked the capacity to support all the migrants who needed it, the Manzo Area Council workers' tireless efforts signaled the queer, feminist catalysts of the sanctuary movement, a movement that may not have existed without them."[65]

Wearing a paisley, button-down tweed jacket, and a silver watch etched with the Tohono O'odham deity I'itoi, Fife elaborates on the ways he and his collaborators navigated the law and legality. Working with the Manzo Area Council taught activists that the legal route was a dead end; efforts to bail migrants out of detention centers only delayed the inevitable. Almost every Central American they supported was denied asylum. Even still, sanctuary practitioners did not describe their smuggling and "evasion services" as acts of breaking the law or as "civil disobedience." Rather, they saw themselves as practicing "civil initiative." Based on the Nuremberg Trials, which determined that officers have a duty to disobey illegal or harmful orders, activists saw themselves as defending rather than violating the law.[66] Sanctuary workers argued they were not committing a crime by harboring fugitives; rather, state agents were the criminals for refusing to respect international human rights agreements. In 1983, the FBI set up Operation Sojourner to infiltrate the Sanctuary Movement. Two years later, sixteen people, including Fife, were indicted on counts of conspiracy and of transporting and harboring fugitives. According to Susan Bibler Coutin, to defend their work after the Sanctuary trials, activists developed more rigid definitions of who counted as a refugee and only smuggled those they deemed eligible—upholding distinctions between economic migrants and asylum seekers. "To validate their understanding of U.S. refugee law," Coutin elaborates, "Tucson border workers assumed responsibility for enforcing the law. In essence, they created a partial substitute for the immigration system."[67] Cunningham similarly explains that the Tucson movement adopted many of the Immigration and Naturalization Services (INS) guidelines when screening and evaluating refugee cases.[68]

Fife confirms that once Central Americans reached the Sonora-Arizona border, sanctuary activists verified their stories with churches and human rights organizations in El Salvador. Once, an immigration officer angrily accused Fife, "You're trying to run your own Immigration Service, aren't you? You guys are making decisions about who crosses and who doesn't. Where the hell do you think you get the right to do that?" Fife chuckles as he recalls his response: "You claim to have half a dozen CIA agents in El Salvador. *I have thousands.* They're called priests and pastors. I've got a much better intelligence system than you could ever imagine." Not all activists saw sanctuary as a form of surveillance, though, nor did they all embrace civil initiative. The Chicago Religious Task Force on Central America, for instance, preferred the radical and insurgent tradition of civil disobedience. "Sanctuary by its very nature breaks the law," read an editorial published in 1985 in the Chicago organization's national newspaper, *Basta!* "All of us in the Sanctuary Movement have chosen to break the law, not as an end in itself, but to defend the powerless, the Central Americans in the U.S. and

REFUGEES: Churches run a 'railroad'

Continued from page 10

On March 24, two years after the assassination of Salvadoran Archbishop Oscar Romero by unknown assailants, the Tucson group ended its secrecy. The Rev. John Fife, pastor of Tucson's Southside United Presbyterian Church, announced he would openly defy the law and provide sanctuary to Salvadoran refugees illegally in the country.

"We decided that we had to change the government policy (of denying asylum) if we were really going to help refugees," Fife said recently. Going public with evasion activities seemed a way to arouse support, he said.

Today 15 churches around the nation — including Catholic, Presbyterian, Methodist, Lutheran, Episcopalian, Unitarian and Quaker denominations — publicly provide sanctuary to Central American refugees. Another 150 churches openly support the sanctuaries with food, clothing, money and encouragement, according to Fife.

None has been raided by immigration agents. Numerous people also offer their homes as way stations and their services as relay drivers to provide refugees with a means of travel — a loosely organized underground railroad.

The railroad takes its name from the Civil War network that helped slaves escape to non-slavery states.

Its hub lies in Tucson.

Its Mexico line, consisting mostly of Catholic churches giving food and shelter, runs from Tapachula in the southernmost tip of Mexico a dozen miles from Guatemala, through Mexico's capital, out to the Pacific coast highway and on to Nogales.

The main U.S. line runs from Tucson to Chicago, passing occasionally through Colorado. Tucson operators expect to have a line to the east

Jim Corbett: Domestic and international law establishes "every person's right to aid the victims of persecution"

Quaker 'coyote' at war with U.S. over refugees

By Carmen Duarte 8-20-84
The Arizona Daily Star

Jim Corbett is a coyote — a smuggler of people.

He's not a money-hungry driver who crams a tractor-trailer with human beings desperate to live in the United States of America.

He's not a sly profiteer who makes his charges pay $400 each before leading them into the searing Arizona desert and leaving them to fend for themselves.

He is a different breed of coyote — a 51-year-old Quaker at war with the U.S. government. He smuggles Central Americans into the country because he believes it is his obligation to do so.

Soft-spoken, partially crippled by arthritis, Corbett works at the risk of being prosecuted if caught, facing up to five years in

See 'COYOTE,' Page 6A

Hondurans Given Aid In Flight
Cleric a Conduit In Underground

By TOM COAKLEY
Denver Post Staff Writer

While other Americans were voting last Tuesday, Brother Marshall Gourley risked arrest by aiding two illegal aliens in their underground journey across the United States.

Gourley, a deacon at Our Lady of Guadalupe Church, 1209 W. 36th Ave., took two fugitive Hondurans — a young man and woman — for pepperoni pizza in north Denver Monday night. He let them spend the night at the Guadalupe parish house and then made sure they had transportation Tuesday to Lincoln, Neb., the next stop on their journey to Chicago.

Through those actions, Gourley briefly joined a group of Christians in several Western states, whose common interest is keeping fugitive Central American nationals in the United States from being sent back to homes where they believe violence awaits them.

Some see their effort as "active resistance" to the United States'

Please See HONDURANS on 4-A

Gourley says his activities will tell

I.3 (above)
1982 Rocky Mountain News headline details sanctuary's mobile strategy.

I.4 (above, right)
1984 Arizona Daily Star profile of Quaker coyote Jim Corbett.

I.5 (right)
1982 Denver Post article describes activist clergy as a "conduit," giving aid to migrants "in flight."

those still in their homelands."[69] And though Fife likens priests and pastors to an intelligence system, Central Americans embraced fugitivity—often refusing to be seen, counted, administered. When they spoke to the press and offered *testimonios*, they typically appeared masked to avoid detection and some even changed their appearance by using makeup or cutting and coloring their hair. Their patterned bandanas and dark sunglasses were fugitive maneuvers even if and when they appeared in public. Migrants used pseudonyms or chose to remain anonymous to prevent harm to loved ones in their home countries. They entered the underground to escape capture and fled sanctuaries when they were no longer considered safe.

○

Though they no longer use the word "sanctuary" to describe their work, Fife tells me that he, Margo Cowan, and other leaders of the 1980s movement returned to the concept of civil initiative when establishing humanitarian aid groups such as the Tucson Samaritans and No More Deaths in the early 2000s. During the George W. Bush administration, activists across the country invoked sanctuary in response to increased workplace raids and deportations. This New Sanctuary Movement (NSM) was catalyzed by Elvira Arellano's flights into and out of sanctuary in Chicago. In 2002, Arellano was arrested for using a false Social Security number at O'Hare International Airport, where she worked cleaning the passenger cabins of commercial planes. Arellano's arrest was part of Operation Tarmac, a post-9/11 series of raids of airport employees and part of a broader escalation of the US security state. Four years later, in defiance of an order of deportation, Arellano and her eight-year-old son fled to Adalberto United Methodist Church in Chicago's Humboldt Park neighborhood. The two received sanctuary at the church for a year, where Arellano credits the Puerto Rican community with protecting her and practicing care as solidarity.[70] She was deported in 2007, after she fled sanctuary to participate in protests for migrant justice in Washington, DC, and Los Angeles. After she was deported, Arellano cofounded Movimiento Migrante Mesoamericano, a network of activists and organizations that works to defend and shelter migrants crossing through and into Mexico and that organizes caravans of mothers of disappeared migrants. Arellano did not merely receive sanctuary while living in a church. Rather, she practiced sanctuary across borders—understanding that, while in transit, migrants are subject to extortion, detention, disappearance, and other forms of violence. She understood sanctuary as a form of collective action, a set of practices to collaborate with people on the run.

The NSM housed migrants at risk of deportation in places of worship, often for years at a time. Activists transformed religious spaces into living quarters, offered legal assistance to migrant families, and hosted press conferences to make public the violences of deportation. The Bush-era movement differed from 1980s sanctuary in its focus on defending long-term US residents more so than newly arrived "refugees." Rather than highlighting state terror in Central America, migrants involved in the NSM focused on the trauma of living in the shadows, lacking a driver's license, and fearing deportation.[71] Unlike the Sanctuary Movement of the 1980s, which encouraged migrants to share *testimonios* as a way of denouncing US foreign policy, the NSM uplifted migrant narratives that sought inclusion in the nation state. Marta Caminero-Santangelo explains that these stories often emphasized family separation and family values.[72] Through storytelling, the NSM sought to convince Americans, specifically white evangelical Christians, to defend undocumented families. Yet, to paraphrase Karma Chávez, the use of storytelling and selective support of deserving, law-abiding migrants often curtailed a critique of the conditions that create "illegality" in the first place.[73] These stories all too often sought inclusion in the state by making appeals to heteronormativity, capitalist productivity, and Christian devotion. They became cleansing rituals of sorts, in which unauthorized migrants who defied the taboo sought to reenter the profane.

Earlier, I described how, in the wake of Trump's election, organizers called for sanctuary everywhere—including restaurants, cities, hospitals, universities, homes, and hotels. Expanded sanctuary affirms a coalitional politics that collaborates with those most targeted by the new administration—especially Black, Indigenous, queer, and migrant communities. Chávez proposes a "queer politics of fugitivity," arguing that sanctuary's ambiguity opens worlds of possibilities. Given that there is no legal definition or precedent for this practice, Chávez embraces being outside of the law or "colluding with the criminalized."[74] A. Naomi Paik's work likewise challenges the liberal frameworks of sanctuary movements that selectively defend the "law-abiding, hard-working, gainfully employed, and normatively reproductive contributors to the economy."[75] Her vision of an "abolitionist sanctuary" dismantles and defunds policing in the present while also imagining and creating otherwise futures. Chávez's and Paik's understandings of sanctuary—as fugitive and abolitionist—shape my thinking around the sacred. Abolition, in the end, is unsatisfied with the routine and the ordinary, seeking escape routes out of the profane's prohibitions.[76]

Alison Harrington, the pastor of Southside Presbyterian Church since 2009, seems to agree with Chávez's call for a sanctuary outside the law. While conducting fieldwork, I meet with the pastor to discuss civil initiative in the 1980s and where the movement stands now. She reiterates Fife's point that sanctuary did not start in North American churches, but rather emerged in El Salvador and in homes across Mexico, along migrant routes. For Harrington, sanctuary is a practice of survival nurtured by people facing state violence and oppression. She says sanctuary comes alive in nightclubs like Pulse, through initiatives like the Black Panthers' breakfast programs and community defense tactics. She mentions Marisa Franco, a cofounder of Mijente—an abolitionist network of Latinx and Chicanx organizers—who defines sanctuary as a "ring of fire" around people and social movements. The ring of fire is hot, fraught with danger. It protects while also setting sanctuary apart.

In Harrington's office, I admire a screen print that reimagines a mugshot of Martin Luther King Jr. as a Byzantine icon and another of the Virgin of Guadalupe clandestinely crossing the border. Noticing these odes to transgression, I ask about the legality of this tradition. Harrington answers that sanctuary has a "conversion effect." By practicing sanctuary, "people are converted to the true gospel of Christ, which allows you to follow a higher authority than a law." She continues: "When we first started doing this work in 2014, we always questioned, is this against the law or not? I used to say no. Some of my colleagues, older white pastors, were concerned about losing their tax status." Harrington remembers one who stunned the room when he blurted out, "Screw our tax status! That's a holdover from Constantine and a merger between Christianity and empire. Who cares about that?" Harrington's understanding of sanctuary shifted when Trump was elected. "As we neared his inauguration, I was like, yeah, it's against the law. We are harboring. We are hiding people. And the closer the church can move out of a legal framework into a framework of illegality, the closer we are to our undocumented brothers and sisters. We need to be a church of illegality."

○

Like many other young migrants, I learned I was illegal when I was a teenager. I remember the morning my parents sat me down at the coffee shop inside our local Barnes and Noble and gently explained that I was ineligible for a driver's permit because I did not have a Social Security number. We had overstayed our tourist visa in the United States and not only could I not drive, I also could not work legally; I was ineligible for financial aid to attend college, and—except for my youngest sister, who was born in this country—my entire family was subject to deportation. I was clutching a copy of Paulo Coelho's *The Alchemist* as my world came crashing down. "There is only one thing that makes a dream impossible to achieve," Coelho writes toward the end of the novel, "the fear of failure."[77] I told myself that Coelho must have never met an undocumented person before.

I am part of a generation who called ourselves DREAMers and came of age before Obama authorized the policy of Deferred Action for Childhood Arrivals. My generation organized politically as young people who loved this country, who had earned citizenship through our diligence and decency. DREAMers staged mock graduations in congressional buildings— donning caps and gowns in front of politicians whose inaction kept us from pursuing our dreams—and campaigned for legislative reform. I was convinced we could redeem this country if only we were given the chance. In December 2010, I watched as the Development, Relief, and Education for Alien Minors (DREAM) Act died in the Senate, five votes short of the sixty it needed to become law. I was eighteen and had recently enrolled at a women's college only a few miles from my parents' house. All I wanted was to contribute to the country I called home. How could lawmakers not understand? I was a hard worker and high achiever. I was not responsible for my parents' mistakes. I did not choose to migrate to the United States, but it was the only home I knew. Argentina existed only in the past, the way a deceased grandmother or great uncle exists, through the stories others tell.

What I did not understand at the time was that the DREAM Act not only excluded my parents, but that it also advocated for "the best and brightest" while leaving behind most undocumented people. The DREAM Act applied only to youth who attended college or joined the military for two years. Those of us eligible for conditional status had to have immigrated to the United States before the age of sixteen, be under the age of thirty, have lived in the country for five consecutive years, and have passed a criminal background test. Had it become law, we could have lost our status if we received a dishonorable or other than honorable discharge from the military or if we became a "public charge"—meaning if we became dependent on the government for financial support. To put it simply, the DREAM Act promoted what Tania Unzueta Carrasco and Hilda Seif describe as "racialized, gendered and class-bound ideas of the 'good citizen.'"[78] The DREAM Act recruited young undocumented people like me to reinforce American exceptionalism, to redeem the nation-state. We unwittingly (some, strategically) reproduced narratives that paint America as a nation built by migrants, one always made better—more diverse, inclusive, and fair—by entrepreneurial and exceptional people. As Walter Nicholls writes in his book on undocumented youth activism, "Rather than being a foreign threat to the country, these immigrants were presented as the exact opposite: extensions of the country's core historical values and a force of national reinvigoration."[79]

Unzueta Carrasco and Seif suggest that, for many undocumented organizers, the DREAM Act's failure "freed us to more publicly challenge the nation state and its definitions of citizenship and deportability."[80] They explain that, after 2010, organizers in Chicago felt more emboldened to challenge "middle class frames of morality, higher education, meritocracy, and individual success."[81] They began to take up deportation defense campaigns for people who would have been ineligible for relief under the DREAM Act, including proposing abolitionist alternatives to detention and deportation for a young person with multiple driving under the influence (DUI) charges and who lacked a high school diploma. They held more public deportation defense actions, challenging the United States to disappear community members in the open. And they refused to participate in the criminalization of their parents, to continue rehearsing narratives that excluded their family members. Unzueta Carrasco went on to cofound Mijente. Having been refused the DREAM Act, she and other organizers began to call "into question citizenship, as recognized by the state, as the determining factor for whether a person has a right to live, work and participate in the nation-state."[82] Being denied the everyday, organizers imagined futures beyond inclusion. Living in the shadows, they saw what was invisibilized in the routine.

At home working on this chapter, I know I am able to write this book because, twenty-one years after landing in Miami, my family became United States citizens. I was able to enroll in graduate school, gain lawful employment at a university, and receive grant funding to conduct research. But citizenship—not having it, the process of attaining it—has caused enduring harm to me and my loved ones. Years of undocumented living haunt our present; I can see the ways my parents still shudder when they see a police vehicle, how they avoid airports, how they continue to bear the weight of the debt they incurred to pay our legal fees. After his naturalization ceremony, my dad cried. He regretted betraying his ancestors, abandoning his dead. He lamented what he had to give up to become incorporated into the everyday. We are always between worlds, the sacred and the profane incompatible and at odds with each other but occasionally, inevitably, coming into contact.

○

The morning after the 2016 election, I attended a gathering of faculty and staff committed to defending undocumented members of our campus. I arrived early enough to find a seat but, within twenty minutes, the classroom was packed with people standing shoulder to shoulder, sitting cross-legged on the hardwood floor, with others overflowing into the hallway. We had two months to prepare for a presidency that had promised to target migrants—especially those who were Muslim, Latin American, "bad hombres." Professors ripped pieces of paper from their spiral notebooks and distributed sign-up sheets to form working groups: one on mutual aid, another on education, and a third on direct action. Angela Stuesse—an activist anthropologist—proposed the word "sanctuary" to describe the solidarity practices we were envisioning and outlining on the whiteboard. That classroom is where I first became curious about these "expanded" understandings of sanctuary.

I could point to that moment as the birth of this book. But there are other origin stories or creation myths for my project, including July 2015, when I first traveled to Tucson and learned about the congregation's insurgent tradition of sanctuary. This project also began on May 1, 2006, when I participated in A Day without Immigrants. Instead of attending school, I joined a community forum at church where we collectively imagined how to defend each other in the absence of immigration reform legislation. Ultimately, this book was also set in motion on December 30, 1998, when, as anthropologists have done since Bronislaw Malinowski, my family left home and immersed ourselves in a distant culture, when we said goodbye to Buenos Aires and remade our lives in Tobaccoville, North Carolina. In the end, what are migrants, if not ethnographers, learning to live in an unfamiliar place and studying its rituals and routines—not only to survive, but to transform the everyday?

I spent several months in 2019 and 2020 conducting participant observation in the Sonoran Desert. When stay-at-home orders were implemented during the COVID-19 pandemic, I returned to North Carolina and continued to conduct interviews online, practicing what Gökçe Günel, Saiba Varma, and Chika Watanabe call patchwork ethnography.[83] I have since returned for weeks or months at a time in 2021 and 2022. During those years, I carried my notebook everywhere—to my citizenship interview, biometrics appointments, and even my naturalization ceremony. Mine is a mobile methodology. I follow Wendy Vogt's proposal for an "anthropology of transit," which highlights the tensions between "the transience of our interlocutors and the ethnographic authority attached to 'being there' in the field." Vogt provocatively asks, "Where, exactly, is 'there' when we are talking about such fluid, transient populations?"[84] Like Vogt, my field sites are mobile and temporary. Migrants are not fixed in place, and neither is my project.

My writing is a practice in the kinds of waywardness and errantry I observed in the field, and I am intentionally on the move on the page, meandering between (auto)ethnographic, historical, and theoretical scenes. This style is inspired in part by Kate Zambreno's novel *Drifts*, which is written in fragments and lacks a conclusive end. "The publishing people told me that I was writing a novel," Zambreno observes at the beginning of the book, "but I was unsure. What I didn't tell them is that what I longed to write was a small book of wanderings."[85] My own book of wanderings does not arrive at conclusions or syntheses, because the fugitive sacred does not and cannot arrive. Nor do I settle in one field or discipline; a migrant, I am on the move, most comfortable in *nepantla* or *lugar entre medio*. I often use fragments and vignettes—gesturing to moments of transgression, interruptions of the everyday. Unlike social movement scholars, I do not track sanctuary's outcomes, goals, or long-term political shifts. I am okay with the interruptions. Indeed, I prefer them.

Sanctuary Everywhere takes place in the Sonoran Desert not because the southern border is the only site of enforcement; I agree with Gilberto Rosas that the "borderlands condition" has "thickened" or migrated across the hemisphere, especially in the wake of the War on Terror following September 11, 2001.[86] Jonathan Inda and Julie Dowling also refer to the border as a "mobile technology," pointing to the regulation of movement across the interior of the United States.[87] Rather, I turn to the Sonoran Desert because of its sonorous histories of flight and fugitivity. Mobility controls in the borderlands have not and do not merely police Latin American migrants. Rather, as Harsha Walia teaches, the southern border has been shaped by the "entanglements of war and expansion into Mexico, frontier fascism and Indigenous genocide, enslavement and control of Black people and the racialized exclusion and expulsion of those deemed undesirable."[88] Though not analogous, the criminalization of migration "has been inescapably structured through" the transatlantic slave trade and anti-Black mobility controls. For instance, Walia explains that, after the annexation of Texas, slave owners in the state organized militias to prevent Black people from crossing into Mexico and to capture those who had successfully fled.[89] There is a different kind of agency in Latin American migrant experiences, however, and I agree with Dionne Brand that "migrations suggest intentions or purposes. Some choice and, if not choice, decisions. And if not decisions, options, all be they difficult."[90]

I am in conversation with Black and Indigenous studies—not to analogize the migrant experience, but to critically examine ongoing histories of flight in the borderlands. Felicity Amaya Schaeffer writes about *vigias*, or watchtowers, used by the Spanish in the southern borderlands to monitor the movements of Indigenous people and argues that the "Indian savage" is the "original threat justifying militarized approaches to border security."[91] Some of the earliest immigration patrols in the desert were formed to detain Asian migrants during the era of Chinese exclusion. As Brandon Shimoda observes, after Franklin D. Roosevelt signed Executive Order 9066 in 1942, southern Arizona became an "exclusion zone" for Japanese Americans. The state housed at least seven internment sites, two of them occupying the Colorado River and Gila River Indian Reservations—both of whom resisted construction on their lands, uninterested in participating in mass incarceration and militarization.[92] Today, Black and Indigenous migrants are disproportionately targeted by immigration policing, detention, and deportation. By dwelling in these ongoing histories, I attempt what Édouard Glissant calls a poetics of Relation—a refusal of roots and rootedness and instead a search for the other, a "modern form of the sacred."[93]

My project follows an emergent tradition of "fugitive anthropology" that refuses anthropology's—more specifically, activist anthropology's— privileging of "masculine domains of the political—aligning oneself with a formal organization, political party, or ideology more broadly."[94] Like the coauthors of the article "Toward a Fugitive Anthropology," I consider practices that escape institutionalization and policy. In chapter 2, I study touch inside detention centers. The last chapter is a meditation on the dead, who stir us to action though they are not recognized as political actors or as organized in struggle. Like these authors, I could not easily enter and exit the field. Noting that their own fieldwork has been shaped by their sexualized, gendered, and racialized bodies, the coauthors insist "the field" is never fully separate from "home." These distinctions are muddled by their political commitments, ancestral histories, and diasporic connections.

This is certainly true for me, as a migrant who lived undocumented in this country for almost two decades, Though, I agree with Kirin Narayan's complication of the outsider/insider binary. Narayan proposes that rather than trying to sort out who is authentically a "native anthropologist," it may be more generative to examine all our commitments, entanglements, and privileges in relation to our collaborators.[95]

Fugitive anthropologists critique the trope of ethnographers as martyrs and rethink activist anthropology's endorsement of "lone acts of bravery" that put collaborators at ease at the expense of the woman of color anthropologist's well-being.[96] For the many years I conducted research as a noncitizen, I was hyperaware of my deportability. There were moments in "the field" when I had to walk away from a scene or practice of sanctuary. For part of the time I lived in Arizona, Scott Warren was on trial and facing twenty years in prison on two counts of harboring migrants for offering food, water, and clothing to border crossers. I knew that a conviction for me would mean deportation. In my field notes, I often question if I am a failure for not engaging in certain activities that could lead to my arrest and deportation. At those moments, I describe feeling "like a fraud—for prioritizing my own safety, for being unable or unwilling to engage in the sanctuary practices that I celebrate in my work. And then I remember my dad's words, that I am no one's hero, and my advisor's reminder—that the trope of anthropologist as savior is tied up in a long history of colonialism." In the following pages, I am not fearless nor am I brave. I am not always willing to lay my body on the line.[97] I often come undone in this work. I frequently fail. Neither I nor my collaborators are martyrs or heroes.

In these pages, I attempt to document the entanglements, itineraries, intimacies, and aspirations of people on the move. I wanted to document with care, refusing to replicate images of violence and brutality, using pseudonyms for people and places—unless my collaborator explicitly asked me to name them in the manuscript. Sarah Horton similarly suggests that ethnographic writing "demands care in deciding which parts of the story to divulge to which audiences and how to package potentially controversial material. It also requires care to ensure that research participants are appropriately represented as complex, sympathetic characters rather than as one-dimensional victims of suffering."[98] This book is not mostly, or even largely, about the violences facing migrants on their journeys. Even when militarization and enforcement are foregrounded, I trace the fugitive sacred that creates alternative worlds in the present.

Leslie Jamison writes about her fears of betraying her interlocutors and notes the limits of the essay form. In her collection *Make It Scream, Make It Burn*, she laments that "representing people always involves reducing them, and calling a project 'done' involves making an uneasy truce with that reduction. But some part of me rails against that compression. Some part of me wants to keep saying, *there's more, there's more, there's more*."[99] I am hesitant to call this project done, because every day I read the news or check my inbox and there are more immigration restrictions, more demonstrations against border militarization, and more escape routes around these controls. My project is mobile, and it wants to keep running. Writing this introduction involves making a truce with this reduction. Sanctuary exceeds this page. There are words I wanted to write and others I could not write. There are times I paused the voice recorder or left my notebook in the glove box of my car. There are experiences I avoid narrating and practices I refuse to detail. Dionne Brand might call these my left-hand pages.[100] This is all to say that, behind the sentence, there is a world I am withholding. *There's more, there's more, there's more.*

o

Chapter 1, "The Desert: Vanishing Time and Sacred Landscapes," imagines how the Sonoran Desert meanders in ways that defy and unsettle PTD, a 1994 strategy that militarized urban entry points and rerouted migrants to less accessible areas. While recent scholarship has identified land as an accomplice in enforcement, I argue that the desert is fugitive—refusing efforts to control and contain its sacred forces. This chapter draws on humanitarian water drops and interviews with Tohono O'odham and Hia-Ced O'odham land defenders to think about the desert as sacred, at odds with the profane's taboos: metal beams, roadside checkpoints, surveillance technologies. I show how the desert, both positive and negative sacred, exceeds state attempts to turn its forces to utilitarian, profane ends. Rather, it poses a perpetual problem to efforts to seal or secure the border. It is too much—one of the lushest deserts in North America—and is inhabited by more-than-human beings that cannot be entirely policed. They offer escape routes and hidden passages, which human beings navigate through fugitive methods.

Chapter 2, "The Detained: Contraband Touch in the Carceral Borderlands," considers how incarcerated migrants pursue what Bataille calls a "lost intimacy" despite prohibitions on contact. Through conversations with a Venezuelan couple detained in neighboring detention centers in Arizona,

I show how contraband touch circulates among the smuggled—a concept inspired by Fred Moten and Stefano Harney's shipped. In these pages, I focus on the fugitive sacred as forbidden, prohibited from contacting the profane because of its contagion and restlessness. Inside the prison, touch is excessive. There are rules that limit how those from "outside" can embrace those "inside" the prison. Upon entry, a metal detector scans visitors and guards pat down bodies, disciplining with a coercive touch. Touch is outright banned between those inside the prison—a contraband intimacy that has the potential to inspire disruption and rebellion. Through interviews with Eva Contreras, I trace the fugitive sacred and its restless, rebellious desire to spread.

Chapter 3, "The Deported: Lines of Flight through Nogales, Sonora" studies sanctuary in the wake of deportation. While most sanctuary campaigns focus on preventing deportation, this chapter travels across the southern border with Panchito Olachea, who was deported from the United States and now operates a mobile clinic in Nogales, Mexico, treating migrants and other residents of the border town. In this chapter, I trace Panchito's many conversions and becomings—arguing that the sacred threatens the profane world of things in its impulse for rupture and change. Panchito says he arrived in Nogales drunk and barefoot. He slept among the dead, making home in a cemetery. I follow his life in this *lugar entre medio*, or *nepantla*. I argue that the fugitive sacred is most comfortable here—in the in-between, not interested in settling down in any single place.

Chapter 4, "The Dead: Scenes of Disturbance and Disarticulation," highlights the mobilities of the migrant dead in the Sonoran Desert and how their fugitive movements prompt us to practice sanctuary as ongoing "wake work," to summon Christina Sharpe. Through fieldwork with Álvaro Enciso—a cultural anthropologist and artist who makes and plants crosses for the migrant dead—this chapter highlights the tensions between the urge of the living to lay the dead to rest and the urge of the dead to resist closure. Largely unidentified and anonymous, spread out over miles on the desert floor, the crowd of the dead is restless and unruly. In their haunting, they prompt us to deal with the ongoing and unending nature of violence in the borderlands and unfinished losses in our personal lives. They escape forensic care and humanitarian desires for closure, suggesting that sanctuary is not an arrival nor a destination. Álvaro himself nurtures this haunting, returning every Tuesday with a shovel and cross in hand. In his words, *"así los chingo."*

A note on language: Throughout this book, I use "Latinx"—a more expansive term that resists the gender binary implicit in Latino/a—to refer to people of Latin American descent. I also use "migrant" to describe people who cross national borders. I do not differentiate between refugees, asylum seekers, immigrants, or migrants. In doing so, I reject hierarchies created to determine who is worthy of migrating and whose entrance is deemed legitimate. I also rarely translate fieldwork material into English. There are select moments when I offer English-language readers excerpts from the Spanish-language material. This is an intentional meandering maneuver, in which I echo migrants' fugitive flights. Anthropologists have compared the ethnographic task to translation and, in these pages, I am translating scenes that often did not take place in English. I am inviting the reader into a world that is not immediately available or accessible. Sometimes, I translate select words to emphasize affect or tone. Other times, I intervene with clarifications or clues. All translations are my own. And though I used to avoid italicizing text in Spanish because I felt the italics othered my first language, I have chosen to employ italics here. This is a poetic and aesthetic choice. Italics make words appear mobile, almost as if they are blowing in the wind, slanted and crooked, running toward an exit. In my eyes, the italics are fugitive. Migrants are on the run in the borderlands, and so are their words on these pages. *Adelante.*

Chapter One

The Desert

Vanishing Time and Sacred Landscapes

If we only track the purview of power's destruction and death force, we are forever analytically imprisoned to reproducing a totalizing viewpoint that ignores life that is unbridled and finds forms of resisting and living alternatively.

—MACARENA GÓMEZ-BARRIS

My arms are raw from brushing through thickets of mesquite to participate in a ceremony for a migrant who died at Ironwood Forest National Monument. Tucson Samaritans volunteers and I hike about a mile to the site of death, carefully weaving through rows of ocotillo. Pastel pink flowers erupt from a pincushion cactus. The yellow plumes of palo verdes bloom even as the heat index soars. I notice a rufous-winged sparrow perched atop a saguaro, calling my attention to white flowers adorning the cactus's crown. Álvaro Enciso—an artist who makes crosses to honor migrants killed during the crossing—encourages me to taste the saguaro's fruit. He picks one up from the desert floor and uses a pocketknife to cut open its husk. I cup the crimson fruit and its pulp stains my fingers almost as if I am gripping a human heart: fleshy, bloody, oozing.

According to the Tohono O'odham—a Native people whose lands extend over what is today the US state of Arizona and the northern Mexican state of Sonora—the first saguaro, or *Ha:sañ*, appeared when a child abandoned by their mother sank deep into the ground and re-emerged as a towering cactus, arms stretched toward the heavens. Tohono O'odham translates to Desert People; saguaros are active participants in the community's ceremonial life. With the help of *k'uipud*, tall poles made of cactus ribs, O'odham harvest saguaro fruit, or *bahidaj*, to make wine to usher in the monsoon season. In a short documentary, Tanisha Tucker—whose ancestors harvested *bahidaj* for generations—specifies that she never collects fruit from every ripe saguaro.[1] "We take as much as we need and give as much back to them," she elaborates as the camera pans to her hands resting a pod next to the saguaro from which it emerged. She thanks the creator for rainfall that bears the fruit, for land that makes life possible.

Seth Schermerhorn points out that saguaros, along with various more-than-human participants in desert life, including coyotes and oceans, are classified alongside saints and devils. These *hemajkam*—meaning "people" or "spirits"—can protect or attack humans depending on a person's righteousness.[2] They are both positive and negative sacred or, to use Gloria Anzaldúa's language, both light and dark, inhabiting upperworlds and underworlds.[3] *Hemajkam* are benevolent and vengeful. They simultaneously fascinate and terrify, inspire awe and repulsion. Devotional rituals—harvesting the saguaro, making "rain magic" by drinking alcohol from the *bahidaj*—sustain sacred relations.[4] Reciprocity and care are crucial when engaging with the sacred, and *hemajkam* can destroy those who disrespect them. Take I'itoi, for instance. Elder Brother, who lives at the base of Baboquivari Mountain, is often described as "very kind. He *is* goodness."[5] Yet the man in the maze is also known as an angry and spiteful deity. A collection of O'odham oral histories observes "the Great Spirit—Ee'-e-toy—can be very terrible, too, when it is necessary for the good of his people."[6]

Álvaro strikes the ground with his shovel, in his words "desecrating sacred land" to mark the site where an unidentified migrant's remains were found that January. All at once, the more experienced volunteers begin searching for stones to place around the cross's foundation—larger ones first for stability, then smaller ones to fill in the cracks. The rest of us follow suit, combing the craggy ground. I quickly become distracted, imagining what this migrant saw in their final moments: the lavender silhouettes of the Silver Bell Mountains, the reedy eyes of a distant surveillance tower, the belly of a Border Patrol helicopter flying overhead. Suddenly, a burning sensation grips my ankles and calves. I look down and shriek as a swarm of fire ants travel up my legs, leaving behind bright red welts. Alicia, a volunteer with whom I bonded over our home state of North Carolina, rushes to my aid as I frantically shake my legs. She offers me ice packs and topical creams to relieve the pain. But Alicia scolds me, saying I could have avoided this by wearing long pants. Álvaro laughs when he sees me and

insists I have to include this experience in my book. "Being vulnerable will make you more relatable," he playfully suggests, "and there's a lesson here. The desert can turn on you *in an instant.*"

When I return to the cross, I notice the team of journalists on today's trip setting up to interview Álvaro. One unpacks his drone to capture aerial shots, while the others unfold a collapsible reflector and test a shotgun microphone. When they point their cameras at Álvaro, he instinctively delivers a speech he's rehearsed many times before: "Look around—the Sonoran Desert is beautiful. But it's a cemetery, full of red dots where bodies were found." He explains that Prevention through Deterrence (PTD) has led to an unimaginable loss of life, with over ten thousand migrants estimated to have died as a result of dehydration, hyperthermia, heat stroke, and injuries sustained during the crossing. "That's why I'm here, pointing fingers at the people and policies responsible for these deaths." Indeed, since 1994, PTD has produced a surge of enforcement agents and surveillance infrastructure—night-vision goggles, surveillance towers, motion sensors, facial recognition software, and stadium lighting—along urban crossing points to intimidate and discourage migrants from traveling through these more populated areas.[7] The Border Patrol's "Strategic Plan" from 1994 details how PTD redirects migration to desert lands that the agency describes as "hostile terrain," where migrants "find themselves in mortal danger."[8] Álvaro references this history repeatedly. He says that the United States is weaponizing the land, turning this "beautiful" desert into a graveyard. Humanitarian groups like the Tucson Samaritans similarly point to 1994 as a turning point in border enforcement. They were founded a few years after PTD took effect, and their training sessions for new volunteers go into detail about its consequences.[9]

While recognizing that the "absolute sealing of the border is unrealistic," the 1994 Border Patrol report claims strategists "found legitimate reason to believe that the border can be brought *under control*."[10] In this chapter, I draw on interviews with Tohono O'odham and Hia-Ced O'odham land defenders as well as fieldwork in the Sonoran Desert with humanitarians. I study these efforts to "seal" and "control" the borderlands, proposing that PTD and other forms of border militarization are ways the profane attempts to control and toolify the fugitive sacred. Militarization aims to contain and capture the desert, to seal off the sacred and its unruly forces. Yet, despite the best efforts of state agents, *coyotes*, and even migrants and activists, the desert cannot be possessed. The Sonoran Desert practices what Leanne Betasamosake Simpson terms "generative refusal," endlessly exceeding settler colonialism's capture and prohibitions on mobility.[11] Land is positive and negative sacred, light and dark—it nurtures and destroys, provokes wonder and terror. In these pages, I make a case for the desert's meanders and inconsistencies, for its life-threatening danger and mind-bending beauty—left and right hand sacred endlessly in flux.

○

Days after leaving Arizona because of the COVID-19 pandemic, I schedule a video call with Tristan Reader, a professor in the Department of American Indian Studies at Arizona State University, who was also involved in the 1980s Sanctuary Movement. He shares that, back then, many disagreements between sanctuary activists in Sonora and others in the interior of the country centered on land. "It wasn't insurmountable," he makes clear, "but it was a divide between those people and places away from the border that largely viewed [sanctuary] as a form of political protest against intervention in Central America. And, along the border, it was more of a humanitarian and immediate practice. People away from the border could choose who they wanted to welcome into sanctuary. Those at the border faced a certain pressure of not being able to be selective in those ways."[12] Unlike activists in the interior of the country, those in the borderlands had to decide whether to cross migrants who had been perpetrators of violence. "That kind of spatiality really played a role in terms of how pressing it is to be physically present in these border spaces versus the luxury of being outside of those border spaces." Reader disagrees with my argument that sanctuary is a mobile practice. During our conversation, he cautions me against falling into the trap of delocating sanctuary, which he insists is a "Western" impulse. Land is essential to sanctuary. By land, he is referring to relations and obligations, that is, between humans and other humans, humans and more-than-human animals, more-than-human animals and earth—its soil, grasses, mountains, canyons—between humans and ancestors, between ancestors and earth.

And, indeed, the 1980s movement was only possible because activists entered into relation with land, because they pursued intimacy with the Sonoran Desert. Jim Corbett, the "Quaker coyote" who guided migrants across the desert, wrote a book titled *Goatwalking,* in which he details how his "errantry" shaped the underground railroad. A self-proclaimed Don Quixote figure, Corbett writes of his own experiences living in the "wildlands" of the Sonoran Desert. He insists that his knowledge of trails, water sources, edible plants, and holes in border fences facilitated fugitive crossings. Corbett explains that, during the early stages of the Sanctuary Movement, the group most involved with aiding border crossers was a goat-milking collective. They named themselves Los Cabreros Andantes, or the errant goat herders. Because of their relation with land, Corbett proposes, "few groups could have been better prepared, bonded together, and predisposed than the Cabreros Andantes to help the refugees get through."[13]

Goatwalking—or a commitment to "hiding in the world," a losing hold of productivity—informed Corbett's theological and political commitments. According to him, goatwalking "participate(s) in life rather than living by possession."[14] The Quaker coyote does not romanticize this practice. At times he refers to it as a kind of madness or dangerous transgression. Goatwalking refuses order, possession, and purpose. "The goatwalker wanders, but rarely hikes. Goatwalkers are not trying to conquer intervening space in order to arrive at a destination."[15] For Corbett, goatwalking is a commitment to errantry and relation with land

and its more-than-human beings. For instance, Corbett describes ways of speaking with goats, given that they "tolerate physical differences and allow properly behaved human beings to become fully accepted members of the herd."[16] Corbett enters into the desert, collaborates with desert life, becomes desert.

"Unlike formal religion," he reflects, "errantry is wanderings and openings, uncertainties and beginnings. From the time I turned Quaker, I've never reached a destination. I know nothing of personal salvation."[17] Errantry does not seek arrival or resolution, but rather dwells in those dangerous and unsettling moments of transgressing the profane. He terms this practice of escape the *cimarron*, or maroon, alternative. *Cimarrones* stand opposed to settled life, choosing instead to be "at home in wildlands." It is this commitment to flight that opens *cimarrones* "to insights unknown to peoples who worship owners-masters because they can live only within the man-made world's make-believe boundaries."[18] *Cimarrones* do not seek to tame land. They do not yearn to master more-than-human life.

In the 1980s, as Corbett goatwalked across Sonora and smuggled migrants across the border, the US and Mexican governments were already strategizing to weaponize the desert against migrants.[19] In *Goatwalking*, Corbett describes "the Mexican government's role as a US agent," detailing the construction of militarized checkpoints and prison camps for processing and deporting Central Americans.[20] Yet land has always evaded becoming toolified, or, according to Georges Bataille, made "subordinate to the man who uses it, who can modify it as he pleases, in view of a particular result."[21] Corbett entered into land, yearning to transgress the everyday or "[sally] out beyond a society's established ways."[22] In other words, he longed to escape the profane in favor of a sacred or fugitive intimacy—what Bataille might call immanence, becoming "like water in water."[23] Of course, Corbett is full of contradictions. He aimed to wander, to become lost in land, to refuse mastery. At the same time, he studied maps that showed the location of water, found edible desert plants, taught others how to navigate less accessible paths. He hoped to know land so he could shepherd migrants across the border. Yet, though he had a purpose and a intended result, he entered into relation with land to facilitate fugitivity, not to protect the profane.

Corbett called for entering into errantry or "go[ing] feral."[24] Migrants and other activists, too, become desert or go feral to survive their journeys. Their guides call themselves *coyotes* and *polleros*. They move through washes, follow mountains as beacons to reach their destinations, memorize trails and water sources, and intuit when to walk and when to rest. In *Solito*,

Javier Zamora describes his mother's journey across the Sonoran Desert, explaining that she drank water from troughs to survive the crossing. As a child, he imagines his mom "in the shape of a cow, then a horse, then in her giraffe costume, kneeling down, drinking dirty water."[25] He details how she blended or disappeared into the night. He pictures her "dressed in black, running to a tree, then a bush, molding into each shape."[26] It is by escaping into or becoming land that migrants are able to deceive and evade enforcement efforts. L/land, as Max Liboiron teaches, is a set of relations.[27]

I learn the importance of cultivating good relations early on during fieldwork, when my unfamiliarity with the desert causes painful scrapes and sunburns. Time and time again, Samaritans volunteers scold me for lacking hiking gear. A swarm of wasps stalks me during one of my first water drops with the humanitarian aid group. One of them stings my forearm as I bend down to leave a gallon of water next to a mesquite tree. Reaching into the first aid kit for Benadryl to relieve my swelling, a seasoned volunteer reminds me to purchase bug spray before the next trip. The hike is exhausting and I grow even more uncomfortable as jumping cholla latch onto my clothing and spines cut into my flesh. The volunteer jokes that nature could not be any clearer that we are not welcome here. "Everything is designed to hurt us," he insists, though when I remember the *bahidaj* I decide I disagree. I slip and fall twice during a hike at Coronado National Forest, my Adidas sneakers no match for slippery gravel and steep inclines. I struggle to stay hydrated in the sunstruck desert. I am a neophyte.

During my first few weeks of fieldwork, Samaritans volunteer and retired teacher Elisa Hauptman invites me to accompany her to a peace fair in Green Valley, Arizona. There, artist Ana Tierra from a collective called Bridges beyond Borders teaches me how to pronounce the Indigenous names of Argentina and the Américas. *Tawantinsuyu*, she repeats as I fumble over the word that denotes the Incan region where my country of birth is located today. Then, she writes Abya Yala on my brochure, which means "land in full maturity" or "land of vital blood." It is the name that the Kuna people gave to the hemisphere that is now known as the Américas. I purchase one of Ana Tierra's screen prints titled "Our Lady of No Borders," featuring La Virgen de Guadalupe breaking through the border wall, tearing open its steel slats with her bare hands. The artist signs it "Para Barbara. Pacha Mama." Determined to enter into relation with Pachamama, Earth Mother, I read a field guide that describes itself as an "etiquette manual, full of names that you can use to greet the Sonoran Desert, the lushest desert in the world."[28] Little by little, I learn the names of a variety of plants and animals. As months go by, I fall in love with the desert's stately saguaros and find that my writing feels most unrestrained when I'm nestled under their arms. I buy hiking boots and nylon pants. I familiarize myself with the land's ecology and history.[29] I grow in awe of the land's extreme violence and extreme beauty, its left and right hand sacred.

○

Following Bataille, I understand the profane as a world of utilitarian things, of subjects and objects. It aspires to order, stability, and purpose. Humans, he writes, in becoming aware of ourselves as subjects—as those who can use, make, and control things—also become separate from other humans, nonhuman animals, and more-than-human beings. For Bataille, through the development of the tool, humankind loses its immanent relationship to the world. Tools—to be clear—are made to achieve an intended goal. They have a design and utility. Humans also make objects or tools of animals by cooking and eating them. As Bataille notes, "to kill the animal and alter it as one pleases is not merely to change it into a thing that which doubtless was not a thing from the start; it is to define the animal as a thing beforehand."[30] Tools enable humans to imagine more-than-human beings, including land, from the start as "controllable things."[31] At the same time, tools alter humans—removing us from a world of immanence, or continuity.

Bataille situates "all the fascination of the sacred world . . . against the poverty of the profane tool."[32] Alongside Roger Caillois, Bataille founded Le Collège de Sociologie—intent on understanding how the sacred shapes (and interrupts) contemporary life. They called their work sacred sociology. Caillois, too, imagines the sacred as fugitive and on the run, like migrants on desert trails, "always ready to escape, to evaporate like a liquid, to discharge like electricity."[33] Caillois writes about the ambiguity of the sacred, the way it shape-shifts and meanders in unexpected ways—ways that are dangerous to the routine functioning of the profane. He warns humans to be careful and to take necessary precautions when approaching the sacred. The world of the sacred, he writes, is an unstable and forbidden one. "The individual cannot approach it without unleashing forces of which he is not the master and against which his weakness makes him helpless."[34] Caillois suggests that sacred forces cannot be tamed; they cannot even be fully known.

Sacred forces are positive and negative; they inspire reverence and fear, both awe and horror. Recall I'itoi. Elder Brother heals and destroys, *for the good of his people*. Bataille is particularly drawn to the negative sacred—to death, excess, eroticism, sacrifice. Caillois also dwells on what he calls the pure and impure sacred. He borrows from Robert Hertz to explain the right and left hand sacred: "To the former belong the clearness and dryness of day; to the latter, the darkness and dampness of night."[35] Yet these forces are not settled. The pure and impure are reversible—after mourning rituals, for example, the impure corpse becomes "a tutelary spirit, beseeched with awe and reverence.... The remains of the cadaver become relics. Horror is changed to trust."[36] In all cases, the two poles of the sacred are opposed to and at odds with the profane world.

Spanish conquistadors described the Sonoran Desert as *El Camino del Diablo* or *Camino del Muerto*. They saw land as treacherous but also otherworldly, as facilitating passage between the worlds of the living and the dead. The land promised adventure and prosperity, but—to return to Álvaro—it could "turn on you in an instant." The desert is demanding. Thorny plants dig into flesh; snakes and scorpions inject venom that attacks nerve cells, and the beating sun burns those unprepared to meet its gaze. During sandstorms, visibility can fall to near zero. And flash floods are known to turn dry washes into rushing streams of water in only a few minutes—with enough force to knock down saguaros and erode border walls. Luis Alberto Urrea writes of ancient religious texts where "fallen angels were bound in chains and buried beneath a desert known only as Desolation." Of the Sonoran Desert he suggests, "This could be the place."[37]

But the desert is lush and the most biologically diverse in the United States. It is, as Bernard Fontana writes, both relentless and forgiving.[38] The climate ranges from extreme drought to torrential rainfall during the monsoon season. The Arizona Upland is home to saguaros and palo verdes and, in the desert valleys, low shrubs such as creosote bushes stretch for miles. Datura, a bridge to the world of the dead, blossoms in washes while jumping cholla, the traveling plant that clings to human skin, thrives in cactus forests. Mule deer stott across dry flats—desert dancers gliding across the land with a distinctive walk that propels them off the ground. They, along with javelinas (collared peccaries that prefer to travel in packs) and antelope jackrabbits (speedy hoppers that use camouflage to escape predators), have fed and sustained O'odham for generations.[39] They also model ways of moving through and hiding among the desert that can prove life-saving for migrants—being unpinnable and imperceptible, embracing the power of the crowd. Land is dizzying, dangerous, excessive, awe-inspiring, and life-threatening all at once. Fontana proposes, "This desert is many little worlds in one," full of "endless contrasts."[40]

Settlers who arrived in the Sonoran Desert saw the land's radiant energies and aimed to repurpose them for productive ends. Put differently, they longed to transform land into a tool. Fontana observes how Father Eusebio Kino's writings in the seventeenth century celebrate the desert's abundance. Kino—a Jesuit priest who established the first Spanish mission in Sonora—refers to the land as "fertile country," and he effusively describes "plentiful ranches" and "rich and abundant pastures." Fontana compares Kino's writings to those of Moses in the Hebrew Bible, noting the similarities between the former's romanticization of the Sonoran Desert and biblical writings about Canaan: "they were the same: parched, semi desolate regions that could be turned to paradise through the grace of God and the labor of man."[41] In both cases, the desert existed to be tamed by humans, rendered useful and profitable. Or, in other words, profane.

While traveling across the Southwest to mark the border after the 1848 Treaty of Guadalupe Hidalgo, members of the Joint United States and Mexican Boundary Commission wrote about the desert as desolate and unforgiving. Rachel St. John cites John Russell Bartlett's journals of his journey through New Mexico, in which he declares that "as far as the eye can reach stretches one unbroken waste, barren, wild, worthless."[42] Even still, Bartlett and his contemporaries agreed that domesticating the frontier was not only possible but profitable. They conjured the desert as an empty land, but one that could be tamed in service of the nation. From Bartlett to the Border Patrol, state agents have sought to make land a tool, to fix the desert's positive and negative sacred energies in the world of the useful profane. Nation-states employ steel slats, coiled wire, and—further east—giant buoys that double as "floating barriers" to render land orderly and subdued, spiritless.

Yet, then and now, Indigenous flight, armed resistance, and land itself thwarts the attempts of Spaniards, Mexicans, and Americans to control and transform the borderlands. St. John elaborates on this argument, noting that the 1889 International Boundary Commission's objectives were obstructed by "troublesome territory" and Indigenous communities who rejected their sovereignty. Notably, the commission was formed to settle the international boundary after the meandering Río Bravo and Colorado rivers shifted land from one bank to the other.[43] St. John continues: "The problems they confronted would threaten their work and their lives, but perhaps most importantly would prove how little control the United

1.2 Ocotillo in bloom.

States and Mexico actually exercised over the land they had fought so hard to possess."[44]

○

In recent years, scholars have described the Sonoran Desert as a "treacherous geography" or "killing field" and "massive open grave," as a weapon that the US government deploys to deter migration.[45] Jason De León describes the desert as an ecosystem where the sun's rays bleach out memory, where flesh is shredded by beaks, where human remains are scattered and disappeared by the elements. In *The Land of Open Graves*, he argues that "nature has been conscripted by the Border Patrol to act as an enforcer while simultaneously providing this federal agency with plausible deniability regarding blame for any victims the desert may claim."[46] In short, De León insists that the US government strategically rerouted migration to the desert to outsource punishment to "nonhumans who act as agents of deterrence."[47] He borrows from Michel Callon and John Law's theory of the *hybrid collectif* to argue that "nonhuman actants"—javelinas, giant centipedes, bark scorpions, coral snakes, red devil's claw, whitethorn acacia, pincushion cacti, crucifixion thorn, monsoons, flash floods, canyons, hot sand, loose gravel—play a key role in border control. Though he does understand land as a set of relations, De León can only imagine the Sonoran

Desert working in collaboration with the state. His book creates a totalizing narrative of landscape as weapon—sharing with the state a desire to bring the desert into profane existence, to render land useful and rational. *The Land of Open Graves* proposes that, when properly managed and surveilled, land can be counted on to capture fugitives.

In the aforementioned excerpt from *The Land of Open Graves*, De León uses "conscripted" to describe the relationship between the state and Sonoran Desert. He does not return to the word again in the book.[48] To conscript is to recruit someone (or, in this case, land) for military service forcibly or compulsorily. De León's use of the word suggests that land is being drafted against its will, that it might possibly resent or resist state orders. *Conscript* comes from the past-participle stem of the Latin *conscribere*, or "to enroll," and from the assimilated form of *com*, "with, together," and *scribere*, "to write." Writing is, of course, another way of taming or toolifying the desert. Treaties, maps, border markers, and land surveys all aspire to know, claim, and establish limits around more-than-human life. Through writing, nation-states declare ownership over land and intend to make that ownership indisputable. *Scribere* derives from the Proto-Indo-European *skrībh-*, which means "to cut, separate, sift." Land is cut open by the state, targeted and wounded. Enforcement agents cut down saguaros. Bulldozers carve through ancestral burial grounds. Contractors blast mountains to make way for switchback roads. As I see it, for the Border Patrol, the desert is not so much an accomplice as it is an obstacle to enforcement. And so the profane world toolifies and pacifies land, aims to make more-than-human beings compliant. But, even when it is conscripted, land rebels. As state agents labor to transform land into a tool of enforcement, sacred energies continue to create escape routes, which migrants navigate through fugitive methods.

While it is undeniable that PTD is designed to deter and disappear migrants, the Sonoran Desert does not only act as a "killing machine" or a landscape that facilitates death, disappearance, and destruction. To return to Liboiron, "Land is a verb," a set of relations "between the material aspects some people might think of as landscapes—water, soil, air, plants, stars—and histories, spirits, events, kinships, accountabilities, and other people that aren't human."[49] Remember *bahidaj*, for instance. Cottonwoods, too, offer shelter to weary travelers—among them the migrants targeted by PTD. Monsoons are overpowering and abrupt; they can drown people crossing the desert, but they also provide much-needed rain and cloud cover. They can make it nearly impossible for the Border Patrol to operate their vehicles on certain routes, to chase and detain people on the run. Erosion from the torrential rains slows down border wall construction. The Sonoran Desert is fully sacred—ambiguously and ambivalently negative and positive, too much to be possessed or controlled. Liboiron insists, "Land never settles."[50]

Though I focus on Sonora, the Río Bravo presents another fugitive opening. Since 1848, the river has routinely changed course and forced state agents to renegotiate boundary lines. Writing in his 1857 *Report on the United States and Mexican Boundary Survey*, William Emory notes the water's unruly movements: "The [river] does not always run in the same bed; whenever it changes, the boundary must change, and no survey nor anything else can keep it from changing."[51] The most radical shift occurred after a historic flood in 1864, which Nicole Antebi calls the river's "last attempt at wildness."[52] Inspired by Harold Fisk's meander maps of the Mississippi River, Antebi created animations of the Río Bravo's meanders from 1827 through 1960. Her shape-shifting map celebrates the river's restless energies and the movements of more-than-human beings. She shows how land is always in flux. Although the National Park Service celebrates dam construction as "the taming of a once wild river" and the Chamizal Convention of 1963 established guidelines for rechanneling the Río Bravo, the river teaches that the project of maintaining and reinforcing a border remains tenuous and incomplete.[53]

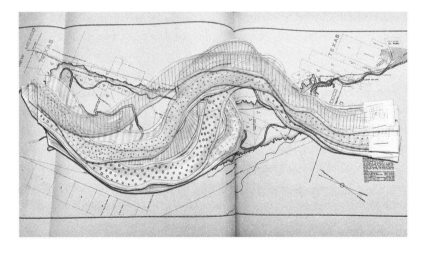

1.3 Nicole Antebi maps the "restless" Río Bravo.

A meander is a bend or curve in a river or stream. After a small interruption creates an initial deviation, the water begins to move at different speeds across the channel. The outer, or undercut, side of the curve moves more quickly and tends to erode the landscape while the slower, inner side deposits sediment collected upstream. As long as water is flowing, though, there is always potential for erosion. The result is a snaking or sinuous pattern that grows more exaggerated over time. Meanders shift in many different ways and they constantly want to expand; they are restlessly energetic. Most rivers meander, though admittedly some more forcefully than others. The term has also been appropriated to mean moving aimlessly without a fixed direction and to be directed in various directions or at multiple objects at once. In the introduction to this book, I noted that my method was a meandering one, and here I extend the term to suggest that meandering is a sacred migration, one that transgresses law and order. Meandering is negative and positive sacred; there is simultaneous erosion and deposition. The land moves and meanders without consideration for authority figures and the state's utilitarian designs. Even the dams that allegedly tamed the wild river have a life span. Concrete wears down. The water will flow again.

I propose meandering as a refusal of lawfulness and stability. To meander is to wander, to become a goatwalker. To meander is to resist being a useful thing, a tool. To meander is to stand in the way of enforcement efforts. To meander is to obstruct the state's plans and projects. It is a refusal of the ordered and orderliness, the settled and settlement. Meandering is a waywardness that is rarely purposeful and never methodical. It is a fugitive escape into the world of errantry. Like the Río Bravo, the Sonoran Desert meanders—interrupting the state's militarized or profane designs.

○

During a visit to Tucson, I meet with Amy Juan of the Tohono O'odham Nation. In a cramped, dimly lit coffee shop, we discuss post-9/11 border enforcement and what she terms "checkpoint trauma"—an awareness of being policed everywhere. I mention that I recently read a profile of her written by Todd Miller where she identified O'odham territory as the "most militarized" in the United States.[54] Though Timothy Dunn traces contemporary border militarization to the Nixon and Reagan administrations and the declaration of the War on Drugs,[55] militarization swelled in the wake of September 11, 2001. Before the attack on the World Trade Center, the Border Patrol employed approximately nine thousand agents. By the end of the Bush administration, the agency had doubled in size.[56] The Border Patrol's ballooning budget made possible the construction of "forward operating bases," where Army and Air National Guard troops are stationed and deployed to apprehend border crossers. With the Real ID Act of 2005 and the Secure Fence Act of 2006, Congress authorized the construction of a virtual wall and granted the Secretary of Homeland Security unprecedented power to "waive in their entirety" dozens of laws seen as an impediment to building a physical wall. This includes the Native American Graves Protection and Repatriation Act, the National Environmental Policy Act, the Endangered Species Act, the Arizona Desert Wilderness Act, and the American Indian Religious Freedom Act. The implication being that land and its multispecies inhabitants—including, and perhaps especially, the dead—pose a problem to state sovereignty. Indigenous ancestral remains, ancient saguaros, endangered Sonoyta mud turtles—all must be tamed and disciplined into submission. That is, made into tools.

In 2006, Customs and Border Protection introduced militarized checkpoints at every exit from the Tohono O'odham Reservation—not only on the US-Mexico border—where O'odham are required to show identification and are subject to interrogation and inspection by armed agents. These checkpoints and other forms of surveillance infrastructure in the desert—specifically integrated fixed towers (IFTs) designed by the Israeli company Elbit Systems and first tested on Palestinians in the West Bank—constitute what Miller calls a "high-tech occupation" on the Tohono O'odham Nation's land. With high-definition cameras, motion sensor systems, and 360-degree ground-penetrating radars, IFTs are designed to catch bodies in motion—Indigenous and migrant alike.[57] Caitlin Blanchfield and Nina Valerie Kolowratnik claim these towers go hand in hand with the construction of detention centers for migrants apprehended at the border. After all, surveillance infrastructure is modeled on carceral logics: Normandy fencing encloses ancestral lands; radio-frequency radars detect movement; communication systems facilitate capture. Blanchfield and Kolowratnik argue, and I agree, that surveillance infrastructure is "a continuation of the settler colonial project that seeks to dominate and control land on registers sensorial, physical, and epistemological."[58] Homeland Security's militarized occupation of O'odham land is designed to undermine the desert and Desert People's mobility. And militarized occupation targets humans and more-than-humans alike. For example, floodlights topping the border wall limit the migration of rare animal species in the area such as javelinas. These collared peccaries have evolved to digest cactus and scatter seeds through their migration. If they cannot travel, they cannot disperse seeds for prickly pears and other cacti, disrupting the migrant and Indigenous food sources these cacti represent. While on a humanitarian water drop near Sasabe, Sonora, I see the ways militarization targets more-than-human beings. Along a dirt road past the area where construction crews blasted Fresno Peak, a lone deer tries repeatedly to find an opening in the border wall. The white-tailed doe sprints up a steep hill, desperate to cross, as a volunteer and I trail behind in our suv. It pauses every time it comes face-to-face with the wall, as if disoriented. About a quarter of a mile later, the deer accepts defeat.

O'odham on both sides of the border report being harassed, intimidated, and assaulted by enforcement agents as they cross the border to visit family, participate in pilgrimages, and gather traditional foods. Testifying before the House Committee on Natural Resources' Subcommittee for Indigenous Peoples of the United States, Chairman Ned Norris Jr. condemns not only the desecration of sacred sites on O'odham lands for border wall construction but also everyday practices of what Gilberto Rosas calls "racialized management." Norris observes that Border Patrol agents routinely detain and deport O'odham members for attempting to travel through their homelands, "engaging in migratory traditions that are an important part of our culture, religion and economy." Norris goes on, declaring that "the border is an artificial barrier to our freedom to traverse our lands."[59] Border Patrol and customs agents have been known to confiscate and prevent tribal members from transporting materials essential to their ceremonial practices—including bird feathers, pine leaves, and sweetgrass. Vehicle barriers keep cattle from grazing or reaching watering holes across the border, and drones monitor rituals intended to remain private. In his remarks, Norris denounces proposals to install ifts on sacred mountains where ancestors and medicine men are buried. Surveillance infrastructure interrupts O'odham ritual practice, which depends on reciprocal, mobile engagements with land.

As I sit with Amy, I ask about practices of care and sanctuary. Before responding, she observes that this perspective is largely absent in public conversations. O'odham "don't really talk about it, to protect each other and to protect the way care works. It's something I rarely talk about, too." Unlike the 1980s Sanctuary Movement, which relied on a politics of visibility to gain public support, contemporary practices are often underground—circulating as whispered gestures, fleeing surveillance infrastructure and smart borders.

Amy explains the importance of sharing food, water, and shelter with others, especially those in need: values that elders pass down to O'odham children at a young age. Despite the criminalization of humanitarian aid and felony charges associated with transporting and harboring border crossers, Amy suggests Desert People continue to practice fugitive care. "I still hear stories. People still like to share with migrants." Her comments are vague for a reason, protecting networks of care that Édouard Glissant teaches should remain opaque or, in other words, sacred.[60] Amy speaks softly, and the growl of the nearby espresso machine sometimes drowns out her sentences. I lean in to catch her words. She pauses when I ask about the criminalization of aid. "It hurts," she finally responds, "because you're raised with these values. Especially in ceremonies and in our traditions. We pray for the whole world. We pray for everybody. We know the world isn't ours." Amy expresses a refusal of borders, a solidarity that transcends checkpoints and surveillance towers. She enunciates a relation to land based on collectivity, not possession.

Amy tells me about an encounter she had with an elder after a ceremonial relay run across the border. "One year, at the end of the run, I was sitting down with a tribal elected official who was helping as a driver, as support. He sat down by me and started crying. He said he hadn't told anyone what happened." Along the way, as the elder drove his truck along back roads, he saw three young women he mistook as O'odham runners. He slammed the brakes as he approached the group, concerned they had strayed from the official route. When he saw them up close, he realized the women were "travelers"—Amy's chosen word for migrants. Their camouflage clothing had been torn apart by cacti and the soles of their shoes were missing. The travelers erupted into tears when they saw him, relieved to see a friendly face who offered them food and drinking water. They had finished the gallons they brought on the journey days before. The women thanked him in Spanish as they crawled into the backseat of his truck, but the elder—aware that he was driving a government vehicle and that O'odham are racially profiled on their own lands—had to turn them away, despite their pleas and tears.

"It broke my heart," Amy confesses as she holds back her own tears, "because it's one thing for young people like me to experience this, but our elders hold on to their values. He didn't say much, but he knew I would understand. [Turning away travelers,] it's not what we're taught. It makes you feel less O'odham, because you're not able to help someone." Border militarization not only polices Indigenous mobility; it also targets *himdag*—the Desert People's ways of life, which Amy translates as Indigenous epistemology or "the way we walk." *Himdag*—the closest word to "religion" in O'odham vocabulary—is marked by an ethic of reciprocity, of living in mutuality with human and more-than-human neighbors. Notably, in Amy's translation, even *himdag* is mobile. It is "the way we walk." Those who remember and preserve *himdag* understand the militarization of the desert as a violation of ancestral values, and Amy notes that when the government held listening sessions regarding IFTs, some of the first to oppose the proposal were elders and healers. "Even without knowing the technology, their first concern was how the towers would affect the pollinators, our plants, the migration patterns of bees, and our medicine." Deserts are not death-dealing machines; borders and their surveillance apparatuses are. Even still, Amy suggests that the Desert People continue to practice sanctuary. "I still hear stories. People still like to share with migrants," she confesses in a hushed tone, as the whistle of milk frothers and the shuffling of feet facilitate her fugitive speech.

○

Days after Donald Trump's inauguration, Verlon José—who, at the time, served as the vice chairman for the Tohono O'odham Nation—went viral on the internet for promising that a wall would only be built on O'odham lands "over [his] dead body." In February 2017, the Tohono O'odham Nation released a video titled "There's No O'odham Word for Wall" in further protest of the proposed border wall.[61] Opening with the image of I'itoi as the man in the maze, representative of life's movements and migrations, the six-minute video asserts that border walls further the violences of the Gadsden Purchase of 1853—which divided Tohono O'odham lands horizontally, splitting the Nation between Mexico and the United States. Jacob Serapo, an O'odham rancher whose water source is in Mexico, wistfully looks away from the camera as he explains how the border wall has disrupted his daily routines. Instead of simply walking into Mexico for water, he has to collect barrels and travel four miles north to fill them for his family's domestic and agricultural use. In the promotional video, Verlon José explains, "We do not own the land, but we care for the land. Every stick and stone is sacred. Every creature is sacred, every creature has a significant part in our way of life."

The vice chairman insists that O'odham foster a relation to land based not on control or ownership, but on care and reciprocity. Yet, although "there is no word for wall," tribal leaders, including José, affirm the need for "smart" border controls, cooperate with the Border Patrol, and provide tribal funds for enforcement. The Nation has also passed a resolution banning outside humanitarian groups from placing water on the reservation. Tiffany Lethabo King might refer to these as the "difficult and agonizing choices [Black and Indigenous people make when it comes] to negotiating and fighting for their existence." She continues, insisting that "'innocence' does not exist within the lifeways of this hemisphere or the modern world. The endeavor of surviving under conditions of conquest is never clean."[62]

In an article for the *Phoenix New Times*, Mike Wilson—a Tohono O'odham member who places water in the desert for migrants—condemns the Nation's cooperation with the Border Patrol. He points out that most migrant deaths take place on O'odham land and criticizes his community for "repeatedly refusing to accept moral responsibility for migrants dying in the desert." Ned Norris responded to the critique by noting that the Nation is cooperating with the Border Patrol to install "eight highly visible beacon towers" that migrants could hypothetically use to signal for help. But Mike Wilson calls that response "hypocritical," denouncing the Nation for banning humanitarian aid groups from accessing their lands while partnering with the Border Patrol to establish "rescue beacons" that double as surveillance towers.[63]

Mike tells me that he first set up water stations along cattle trails in the Baboquivari Valley in 2010, while serving as a lay pastor of a Presbyterian church on the reservation. He was called to do so when he noticed the overwhelming number of migrant deaths south of Ajo Road and near the international border marked on the Humane Borders Migrant Death Map—a "cluster of deaths, like grapes on a bunch stem." "Anyways," he continues, "it didn't take a theologian to look at that map and notice that something was very wrong. People were—and are—ignoring human suffering and death." At first, he would place about three hundred gallons of plastic water jugs along migrant trails. Mike dedicated one day every week to refilling the stations. He walked with a wooden stick outfitted with a string, which he used to attach empty water bottles. "I probably looked crazy," he cackles, "walking with a pole full of dangling water bottles, like a fisherman." Then, like any well-trained pastor, he finds a biblical parallel—"God *did* say, 'I will make you a fisher of man.'"

With the support of Humane Borders, he installed four two-hundred-and-fifty-five-gallon drums of water—one at each "station." At the time, he could not publicly collaborate with the organization because they were banned from entering the reservation. Mike baptized the stations "Matthew, Mark, Luke, and John," a reference to the biblical gospels. Not long after partnering with the organization to install the water drums, Tohono O'odham tribal police began confiscating them, draining them, or piercing them with bullet holes. "I couldn't keep asking for replacement barrels from Humane Borders, so I went back to using plastic jugs," he shares during our conversation. Mike arranged the plastic jugs on the ground, in the same place the barrels used to be—always in the shape of a cross. The slashing and emptying continued. The few times that he did come across police officers and others sabotaging his stations, they would typically ask Mike who authorized him to put water in the desert and to violate the Nation's laws. He would point to the sky and respond, "That's my authority."

○

I reached out to the Nation and went through the formal process of applying to interview members of the Environmental Protection Office, explaining over email and voicemails that I hoped to study O'odham struggles against border wall construction. However, I was turned down with very little explanation offered. Their hesitation to speak to a researcher with no connection to the Nation makes sense, especially given anthropology's complicity in colonialism and ongoing extractive fieldwork practices. When I tell Mike that the Nation refused my request, he faults the Nation's "propaganda machine," sharing that anyone—including himself—who says anything contrary to their messaging "disappears into the abyss." He suggests that it is paternalistic to not critique the Nation, to not call out tribal leaders for their complicity in migrant deaths. He points out that activists are quick to hold the Border Patrol and Homeland Security accountable for migrant deaths. "You condemn them, and yet you don't do the same for Tohono O'odham leaders? Your refusal to criticize is not a neutral position. Silence should not be a comfortable position."

Nations and nation-states aim to transform land into a thing that can be divided, mastered, and used for productive ends. But, as Mike shows with his pole of dangling water bottles, sacred activity violates the everyday, posing a threat to sovereignty and mastery. Despite the Nation's cooperation with the Border Patrol, many O'odham—including Tohono O'odham, or Desert People; Hia-Ced O'odham, or Sand People; and Akimel O'odham, or River People—insist on offering care to migrants, practicing solidarity across borders.

1.4 View of Baboquivari, where I'itoi lives in a cave below the mountain's peak.

According to Nellie Jo David, a Hia-Ced O'odham water and land defender, "Our people have never known borders. We've always treated people that are crossing as our relatives." Born in the 1980s, Nellie Jo tells me she belongs to the last generation that moved freely without the imposition of interior checkpoints, roving patrols, and surveillance infrastructure. After leaving her hometown of Ajo, Arizona, to attend law school in 2011, Nellie Jo returned three years later to fight the construction of checkpoints in her *jewed*, meaning land or earth. "But I came back home, and it's no longer home." Now, she is actively resisting militarization as part of the O'odham Anti-border Collective—a group of Indigenous youth intent on breaking down "borders, states, settlements, mines, dams, extractive and invasive agriculture, bombing ranges, and freeways" occupying unceded O'odham territory. Nellie Jo is convinced that border militarization works "to regulate our people's cross-national citizenship, which is really crazy to think that our people who have been here since time immemorial have such limitations on our own land." Border militarization, she reiterates, works to discipline O'odham into United States citizenship, to sever practices of care between Indigenous communities in Sonora and those migrating from the Global South—whom Edward Brathwaite might refer to as "arrivants."[64]

When I share my frustration with the ways the desert is described by scholars, Nellie Jo tells me she has long wanted to write a piece on Luis Alberto Urrea's *The Devil's Highway*, the bestseller that follows the journey of twenty-six migrants who died crossing this land in 2001. In the book's opening pages, Urrea insists "desert spirits of a dark and mysterious nature have always traveled these trails."[65] Long associated with negative sacred energies, land is depicted as unforgiving and hostile to travelers. Urrea continues by insisting there is nothing "soft" in the desert. To the migrants who died, the "world of spikes and crags was as alien to them as if they'd suddenly awakened on Mars."[66] Urrea only notices negative sacred energies, describing land as dark and capricious. But Nellie Jo continues, "All that land has a Hia-Ced O'odham history. And it wasn't known as deadly. And it wasn't known as hostile prior to settlement. Because we knew the waterholes, we knew all those things. And so it wasn't deadly until the imperialists forced these policies on people. Because, otherwise, we were always willing and able to help folks that were traveling." Unlike Desert People, who are taught from an early age that I'itoi provides for humans and more-than-human neighbors, migrants are almost always unfamiliar with the land's rhythms and movements. Border enforcement sets up migrants in an antagonistic relationship with the desert, and with the O'odham, whose tribal leaders often cooperate with the Border Patrol in order to defend their sacred lands from militarization.[67] States criminalize O'odham ways of life—*himdag*—and these ancestral practices of care that shelter migrants across borders precisely because they pose alternatives to policing and surveillance. And, so, migrants are often locked out of relationships of mutuality with the desert. On the contrary, they are made to fear and mistrust land and its more-than-human inhabitants.[68] Nellie Jo insists this was not always the case and that historically O'odham have aided travelers.

National Park Service officers arrested Nellie Jo in September 2020 when she and Amber Ortega, a fellow Hia-Ced O'odham water and land defender, sat atop construction vehicles used for wall construction and told crew members they were not welcome on sacred lands. The two women forced work to a halt at Quitobaquito Springs—an oasis and sacred site where water flow is reportedly at an all-time low due to extraction for wall construction. Nellie Jo and Amber were strip-searched, shackled, and incarcerated in a private prison without access to a lawyer for twenty-four hours. The two say they risked their lives—and Nellie Jo was forced to take a leave of absence from her doctoral program—"to enact their sacred responsibilities to protect their homelands."[69] As she was being handcuffed, Nellie Jo overheard a park ranger telling the media that she and Amber had no legitimate claim to the land.

Only a short month later, on Indigenous People's Day, the O'odham Anti-border Collective held a direct action at the Border Patrol checkpoint near Lukeville, adjacent to Quitobaquito Springs. They demanded an end to the desecration of O'odham homelands and sacred sites and an end to the harassment, incarceration, and deportation of Indigenous people on Indigenous land. This includes the targeting of both Indigenous O'odham and Indigenous Central Americans increasingly migrating north. They called for an end to sexual and gender-based violence perpetuated by the Border Patrol, and the dismantling of the border wall and surveillance towers terrorizing Indigenous communities. Carrying a banner that read "Borders = Genocide," the group of thirty O'odham (Hia-Ced O'odham, Tohono O'odham, and Akimel O'odham) performed prayers and held a ceremony, blocking traffic in both directions on Highway 85 for over two hours. With their handheld drums and gourd rattles, land and water defenders chanted "Shame on You, Your Ancestors are Looking Down on You" as Pima County sheriffs and state highway troopers wearing riot gear lunged toward the group. The O'odham Anti-border Collective presents alternatives to militarization, and their struggle—informed and inspired by Palestinian liberation movements, taking place in another occupied desert—calls for Indigenous solidarity across borders. So far in this chapter, I have drawn on secondary sources and interviews with O'odham activists to demonstrate the ways state agents attempt to tame the land and its sacred energies, and how O'odham propose alternatives to extraction and militarization. In the next section, I turn to the ways the desert poses a problem for enforcement—its excess an obstacle to policing.

o

"*Mi cuento comienza en la autopista 85, poste 67*," Dora Luz Rodriguez tells me during our drive to Sonoyta, Sonora. From the passenger's seat, I notice the Salvadoran social worker admiring the mountains in the distance, imagining the desperation of migrants journeying for days under the broiling sun. She recognizes herself in their movement. In the summer of 1980 during a historic heat wave, she crossed the desert with a group of twenty-six fellow Salvadorans fleeing civil war. Her companions were mostly students, housewives, and young professionals. "*Sobrevivimos trece y murieron trece. Extraño, ¿no? Los dos números.*" Dora finds it strange that thirteen survived and thirteen died in the desert, that number associated—at least biblically—with the betrayal of Judas (the thirteenth disciple), with evil and lawlessness. Her coppery eyes scan the wide expanses of the desert and she recalls how saguaros take on human qualities at night: "their arms, predators ready to capture you at any moment." Dora points out a vacant gas station where two fellow migrants hid while the rest of the group wandered in the desert. When the couple was found by the Border Patrol, they refused to share the group's whereabouts, worried their confession—like that of the treasonous disciple in the gospels—would lead to their friends' deportations and deaths. Twenty-four hours later they caved. Dora wonders what might have been if the couple had spoken earlier; perhaps some of her companions might still be alive.

Coyotes told Dora's group that it would take about thirty minutes to cross Organ Pipe Cactus National Monument, so most travelers only brought one gallon of water. Some of the women even crossed while wearing their church dresses and high heels. After several days, their guides abandoned the group—claiming they were going to look for help and disappearing altogether. At this point, migrants began to drink their own urine, hand lotion, melted lipstick, and any other liquids they could salvage from their duffel bags. They doused their lips in toothpaste to avoid burns. "*Parecíamos monstruos, porque teníamos todo blanco nuestras bocas.*" The beating sun made the men go mad, and one of them suggested killing the women so they could feast on their blood. Dora survived by hiding under a palo verde, her sanctuary away from the apocalyptic scene unfolding around her. Three sisters who had adopted Dora as a parental figure died shortly before the group was found. As we drive past the milepost that marks the place where her group was "rescued" by the Border Patrol after six days in the desert, Dora tells me—tears staining her eyes—"*Lo triste es, Bárbara, que estábamos a una milla de la calle. Pero el desierto es tan engañoso que todo se ve igual.*" The desert is deceptive, says Dora: a branching maze that leads you in endless circles, where everything looks the same and nothing is an exit. For Dora, rescue also meant detection. Enforcement agents airlifted survivors to hospitals and almost immediately transferred them to the county jail in Tucson, until sanctuary churches paid their bonds. Dora was one of the first Salvadorans supported by the Sanctuary Movement and—soon after being released from detention—she began attending their clandestine meetings. Later, when the movement went public, she transformed her home into a sanctuary for a Guatemalan family. They lived with her for about a year.

Our conversation is repeatedly interrupted. Dora's phone constantly buzzes with phone calls and text messages from Salvadorans seeking aid or solace. Some calls come from migrants in detention centers, others from folks in Mexican migrant shelters. In 2016, Dora founded SalvaVision, an organization that provides material support and legal aid to migrants waiting for asylum at the US-Mexico border, incarcerated in Arizona, and those deported to El Salvador. Dora once told me that aid work is how she heals. After hanging up a call, Dora continues her story: "*En el camino veníamos platicando y riéndonos. José, quien aún vive—tiene ochenta años y está aquí en Tucson—traía su guitarra y cantábamos todo el tiempo con él. Nuestra tragedia empezó cuando nos dejaron tirados. La tragedia no fue cruzando el desierto.*" Dora's story highlights the desert's fugitive refusals; the tree hid Dora from her murderous companion and offered her shelter until her group was found. With guidance and a knowledge of the desert, crossing the territory is not a death sentence. The Salvadoreña social worker stresses that the tragedy was—and continues to be—being abandoned and left to die. She and her group sang and danced along the journey. They laughed and found joy in each other's company: "our tragedy began when they left us stranded." The desert is not a killing field or an accomplice in border control. The desert is both positive and negative sacred, and it refuses state

1.5 Dora Luz Rodriguez describes the desert's deceptions on the way to Organ Pipe Cactus National Monument.

efforts to appropriate its energies for profane, utilitarian purposes. Time and time again, the desert obstructs enforcement efforts. It meanders.

The state and its enforcement agents see the desert as a problem to be managed, Laiken Jordahl tells me. While working as a wilderness fellow at Organ Pipe, Laiken had many conversations with Border Patrol agents. He recounts, "The way that they view the landscape, it's like every cactus or every strand of trees is an obstruction. So life itself is an obstruction, a distraction." To the Border Patrol, the desert is an obstacle to catching migrants. Saguaros stand in the way of walls. Cottonwoods shelter migrants. Creosote bushes are both an antioxidant and anti-inflammatory, useful for treating bites and cuts in the desert. Desert People, too, are an obstacle. They represent alternatives to militarization and enforcement. O'odham solidarities and kinship ties with Indigenous people on the other side threaten the nation-state's sovereignty. Their relationships with land and more-than-human beings disrupt wall construction. Laiken continues: "Border Patrol sees all of life in the desert as a problem. And I think it does serve their interests to actually make the desert a lifeless place."

Laiken mentions that "vanishing time" is a phrase commonly used by enforcement agents to describe the window between the moment a migrant crosses the border and the time they reach a hiding place. For instance, when someone has fled to a brush, *arroyo*, or a safe house, they have escaped into vanishing time. To paraphrase Laiken, the Sonoran Desert—its meandering paths, shape-shifting *arroyos*, treacherous slopes—is an obstruction to policing. It can serve as an accomplice to unauthorized crossings. Here, my thinking departs from scholars like De León. Vanishing time is both a death sentence and a fugitive maneuver. The desert not only eliminates, but also nurtures life. Its positive and negative sacred energies cannot be contained and—despite the obscene amount of money and resources poured into this project by the US and Mexican governments—the desert cannot be possessed, that is, borrowing from Bataille, rendered useful or spiritless: operationalized.

Vanishing time is a fugitive and queer time, which José Esteban Muñoz describes as living within but existing outside the straight present.[70] In *Cruising Utopia: The Then and There of Queer Futurity*, Muñoz describes straight time as the here and now; it is normative and rational—"being ordinary and being married."[71] Queer time is a critique of the present. It is still forming (formless): illegible, unreadable, not able to be caught, caught up to, or captured. Locating queer time in gesture and ephemera—the cool look of a street cruise, the ecstasy of the dance floor—Muñoz teaches that what is queer is hard to catch. Migrants and *coyotes* are likewise hard to catch. They camouflage themselves in the desert and move clandestinely through granite mountains and deep canyons. Land, too, is out of reach and out of grasp. The Sonoran Desert resists by being too much, inhabited by diverse species of mammals, birds, amphibians, reptiles, native fish; it is shaped by wide valleys and mountain ranges and shape-shifting arroyos that overflow with water. It is unpredictable, unsettled. And, so, militarization works to make the land profane, or spiritless.

In the seventeenth and eighteenth centuries, the Great Dismal Swamp sheltered maroon communities, similarly functioning within vanishing time. The vine-entangled swamp remained outside the reaches of colonial surveillance, too much to be managed or controlled. The expansive morass is heavily wooded with cypress, juniper, and water ash, overgrown with honeysuckle and woodbine. It escapes through excess.[72] Similarly, from the late nineteenth century, when the desert harbored Apache fugitives and Chinese border crossers outmaneuvering migration bans, land has exceeded and escaped the will of state agents, *coyotes*, prospectors, surveyors, and narcotraffickers who attempt to tame its sacred energies.

The Sonoran Desert is sacred, not only because it houses ancestral remains or facilitates pilgrimages and other devotional rituals. Rather, the desert is set apart from the profane, subject to taboos and prohibitions: checkpoints, vehicle barriers, surveillance towers. Because of the desert's restlessness and unpredictability, the state seeks to make land "a lifeless place." *Coyotes*, too, seek to control and capture the desert's sacred energies, promising safe passage precisely because they assume to have tamed the wild. Yet land moves and meanders in unpredictable ways. The desert slips out of the control of all who attempt to govern it: it is too much, a landscape defined by excess and movement. The desert nurtures and destroys. It is respectful and vengeful, ambiguous and ambivalent. Caillois insists that it is for this exact reason that prohibitions are in place, to prevent the unruly sacred from destabilizing the profane world of rules and order.[73] Even as the state attempts to stop all movement in the desert, land refuses colonial occupation. Even as bulldozers plow over cacti and crews extract millions of gallons of precious groundwater, destruction is never total.

On our drive back to Tucson from Sonoyta, Dora and I enter the United States through the Lukeville port of entry located within Organ Pipe, the same checkpoint where Nellie and Amber were arrested in September 2020. Dozens of mangled saguaros lie next to bulldozers, coated in dust. I am reminded of a story about an ancient saguaro standing in the way of the planned site of the Himdag Ki—the Tohono O'odham Cultural Center and Museum. Elders say that the footprint for the Himdag Ki was moved to spare the lone saguaro. When asked about the decision to relocate the construction project, an elder scolded a young boy: "The saguaros—they are Indians too. You don't EVER throw ANYTHING at them."[74]

Saguaros marked for removal are spray-painted with red dots, echoing maps created by Humane Borders that also use a red dot to mark every dead migrant recovered in the desert. Saguaros, too, are corpses haunting the borders of nation-states, casualties of PTD. Yet, even as human beings destroy and disappear more-than-human inhabitants, white flowers peek out from the cacti's bristly husks. Maggie Nelson opens her poetry collection *Bluets* with a confession: "Suppose I were to begin by saying that I had fallen in love with a color. . . . *It began slowly. An appreciation, an affinity. Then, one day, it became more serious.*"[75] Suppose I were to begin this book by saying that I had instead become obsessed with a color. As a child, the color red evoked the sacred blood of Jesus. His body mutilated, his side pierced by a spear. In Sonora, red marks the sites where migrants die and saguaros lie prostrate. At the same time, the color is reminiscent of the *bahidaj* I enjoyed on a scorching June afternoon. It speaks to life that moves, life that is excessive, that seeks transformation, that radiates potential.

Even now, as they are marked for removal, saguaros bear fruit. Yet the *bahidaj* is not immediately visible. To catch a glimpse, we must first squint. As Muñoz proposes, "To access queer visuality we may need to . . . strain our vision and force it to see otherwise, beyond the limited vista of the here and now."[76] The Southern Arizona Sanctuary Coalition's logo features a hand-sketched image of *bahidaj* growing from a saguaro's crown and morphing into monarch butterflies, the more-than-human allies of migrant justice movements. In this drawing, *bahidaj* sustains and nurtures butterflies; the desert and its more-than-human relatives provide sanctuary. The monarchs are in motion, fluttering their wings toward otherwise possibilities, offering alternatives to the present. The logo suggests that sanctuary is mobile. That it flees the present.

○

While on a humanitarian water drop at Kino Springs—a community whose golf club claims to be the place where Father Eusebio Kino "found sanctuary" in 1691, a volunteer shows me a tweet posted by CNN: "Hundreds of vultures have made a perch out of a Customs and Border Protection

(CBP) radio tower, and the government has had enough."[77] For weeks, the flock of birds coated the structure with feces and vomit, effectively limiting CBP's ability to patrol the border. The two of us burst out in laughter, amazed by how animals mock enforcement efforts, effortlessly outwitting billions of dollars' worth of technology. As we continue along the dirt and gravel road that runs parallel to the wall, I spot a section where the Santa Cruz River meets the thirty-foot-high steel panels. Undeterred by the towering fence, the water continues to run its course—its constant rush a protest against wall construction. A movement adjacent to meandering. Suddenly, another volunteer draws my attention to a decomposing coyote caught between the steel bars. Unable to fit through the four-inch-wide gaps, the animal likely starved to death. To return to Laiken, the profane world works to render the desert lifeless, to pacify the threats land poses to militarization.

Borders—their walls, surveillance towers, "smart" technology, for-profit prisons, and enforcement agents—seek to control or tame people and landscapes in motion. Yet land is sacred, teeming with fugitive activity and otherwise possibilities—too much to be managed or controlled. The Río Bravo meanders and the Sonoran Desert facilitates vanishing time. The desert is unfit for the profane and productivity. It is sacred—fugitive, unsettled, uninterested in being a fixed, *controllable thing*. In chapter 2, I discuss how women in migrant prisons resist these carceral techniques of border enforcement, practicing sanctuary through touch: a linger, a graze, a caress that exceeds capture.

Chapter Two

The Detained

Contraband Touch in the Carceral Borderlands

To touch sets something in motion.
—JEAN-LUC NANCY

I meet Zaira Livier at Eclectic Café. Bright paintings by local artists hang from the walls and "Humanitarian Aid Is Never a Crime" posters peek through the café's windows—a statement of solidarity with Scott Warren, who faces felony charges for offering migrants water and shelter. Zaira wears a long dress and gold hoop earrings. Her voice is soft and soothing—reminding me of a lecture by Leanne Betasamosake Simpson I once attended. When asked about her tone, Simpson responded that Anishinaabe elders are known to speak softly. Colonialism, according to Simpson, is loud—invasive and abrasive. To be gentle is a deliberate gesture.

Zaira is the executive director of the People's Defense Initiative and lead organizer for Tucson's sanctuary city campaign. The ballot initiative, Tucson Families Free and Together, was designed to finally dismantle SB 1070, the infamous "show me your papers" law passed in Arizona in 2010, which—in Zaira's words—turned "every police officer into a de facto immigration agent." Although major elements of SB 1070 were struck down in court, police are still permitted to ask anyone they stop or detain to show proof of their legal status. The sanctuary initiative would prohibit Immigration and Customs Enforcement (ICE) and Border Patrol agents from stopping people for routine traffic offenses and make it illegal for local police to ask about immigration status in "sensitive locations" like schools, hospitals, and places of worship. However, section 2 of the ordinance stipulates that "an officer may seek to determine the immigration status of a detainee or arrestee, and of no other person." Campaign materials insist that this initiative would "improve community relations with police" by prioritizing their role as first responders when investigating domestic violence and sexual assault crimes (although sexual and domestic violence is notoriously pervasive among police).

When I ask Zaira why organizers chose the name Tucson Families Free and Together, she says that "sanctuary is a triggering word." According to her, the Trump administration made sanctuary synonymous with crime and lawlessness, with "giving all people papers." The word *sanctuary* is misleading. It suggests the ballot initiative would legalize all migrants when, in reality, it would only prevent police officers from asking people about their status in certain instances. The ordinance would not stop an officer from sharing a person's legal status with federal authorities when they do obtain such information, nor would it affect the police's ability to pursue criminal investigations. It "would not affect how prosecutors will prosecute a crime, what type of criminal sentence is ordered by a judge, the terms of a person's probation, or how someone might be treated while in prison or jail."[1] Tucson Families Free and Together, like other sanctuary cities, does not protect "criminal," or suspected "criminal," migrants, nor does the ordinance call for an end to detention and deportation. Instead, by affirming the role of the police in keeping communities safe, sanctuary cities aim to make policing more efficient (read: profane). While they do seek to create safer and healthier communities for migrants, sanctuary cities—as A. Naomi Paik shows—operate within the framework of law and order.[2]

If sanctuary is a sacred practice, then it must be set apart from the profane—the world of order and orderliness, projects and objects. Georges Bataille describes the sacred as contagious, and "its contagion is dangerous."[3] And because the profane world is understood as settled and steady, as ruled by law and reason, it places taboos and prohibitions around sacred forces. In *Theory of Religion*, Bataille describes the profane world of individuation as one in which humans alienate ourselves from animals and "nature" by demystifying and transforming them into things or tools. "Nature becomes man's property but it ceases to be immanent to him."[4] For Bataille, toolification also distances us from other human beings. Here lies the danger the sacred poses to the profane world: human experience is mediated by an awareness of the loss that comes with toolification. We yearn to cross the limit, to enter into an ecstatic intimacy only made possible through transgression. Bataille proposes that "the sacred is the fusion of beings in place of their separation."[5]

In these pages, I focus on practices of touch in migrant detention centers. Historically, touch has been interpreted as an inferior mode of perception, linked with irrationality, with women and racialized populations, with the left hand sacred.[6] Touch is too messy for the profane world—too unsettling and slippery, ambiguous, and violent. For Jean-Luc Nancy, touch does not necessarily do away with distance—after all, to touch someone else presupposes our separation—but it does rattle and disturb the surface of the skin. Nancy suggests that the motion of touching another displaces them, and the other displaces me in return.[7] Touch unsettles the everyday, arousing and endangering us all at once.

For the profane world of law and order—which creates and upholds boundaries between citizens and outsiders—people who cross borders without authorization are negative, or left-handed, sacred. We arrive in waves, pouring in or flooding the interior, overwhelming and destabilizing communities. We are cast as unruly and disruptive, a viral threat to the nation's imagined purity and stability. Indeed, as David Manuel Hernández argues, during the era of Asian exclusion, fears of contagion motivated the detention of "non- and lesser-white migrants whom Americans feared would contaminate the health and racial composition of the nation."[8] At Angel Island, immigration agents inspected Asian migrants for contagious and/or sexually transmitted infections. Migrants were often required to provide stool samples and undergo strip searches. They were coercively touched and managed to ensure the stability of the everyday.[9] César Cuauhtémoc García Hernández further suggests that immigrant detention emerged through offshore processing centers like Ellis and Angel Island, where migrants were processed and quarantined, often for months or years at a time.[10]

Sacred beings are monitored and policed and can only be approached with an abundance of caution. To return to Émile Durkheim, migrants (especially those who are nonwhite) are set apart because of their extraordinary contagiousness, because sacred beings restlessly spread "to everything that closely or remotely has to do with [them]."[11] Most often, the sacred—positive and negative, healing and harming—spreads through touch and proximity. Police and prisons, then, exist to establish and restore social order, to maintain borders between the sacred, or the escape-bound, and the profane, meaning that which is imagined to be fixed. Indeed, as Daniella Gandolfo explains, *policía* in the Spanish colonial Américas referred to "a broad range of attributes of civilized life." Gandolfo turns to Jesuit missionary texts to explain Indigenous peoples' "supposed lack of *policía*," and she notes that the forced resettlement (and incarceration) of Indigenous communities into *reducciones* was seen as a prerequisite to acquiring *policía*—purity, civility, orderliness, and correct moral conduct.[12] A 1611 dictionary outlines the *policía's* duty to enforce a city's "adornment and cleanliness," or in other words, to serve as purity officials.[13]

The creation of the US Border Patrol in 1924 was motivated at least in part by eugenicist anxieties and racialized notions of migrants as impure, as carriers of contagious diseases. According to Kelly Lytle Hernández, early Border Patrol tactics included kerosene baths, delousing procedures, and head shavings that doubled as "hygienic rituals" and "buried a mechanism of social subordination within a public health program."[14] Immigration officials continue to use coercive touch to discipline migrants, to reinforce boundaries between the sacred and the profane. Enforcement agents chase and tackle migrants on the run in the desert; they shove people into prisoner transport vans and shackle them at the wrists and ankles to prevent escape. Taboos are in place to protect against the unruly sacred, which knows no bounds. They exist to ensure the stability of the everyday, to defend against disorder waged by border crossers. But, then again, taboos need transgression to authorize their existence. And transgression thrives on the ecstasy of crossing the limit.

Drawing from conversations with Eva Contreras—a pseudonym for a Venezuelan asylum seeker I befriended at Eloy Detention Center—this chapter argues that migrants caught in the carceral borderlands practice sanctuary through a contraband, or forbidden, touch. This sensory experience is different from the ones I detailed in the previous paragraph, where migrants are on the receiving end of coercive touch—made to feel a texture, heat, force, or vibration on their skin. Contraband touch involves the illicit *movement* of the hands and body; it is a way of pursuing, embracing, attaching oneself to the other. Like the contagious sacred, touch is mobile. Physiologically, it moves information from mechanoreceptors in the skin to the brain. Nancy differentiates touch from contact, the latter having a more bureaucratic or technical meaning, often reduced to a connection. I agree with him that touching is more than contact; it is "a commitment to or evocation of intimacy."[15] Following Eva's movements from Maracaibo to Eloy, I show how migrants warehoused in detention centers energetically reach out and touch, setting into motion sacred worlds. As Karma Chávez observes, detention centers are spaces where migrants "unravel and become unhinged . . . perpetually beside themselves."[16] Chávez terms this condition one of ecstasy, which is also the language used by Bataille to describe the sacred. It is through contraband touch—a pursuit of ecstatic intimacy, an illicit way of encountering the other—that Eva practiced sanctuary while incarcerated.

○

In the late nineteenth century, the Southern Pacific Railroad built the East Line of Yuma across southern Arizona, using the acronym ELOY in maps and blueprints to refer to a section house, meaning a building for railroad workers and equipment. A 1903 Southern Pacific timetable lists Eloy as a train stop and a 1909 railroad map is the earliest showing the Town of Eloy, located six miles west of Picacho Peak. The town's website, on the other hand, claims that Eloy is derived from a European name meaning "chosen," suggesting that European settlement was not only destined but divinely ordained. Local tradition offers yet another origin story. A railroad conductor despaired when he saw the Sonoran Desert, wailing *Eloi, Eloi, lama Sabachthani*—a reference to Jesus Christ's ninth hour on the cross, when the Messiah cried out "My God, My God, why hast thou forsaken me?"[17]

Ethan Blue draws a correlation between the transcontinental railroad and the emergence of more effective and extensive immigration enforcement techniques, including "deportation parties" sponsored by Southern Pacific starting in 1914. Blue compares deportation trains to "prison cars," because they isolated migrants and employed armed guards to prevent escape. Guards sat in "modified, elevated seats that allowed better lines of sight and bars across the windows meant passengers could leave only by getting past guards stationed at each door."[18] Today, CoreCivic, formerly known as Corrections Corporation of America (CCA), is the Town of Eloy's largest employer, providing 1,600 jobs at four of its private prisons: Eloy Detention Center, La Palma Correctional Center, Red Rock Correctional Center, and Saguaro Correctional Center.[19]

Eloy Detention Center borders miles of fallow cotton fields. In the car after my first visit, Bob Kee, a Samaritan who organizes weekly prison trips, gestures at the entangled histories written in the landscape. "It's a little ironic," he observes, "that the road leading to these prisons is lined by cotton fields." I nod along, thinking of Édouard Glissant. After all, cotton weaves together a poetics of relation between the Middle Passage, the plantation, and the exploitation of migrant labor. In the mid-twentieth century, for instance, *braceros*—Mexican workers granted short-term labor contracts in the United States—were often recruited in Arizona to harvest cotton, one of the state's major agricultural commodities. Terrell Don Hutto, one of CCA's cofounders, began his career as a warden at a plantation-turned-prison in Ramsey, Texas. There, Hutton oversaw imprisoned Black men, who were forced to pick cotton without pay.[20] It was at the Ramsey Plantation where Hutto experimented with disciplinary techniques that he later deployed against migrants. In 1984, CCA opened the country's first private prison in Houston, a motel remodeled to incarcerate unauthorized migrants.

When he calls me with instructions for visiting Eloy, Bob explains that I must wear closed-toe shoes, ankle-length pants, and a long-sleeved shirt. Jewelry and other accessories are also banned. He has seen women turned away for wearing underwire bras, and Bob sheepishly suggests I consider wearing a sports bra instead. He encourages me to bring a thick sweater since prisons are intentionally kept at colder temperatures. Some migrants refer to their cells as *hieleras*, another way detainees experience coercive touch—made to tremble and quiver in response to the environment.

Before that first visit, Bob and I meet at 9:00 a.m. in the parking lot of Southside Presbyterian Church, home of the 1980s Sanctuary Movement. Bob wears khaki pants and a button-down shirt around his thin frame. His face has been weathered to a rusted peach from the hours spent under the desert sun as a Tucson Samaritan. During the hour-long drive, he patiently explains the workings of the private prison system, remaining even-keeled even as he details the slow, everyday violences of detention. For example, he shares that migrants are fed meat only twice a month. They frequently complain that CoreCivic's nurses dismiss their symptoms and prescribe aspirin for every ailment. As Bob merges onto Interstate 10, he motions for me to reach for a clear box in the backseat where he keeps files for every detained migrant he has interviewed. The files include letters migrants write him, intake forms listing their needs, and other miscellaneous notes. Bob explains that today I'll visit a Venezuelan asylum seeker and hands me a manila folder with information about Eva Contreras's case. I learn that she is two years older than I am and that she has been at Eloy for three months. I close the folder as we approach the detention center, a series of concrete buildings enclosed by a wire-mesh fence.

Prisons hope to capture the negative sacred, the dangerous forces separated from the profane through barbed wire and mesh fences. To access these sacred forces, visitors must submit to certain cleansing rites; according to Roger Caillois, "the point above all . . . is to become separated from the profane world in order to make possible the penetration of the sacred world without peril." After all, the sacred, for Caillois, is "more or less 'what one cannot approach without dying.'"[21] Prohibitions are in place to protect the cosmic order. When we arrive at the prison, Bob instructs me to leave all of my belongings in his gray hatchback, except for my driver's license and a fluorescent yellow Post-It note listing Eva Contreras's name and Alien Registration Number. He points to my forehead and shakes his head: "I told you over the phone that you cannot wear any accessories here." When I complain that my bangs will misbehave if I remove the headband, Bob replies curtly, "These aren't my rules." I quickly jot down this exchange in my notebook before leaving it behind—making the connection to Caillois: to access the sacred, I must abandon the human, disrupt daily routines.

I straighten my posture as we approach the entrance, aware that someone, somewhere, is watching my every move. The fence running around the perimeter of the prison reminds me of the border wall, where thirty-foot steel slats similarly divide inside from outside.[22] At the first gate, Bob presses the intercom and announces our presence to an unseen guard: "We're here for a friend visit." A buzz unlocks the first door, and we repeat this ritual twice more. As soon as we are granted entrance to the prison, my body shivers from the shocking cold and I instinctively wrap my gray cardigan around my torso. When we reach the lobby, a guard hands Bob and me numbered pieces of paper and instructs us to watch a small television screen for our turn. In the meantime, we complete visitor forms—listing our names, birthdates, and driver's license numbers. The back of the form lists prohibited items: firearms, explosives, cameras, food, cell phones, recording equipment, prescription drugs, narcotics, marijuana, alcohol. Substances that can be shared and objects that facilitate spread such as phones and cameras are banned.

Families embrace and catch up in the waiting room. Bob tells me people get to know each other here, spending every Saturday participating in a shared ritual. Toddlers run outside, periodically peeking their heads in through openings in the bulwarked door. The woman sitting in front of me is radiant. She wears cheetah-print platform heels and bright red lipstick—finding a way around the limits placed on her wardrobe. The woman's toddler leans his head on her shoulder and takes a nap, clearly accustomed to this routine.

When my number is called, I surrender my driver's license to the guard. "Family or friend?" she asks, and I respond that I am Eva's friend, though

2.1 Freight train whizzes past the road leading to Eloy Detention Center.

we have never met and I could not recognize the young woman in a room full of people. When I remove my cardigan to walk through the metal detector, the guard notices I am not wearing a bra and instructs me to keep the sweater wrapped around my chest at all times. She repeats "at all times," making me self-conscious about my body and its exposure. I nod my head, enter another waiting room, and take a seat on a pallid green, molded plastic couch. A television screen plays *Toy Story*. Periodically, an employee announces detainees' last names. After twenty minutes, I hear "Contreras" and walk through two more secured doors.

Eva, like her fellow incarcerated women, wears dark green scrubs. Her silky black hair is gathered tightly in a bun and she sits dutifully with her arms on her knees. As I approach the table, her tired eyes narrow into a wide smile. One visit at a time, Eva shares how she arrived here.

○

Maracaibo, a city in northwestern Venezuela that borders Colombia, is home to the largest body of freshwater in South America. *Palafitos*, stilt houses made of wood and topped with straw, hover above Lake Maracaibo—giving their residents front-row seats to the world-famous "eternal thunderstorm." According to Eva, Maracaibo was once a prosperous petroleum capital, but it now seems as unstable as the stilt houses.

Though it was the first city in Venezuela to have phone lines, a regular electrical supply, and public transportation, today, oil rigs lie fallow and petroleum leaks into marshlands and fisheries. The lake's shores are littered with dark muck and its surface is covered with duckweed—a bacterial infestation made worse by chemicals used to clean up oil spills. Eva attributes the city's demise to Hugo Chávez's mismanagement of the oil industry and his successor's corruption.

Eva and her husband, Alberto, are members of Venezuela's opposition party Acción Democrática. When Alberto signed a petition calling for a recall election against Hugo Chávez in 2003, he was blacklisted by the government and added to the Tascón List, a database used to identify dissidents and deny them work, loans, education, housing, and food programs. After the couple participated in a protest in support of right-wing opposition leader Juan Guaidó, a *colectivo*—or paramilitary group that supports Nicolás Maduro—broke into the couple's home in search of Alberto. When they did not find him, the armed men kidnapped Eva, blindfolding and dragging her into an unmarked white van. They locked her in a dark room with no windows, depriving her of water and food for over thirty-six hours. After Alberto surrendered all of the money he could find, equivalent to US$1,800, the kidnappers left her on the Lara-Zulia Highway, twenty miles from their home. She walked for hours covered in her own urine. Eva and Alberto fled to Colombia within days of her release—joining over three million Venezuelans who have escaped the country in recent years.

From Colombia, Eva and her husband purchased flights to Cancún and arrived in the Mexican coastal city as tourists. After reviewing their documents, a customs agent instructed the couple to step aside and confined them in a separate interrogation room. He boasted that his team had been contracted by the United States to detain asylum seekers, a phenomenon Todd Miller calls the "empire of borders," or the outsourcing of militarized bordering practices around the world.[23] The officer demanded four hundred dollars to admit the couple into the country. Amarela Varela Huerta identifies Mexico as a "vertical border" between the United States and Central America. To prevent migrants from reaching their destinations in the Global North and to deter unauthorized migration in the region, the "entirety of Mexican territory has been converted into a vertical border crossing for thousands of migrants and refugees from Central America who transit through Mexico on their way to the United States."[24] Enforcement agents in Mexico patrol train routes and bus stations, use drones to surveil movement, and stage highway checkpoints to capture migrants. Like Prevention through Deterrence, Mexico's Southern Border Plan—first implemented in 2014 in response to political pressure by the United States—focuses on apprehending, detaining, and deporting migrants along the Mexico-Guatemala border. Huerta explains that the Southern Border Plan pushes migrants into more clandestine spaces and leaves them more vulnerable to organized crime.[25]

Eva and Alberto then boarded a six-hour flight to Hermosillo, Sonora. There, they met and lived with a community of Venezuelan exiles. Hermosillo reminded Eva of her hometown—heavily influenced by American culture and inhabited by *mestizos* and other in-between people. When one of their roommates witnessed a drug-related murder at the local Oxxo, a popular Mexican convenience store, they all became potential targets of the local *mafia*. The group immediately fled their shared apartment and dispersed to other cities. Eva and Alberto left Hermosillo without saying goodbye to her coworkers at an Italian restaurant, cooks and waitresses who had quickly become family. Eva tells me she was unable to bear another separation. The couple escaped to Reynosa—a border city in the state of Tamaulipas, where Los Zetas and Cártel del Golfo compete for control of migrant routes. After landing there, Eva and Alberto were almost immediately kidnapped by a taxi driver. The man insisted on knowing their country of origin, raising his voice with every repeat question. Eva refused to answer at first, but when the man retrieved a weapon from his glove box, she tearfully confessed that they were Venezuelan. Almost as if sounding relieved, the driver told the couple they were lucky. If they were Cuban, he would have no choice but to deliver them to the *maras*. Cubans are known to have wealthy family members in the United States, and criminal networks can extort ransoms of around ten thousand dollars per person.

There is a glimmer in Eva's eyes as she tells me about a Venezuelan boy she and her husband met in Reynosa. He was traveling alone, an unaccompanied minor who dreamed of the United States despite having no family or friends in the country. The three of them formed a makeshift family while living at Senda de Vida shelter on the banks of the Río Bravo, making kin in spite of being strangers. They fashioned a home out of a tent, joining hundreds who live for months on end in the overcrowded shelter's courtyard. They shared food, huddled together at night for warmth, and imagined their futures in the United States. The boy crossed the river alone although Eva warned him against it. He was driven to desperation after discovering a friend had sold him to the *maras*—which Eva likens to Judas

Iscariot's betrayal of Jesus for "thirty pieces of silver." Last she heard, the boy was being held at a detention center in Douglas, Arizona.

Many who attempt to cross the river by swimming do not survive. A Cuban family they met at the shelter was also eager to cross the border. Restless after waiting for months at Senda de Vida, a mile away from the Reynosa–Hidalgo International Bridge, *los Cubanos* almost made it to the US side of the river before they were spotted by Border Patrol helicopters and forced to turn around. The following morning, armed *maras* came looking for them at the shelter, threatening to murder everyone if the minister did not surrender the family. I interrupt Eva: "*Pero no entiendo, ¿porque los buscaba la mara?*" She teaches me that migrants cannot cross the river without paying the cartel with jurisdiction over the area—a case study in Peter Andreas's argument that an increase in enforcement leads to an increase in corruption.[26] The minister acquiesced to their demands, and the three disappeared. Alberto and Eva never saw them again. The couple made the difficult decision to once again pick up and move to Nogales, Sonora—frightened that they would be the *maras'* next *desaparecidos*. When Eva called her former coworkers in Hermosillo and told them she and her husband had to relocate once again, they cobbled together the money for the two to rent an apartment when they reached Nogales. They also received sanctuary from a nun at the Kino Border Initiative who met the young couple at the bus station in Nogales and helped them file a police report for evidence of corruption and extortion in Mexico. The nun took the couple step-by-step through the process and encouraged them to report the attempted kidnapping and the agent who charged the couple a bribe to enter Mexico. These documents have now become the center of the couple's legal argument that they cannot settle in Mexico due to the threat of violence.[27]

In Nogales, they placed their names on the asylum waitlist and remained for months until their numbers were called by immigration officials. This practice is known as metering, in which Customs and Border Patrol agents limit the number of migrants allowed to seek asylum at the border. The Trump administration implemented metering as a policy in April 2018, though it was first applied by the Obama administration to turn back Haitian asylum seekers at the Otay Mesa and San Ysidro ports in San Diego, California, in 2016. After the couple passed their credible fear interview, which determined there was a "significant possibility" they would be persecuted in Venezuela, Eva and Alberto were loaded onto a van and smuggled to Eloy, Arizona. When the van stopped at Eloy Detention

Center, only Eva's name was called. She was instructed to exit the vehicle, without warning that she would be separated from Alberto. He was taken to La Palma Correctional Center.

Touch is inevitable among the smuggled, those made to flee their homelands and those crossing borders clandestinely, just as it was inevitable among those Fred Moten and Stefano Harney call the shipped. The shipped refers to Africans confined in the bowels of slave ships, human cargo pressed so close together that there was no possibility of stretching out or repositioning their bodies. Africans trapped during the Middle Passage were often kept alive by the warmth of bodies sealed next to them, a tactile experience that Moten and Harney term *hapticality*, or "the capacity to feel through others, for others to feel through you, for you to feel them feeling you, this feel of the shipped is not regulated, at least not successfully, by a state, a religion, a people, an empire, a piece of land, a totem."[28] The shipped developed an insurgent and ecstatic intimacy that enabled them to survive. "Though forced to touch and be touched, to sense and be sensed in that space of no space, though refused sentiment, history and home, we feel (for) each other."[29] For Moten and Harney, the feel of the shipped unleashes an unruly; in the slave ship, there was no such thing as individuation or separation.

During the border crossing, migrants are often packed together, crammed in cargo trucks without ventilation, warehoused in detention cells where they are forced to sleep atop each other, held in safe houses alongside hundreds of strangers standing shoulder-to-shoulder. However, they access a different kind of agency than enslaved Africans who were abducted and containerized across the Atlantic—who were made into property and entered what Frantz Fanon called the "zone of non-being."[30] While migrants are often seen as powerless or victims of global capitalism, whose leaving is a forced displacement, I agree with Sandro Mezzadra that, "for migrations to exist, there must be an individual motion (made concretely [by a person] capable of *agency*), of desertion from the field where those 'objective causes' operate, a reclaiming precisely of a 'right to escape.'"[31] Migrants also have a certain degree of agency over their routes and often meander and spread out over land in an effort to get around checkpoints and circumvent thieves or kidnappers. There are undeniably economic and political motives that prompt migration, including neoliberal interventions, state violence, war, persecution, and environmental crisis. Even still, migration is an active and intentional practice of making life.

Given these important differences, I propose that Eva and her husband were not shipped but smuggled—their movements prompted by nation-states that simultaneously expel and recruit workers. And while shipping often takes place within a legal framework and inside the borders of empire (including from periphery to center), smuggling is at its core contrary to the law. Smuggling is transgressive and, by definition, implies the crossing of borders, the illegal or illicit movements of people and goods into and out of a country. The smuggled disregard the law; they use fraudulent documents, cram into the trailers of semitrucks, crawl under vehicle floorboards as they transgress customs checkpoints. Touch is part of all of these movements. Indeed, an obsolete use of the transitive verb *smuggle* means to fondle, cuddle, or caress. While being cuddled or caressed tends to evoke feelings of warmth and pleasure, the term *fondle* is vaguer. Fondling could be consensual or welcome; it also denotes being grasped, clutched, held against one's will. This volatility defines the sacred, that which refuses to settle, to stay in place.[32] And while the passive verb *smuggled* suggests someone is being made to touch, as a noun, the smuggled become the ones who pursue touch and intimacy. At Eloy, where Eva was warehoused, touch sets in motion fugitive, or contraband, possibilities.

○

I became a US citizen in the summer of 2019, months after I began field-work for the project that would become this book. My mom, dad, sister, and I were all naturalized that year but each of us on separate occasions. The agent officiating my dad's June 6 ceremony quizzed the crowd on D-Day, which he celebrated as an example of "American exceptionalism" and this country's duty to the rest of the world. During my sister's ceremony, a chorus of ICE employees led the crowd in a chant spelling out "U-S-A." They repeated the chant over and over again, each time with more vigor, until they were satisfied with our enthusiasm. We all received the same welcome letter signed by President Trump, congratulating us for pledging our hearts to this country. "And when you give your love and loyalty to America, she returns her love and loyalty to you."

As soon as we arrived at the US Citizenship and Immigration Services field office for my ceremony, my family and I walked through a security scanner and handed our belongings to an officer for a separate inspection. Almost immediately, I was corralled into a waiting area with the rest of the candidates, while my family was ushered to the auditorium. As the prospective citizens lined up single file to enter the auditorium, we were made to surrender our green cards. I was hesitant to let go of the plastic document, the same one I used to apply for work, to travel in and out of the country. And so I protested, explaining to a tall, stone-faced officer that I would prefer to hold on to it. "Ma'am, that's not possible. We do this to prevent fraud," he replied, dismissing my attachment to the document. My facial expression must have hinted at some discomfort. "Come on," he continued, now tauntingly, "you wouldn't want someone to steal your identity, would you?" In exchange, he offered me a miniature American flag, a citizen's almanac, and a pocket-sized Constitution.

The ceremony opened with a four-minute video titled *Faces of America*, a slideshow of grainy images and inspirational quotes attributed to naturalized citizens. Black and white portraits showed European migrants arriving on America's shores aboard steamships and toddlers dressed in navy uniforms, saluting the American flag. The video highlighted iconic landmarks: a rainbow over Niagara Falls, panoramic views of Mount Rushmore, a close-up of the Statue of Liberty's copper flame. The triumphant score added reverence to each image. A quote attributed to a Russian immigrant stated "America is my peaceful refuge," and a Bangladeshi immigrant celebrated that "whatever I have dreamed, America has always fulfilled." Romantic scenes of migrants with crooked teeth and tattered clothing suggested that the United States is a sanctuary, a safe haven for the masses. Freedom is a place, from sea to shining sea.

An immigration agent welcomed the crowd with brief remarks. She explained that the climax of the ceremony was the oath of allegiance. According to her, we would become citizens the very moment we uttered those words. "Pretty cool, huh?" I was taking field notes during my ceremony and missed the cue to stand for the oath.

According to the agent, I became a citizen the moment I disavowed my country of birth and agreed to protect this country's laws and Constitution. The oath invites each prospective citizen to "absolutely and entirely" renounce all allegiance to "any state or sovereignty of whom or which [they] have heretofore been a subject or citizen." I vowed that I would bear arms on behalf of the United States and perform service in the armed forces when required by law. I was asked to state that I took this obligation freely and without any mental reservation. The oath refuses ambivalence, the messiness of migration. But, of course, the profane is never fully able to impose order on such an unruly process.

Donald Trump addressed us new Americans via a prerecorded video message. He told us there is no greater honor and no greater privilege than becoming a United States citizen. He reminded us of the "sacred rights, responsibilities, and duties" that come with citizenship and instructed the crowd to "uplift America by following its laws." But I was standing in that auditorium precisely because I failed to follow America's laws, because—for twenty years—my very presence in this country was an illegal act. In *Black and Blur*, the first in a trilogy titled *consent not to be a single being*, Fred Moten writes that citizenships are "(like) a set of performances."[33] In a journal entry from the night after I became a citizen, I question which set of performances made me an American. Was it when I memorized and performed "This Land Is Your Land" in the second grade? Was it the day I graduated from English as a Second Language? Or was it the day when I tried to sing Argentina's national anthem and realized I had forgotten the words? Was it when I uttered the oath of allegiance alongside a crowd of strangers? Was it, perhaps, when I lit my miniature American flag on fire after becoming a citizen, exercising my new constitutional right? The point is that the process of becoming a citizen began years before I pledged allegiance to the United States. Or perhaps the point is that the project of becoming a citizen is an unfinished one, a failed one. Or, lastly, that the condition of being a migrant is—to return to Moten—a fugitive one, being in but not of the state, *absolutely* and *entirely* pledging our love and loyalty to each other.

Safia Elhillo's "self-portrait with no flag" reimagines the Pledge of Allegiance. Rather than showing loyalty to a flag or a state, the poet pledges allegiance to her "homies" and "mother's small & cool palms," to her "grandmother's good brown hands / good strong brown hands gathering my bare feet in her lap."[34] Elhillo's archive of feelings honors touch; it centers the labor of women's hands in creating refuge. The poet honors her homies, that label being one typically associated with Black and Brown men, the communities rejected by the sanctuary city. Her poem continues: "i come from two failed countries & i give them back / i pledge allegiance to no land / no border cut by force to draw blood."[35] She rejects the United States, referring to it, too, as "failed" and challenging narratives of American exceptionalism saluted at my citizenship ceremony. Instead, her loyalty lies with the table at the Waffle House "with all my loved ones crowded / into the booth / i choose the shining dark of our faces through a thin sheet / of smoke / glowing dark of our faces / slick under layers of sweat / i choose / the world we make with our living / refusing to be unmade by what surrounds us."[36] In these lines, the poet refuses narratives of inclusion

2.2 and 2.3 The author lights a miniature American flag on fire after becoming a US citizen. From Alex Morelli's short film *Becoming*.

and citizenship, choosing instead to commit to excess intimacy: bodily fluids that drip and saturate clothing, crowded booths where it is hard to tell where one body ends and another begins, smoke that fills the air and travels recklessly. These contraband movements are inevitable among the smuggled. The poem ends, affirming "& this is my only country."

○

By my third visit, I am more familiar with Eloy's policies. I know what to bring, where to park, how to dress. I am curious about which Disney animated movie the CoreCivic employees will choose to screen in the waiting room and am disappointed when I arrive to find the live-action remake of *The Lion King*. "This version just doesn't have the heart of the original, right?" I grumble to a stranger seated next to me. Despite my reservations, I sit entranced as Mufasa rescues his son from a wildebeest stampede, only to be pushed off a ledge and murdered by his brother, Scar. Convinced that he is responsible for his father's death, Simba escapes his homeland as Scar orders hyenas to kill the cub. It is only during this viewing, while waiting to visit a friend who abruptly and desperately fled her country, that I read *The Lion King* as a story of exile and asylum. Simba flees his homeland because of civil strife and the extrajudicial murder of his father. Journeying for days on end in the African savanna, the cub collapses in the desert and is rescued by Timon and Pumba. He receives water and shelter. He is offered sanctuary. A guard calls the name Contreras as Nala finds Simba and pleads with him to return home.

Eva and I bond over our similarities despite the worlds that separate us. I laugh when she confesses that her competitive streak got the best of her during a kickball game in the prison courtyard, earning her some enemies as a result. Eva describes herself as cutthroat and hotheaded. I assure her that I can be competitive, too, and that this trait has gotten me into trouble on more than one occasion. We bond when she asks me how I met my partner and I share that he's in North Carolina while I'm in Arizona conducting research. Eva tells me she met her husband when he messaged her on a chat site but, at the time, they were both dating other people. Eva replied on a whim one afternoon, not taking the friendship seriously until they met in person three years later. They dated privately for years, and she did not even tell her parents they were getting married until a week before their nuptials. Eva was not particularly ready to get married. Her bed frame broke one November and, when she went to the furniture store with her now-husband, he insisted on also purchasing a living-room set. He said it was time for the two of them to begin to build a life together. "*Siempre fui una persona muy independiente,*" she tells me. That is, until she was exiled from her home, which forced her to become dependent on the only person she had left—her new husband. Both Eva and I are apart from our loved ones, the difference being that my separation has an expiration date while hers has no end in sight. Eva and Alberto have, however, devised a method for speaking to each other—they each call one of his sisters, who in turn hold their phones up next to each other so the couple can speak directly. Theirs is a fugitive strategy that somehow, always, escapes.

We discuss movies, and all of her favorites are romantic dramas from the United States—*The Notebook, Me without You, Forrest Gump*. I ask her about Venezuelan cinema, and she recommends a film about a young man who engages in illegal activity to buy his mother a house and is killed during a drug deal. The moral of the story is that his mother never wanted luxury goods; she simply wanted a happy and healthy son. Eva has not been able to watch television in detention, not because it is forbidden but because it would seem like a betrayal of her husband, an acceptance of their separation. She recalls that, in Nogales, they huddled together under the covers in their rented apartment, watching Netflix on her smartphone's six-inch screen.

The week before Eva and I met, her asylum hearing was postponed because immigration agents allegedly forgot to collect her biometrics. She claims they intentionally delay hearings and fail to collect the necessary paperwork. "*Sigue el dinero,*" Eva tells me, aware that powerful people are profiting from her incarceration. Indeed, in 2021, the Arizona Department of Corrections granted CoreCivic a five-year contract, guaranteeing the company $85.12 per detained person per day, as well as a minimum 90 percent occupancy rate.[37] I visit Eva after her second asylum hearing is scheduled and notice that she seems aloof. At first, she chalks it up to exhaustion: she was hired to clean the prison's hallways, which pays a dollar a day for five hours of work. Her calloused hands, prevented from touching others while incarcerated, make the prison more pristine, more bearable, more humane. She tells me of the hours she spends on her knees, scrubbing blood, removing hair, wiping away dirt.

After forty-five minutes, as we near the limit for the visit and a guard informs us our time is almost up, Eva tells me that the judge assigned to her case—who has a decent reputation for granting asylum—is away on vacation and that her case has been reassigned to another one. Within a span of five years, this new judge denied 93 percent and granted (including conditional grants) 7 percent of asylum cases. They approved two cases in the past six months. Eva says her world came crashing down, and she blames only herself. "*Es mi culpa por estar de tan buen ánimo la semana pasada, por estar tan confiada,*" she confesses, imagining she cursed herself with positive thinking. For hours, Eva struggled to breathe.

I repeat "*que cagada,*" over and over again, not knowing how to react or how to console her at this moment. My jaw is stiff and my breath agitated. After processing my disbelief, I encourage Eva to be positive. "*Tenés un caso tan fuerte. Incluso tenés registros policiales que muestran que no podés regresar a México,*" I say—scrambling to find words of encouragement, struggling to believe them myself. She nods along, but her eyes look downward, unable to meet mine. Eva finally looks up and tells me she's sure this is a test from God. A few nights ago, when she couldn't sleep, Eva opened her Bible to a passage in Romans that said, "*Somos más que vencedores por medio de aquel que nos amó.*" Eva imagines herself as David prevailing against Goliath, a monster of comparable size to the US immigration system. After hearing her talk about David and Goliath, I remember my dad's church in North Carolina and how often he references that story to describe migrants facing US empire. As soon as I leave the prison, I call and ask if he can invite church members to write letters to Eva in prison, encouraging her to keep the faith. She calls me the following week to ask me if I had anything to do with the letters flooding her mailbox, all from names she does not recognize.

Eva spontaneously bursts into song, a hymn that I instantly recognize from my childhood. "*Si tuviera fe como un grano de mostaza,*" she begins to chant softly, "*yo le diría a la montaña, muévete, muévete.*" I notice myself joining her poetic murmur, forming a choir of two: "*Y esa montaña se moverá, se moverá, se moverá.*" Eva tells me that song hasn't crossed her mind since she was seven or eight years old, but she now realizes that God has been preparing her all along. He always knew she'd face Arizona's mountains—the distant peaks visible from her jail cell and the ones taking the shape of a dismissive judge or an abusive guard. As the song goes, all she needs is faith the size of a mustard seed. For the first time, I see Eva weep. When I reach across the table to hold her hand, a guard says we are not allowed to touch. "Only at the beginning and close of the visit," he explains. Jean-Luc Nancy insists that, out of all the senses, touch is the one subject to the most taboos. He goes so far as to say that "'taboo' means 'do not touch.'"[38] I suddenly become aware that I have not hugged anyone for weeks and have not been physically comforted since I held my partner at the airport and kissed him goodbye.

For Hortense Spillers, the institution of slavery haunts the present (certainly prisons) and poses a paradox—forms of touch associated with intimacy also engender violence. In a lecture on touch, Spillers cites a sermon from Toni Morrison's *Beloved*, in which Baby Suggs preaches from the hush harbor: "They do not love your hands. Those they only use, tie, bind, chop off and leave empty" and instructs freed Black folks to "love your hands! Raise them up and kiss them. Touch others with them, pat them together, stroke them on your face," suggesting that there is a difference between touch that is curative and touch under the conditions of coercion.[39] According to Spillers, the ability to thwart unwanted touch is what distinguishes bodies—"citizen belonging"—from flesh, or "alien entities."[40] Immigrant aliens certainly are marked by a lack of consent; in this case, to touch and be touched. Spillers associates bodiedness with "rights-bearing historical actors" who have access to "what constitutional law calls due process." On the other hand, flesh—or alien entity—is an "expendable figure . . . [who may be] invaded, entered, penetrated by coercive power."[41] Coercive touch marks life at Eloy—pat-down searches, strip searches, being handcuffed and placed in shackles. Incarcerated migrants cannot prevent or ward off another's touch. At the same time, consensual touch is banned, limited, and legislated. Incarcerated migrants are subject to be touched but forbidden from embracing or seeking out another's touch. Spillers closes her lecture with a provocative statement, one that questions whether healing touch can exist under conditions of capture. For Spillers, "without freedom, love and intimacy don't matter."[42]

At Eloy, however, confinement is precisely what prompts—or demands—touch. Coercive conditions incite the longing to come closer, to pursue intimacy. According to official policy, touch is banned or restricted in prison because of its potential to transfer and smuggle contraband. Touch is legislated because it is disruptive, setting the sacred in motion. Disruption happens, as Nancy explains, at the "zone" of the skin, which opens up and exposes itself to the other. "A zone sets up the possibility for disturbance," he writes in an essay rethinking his most famed work, *Corpus*. Through touch, "skin is as dissociated as it possibly can be from its nature as a sort of envelope or boundary: instead it has the appearance of dough, paste, or mortar, of ribbons, laces, straps, bands, or liana, or of banners, and sails that are unfurled, along with the rigging used to haul them down. Skin soars and is heaped up; it is lustrous, creased, and moist."[43] Touch opens up the body—the zone of the skin—to another, sets in motion sacred possibilities that disrupt the profane world of individuation and separation.

In the biblical Gospel of Matthew, Jesus stretches out his hand and touches the leper, his caress a healing force. In John, the Messiah kneels to the floor, pours water into a basin, and washes his disciples' feet. This scene takes place before the Last Supper, the washing of the feet—the rhythmic, tactile ritual—an invitation to enter into intimacy with the divine. Upon his return from the world of the dead, Jesus proves himself to Thomas by asking the doubting disciple to "put your finger here; see my hands. Reach out your hand and put it into my side."[44] In each story, touch facilitates conversion and communion. In each story, touch is mobile: requiring kinesthetic movement and moving or stirring into action. It is, as Nancy writes, both motion and emotion. In prison, the ultimate form of punishment is punitive segregation, also known as solitary confinement: a place stripped of touch and intimacy with others. For Lisa Guenther, who writes about solitary confinement, "there is something about the absence of regular bodily contact with others, the absence of even the possibility of touching or being touched, that threatens to *unhinge* the subject."[45]

Eva describes her cellmates. Although the first was Cameroonian and only spoke English, Eva was instantly drawn to the woman's dark brown skin: a reminder of her own Afro-Latina mother. Eva and her roommate often prayed together, the Holy Spirit making it possible for the two to understand each other. "Like speaking in tongues?" I ask and she nods in agreement. Theirs was an intimacy without, or beyond, intelligibility. Cellmates comfort and console one another during difficult moments, such as when a fellow migrant loses their asylum case or is denied bail, or when someone misses their family. "*Tu compañera de cuarto, esa persona es la que ve tus tristezas, tus dolores, tus alegrías. Esa persona es la que vela por ti, y tú por ella. En momentos difíciles, entras como en una burbuja donde empiezas a olvidar hasta como es afuera y solo se puede recrear algo a través de las palabras de tu compañera que son alimento para tu alma.*" For Eva, incarceration can feel like "entering into a bubble where you begin to forget what the outside is like, and you can only re-create the outside through the words of your roommate, which are like food that nourishes the soul." There's an intensity of feeling among the women, which Eva describes as an intimacy that draws people closer—that disrupts the prison's bubbles of isolation. Words are material; they re-create the world outside the prison, sparking the imagination and transporting people out of incarceration. Eva compares words to food; they can be tasted and sensed. They metabolize and create movement.

At Eloy, women organize a prayer group and gather in the courtyard for two hours daily, singing hymns and seeking revelation. Eva shares, "*En ese momento ese era nuestro más grande alivio, pues sentías como Dios te abrazaba a través de la naturaleza. Eran dos horas de oración donde salíamos renovados pues el espíritu santo sacaba a flote todos tus sentimientos y quedabas en paz.*" For Eva, prayer feels like God embraces the women through nature; she describes prayer as a hug or healing touch. Prayer is a renewal and an *alivio*—a word that translates to ease, to a brief moment of reprieve or refuge. The Holy Spirit "*sacaba a flote,*" or brought to the surface feelings the women had buried or avoided. A more literal translation of her statement might be "the Holy Spirit made my feelings float." Which is to say, the sacred made it possible to move, to escape.

In crafting a theory of "otherwise possibility," Ashon Crawley insists that prayer is fundamentally a breathing practice. Crawley notes that the word *enunciation* comes from the Latin *ex* meaning out and *nuntius* meaning messenger and affirms "The fugitivity of escape as the showing forth of the 'out messenger,' the one that carries a word, a phrase, a plea, a praise, a prayer, a psalm. . . . The fugitive enacts by enunciative force, by desire, by air, by breath, by breathing. Breath and breathing of air, in other words, not only make possible but sustain such movement."[46] Eva's and her companion's prayers are narratives of escape, or fugitive enunciations. With each repetition of their desire to escape the prison, the women insist on another world. They announce their unrest. They denounce the present, and their prayers flee the prison. According to Eva, praying as a collective is an embrace from God, *un abrazo*, a tactile and haptic experience, being touched despite policies and procedures that ban such relationality.

o

Upon Eva's request, I visit her husband at La Palma Correctional Center, which imprisons asylum seekers alongside migrants awaiting deportation after having served sentences for criminal charges. Many lived in the United States for years before being detained during a workplace raid or arrested for offenses such as drunk driving. A young woman tells me she visits her boyfriend here every Sunday. A police officer stopped him at a checkpoint on his way home from work; his visa had expired four days prior.

Foothill palo verdes line the prison's parking lot, their effulgent flowers interrupting the muted surroundings. Banners hang from the prison's entryway, spelling out the acronym PRIDE for CoreCivic's "core values": professionalism, respect, integrity, duty, and excellence. Dozens of families gather outside the main entryway at 2:00 p.m., awaiting further instructions. A young officer instructs the crowd to form a straight line and distributes thirty-three registration forms, the limit for visitations in one day. The young woman I spoke with earlier tells me that last week, she was visitor number thirty-four. Turned away, she cried for the entirety of the five-hour drive back to her hometown.

We are told to complete the required paperwork inside our cars and return at 2:30 p.m. The form is identical to the one I have memorized from Eloy, listing prohibited items and collecting personal information. At 2:25 p.m., an impatient crowd gathers outside the doors to the detention center. When a guard announces we can enter the building, the crowd becomes denser—jamming our bodies through the narrow entryways, pressing into one another without being concerned about touching a stranger. As Elias Canetti suggests, it is only in the crowd that human beings become free of the fear of being touched. In *Crowds and Power*, he writes that humans tend "to avoid physical contact with anything strange. . . . All the distances which men create round themselves are dictated by this fear."[47] This fear is one of contagion, of allowing the sacred to unsettle the everyday and to disrupt our worlds.

Unlike Eloy, where families are called in individually, here we enter as one. The crowd does not disintegrate. Mothers struggle to hold their newborns and place their belongings in plastic bins. They hold their toddlers' hands as they walk through metal detectors. Children lose their balance as they struggle to tie their shoelaces, while guards yell out instructions that go largely ignored. The crowd refuses to be domesticated. To return to Canetti once more, "all ceremonies and rules pertaining to . . . institutions are basically intent on capturing the crowd," or—to put it in other words—controlling the dangerous sacred.[48] At La Palma, there are forms that collect visitors' personal information, full body scanners that detect items under clothing or inside body cavities, and protocols that dictate how many people can enter the prison at once. These are attempts to establish order, to prevent the crowd from growing any further or becoming disruptive. The crowd, however, is largely uninterested in the choreographed ritual.

I scan the room for an empty circular table and wait for Alberto to find me. Unlike Eloy's ascetic white walls, the surroundings here pulsate with murals depicting skyscrapers and landmarks like the Hollywood sign, sports teams including the Oakland Raiders and San Francisco 49ers, and political figures like César Chávez—all painted by incarcerated men seeking escape routes. At the same time, like Eva scrubbing Eloy's floors, the men's labor, their creative touch, makes the prison more bearable and beautiful. The visitation room is loud, pulsing with confidential whispers and unrestrained laughter. I look for the young woman I met outside and notice she and her boyfriend are pressed together; her face so close to his that the two disappear into each other. An incarcerated man radiates as he holds a newborn, presumably for the first time, his cheek against the baby's chest, maybe to feel a heartbeat, to approach the life he has helped create. The crowd's murmurs create an echo in the visitation room, facilitating a fugitive speech.

I am unsure how Alberto will recognize me, curious if Eva has described my appearance and, if so, what she has shared. Guards direct all visitors to sit with their backs turned to the doors that lead to the men's quarters. I do not see him approaching, and when I ask how he found me, Alberto explains that he waited until everyone else sat down with their visitor. That is when he saw me sitting alone. Before asking about conditions inside the prison, I offer to purchase snacks from the vending machines, another luxury afforded to families at La Palma that is prohibited at Eloy. Alberto asks for a soda, chocolate bar, and Doritos chips. This is the first time he has had a visitor since being smuggled to La Palma three months prior, and Alberto takes the opportunity to *desahogarse*, a word in Spanish that translates to "vent," "unload," or more literally "undrown." Some of his complaints echo stories Bob has shared with me, including that migrants are rarely fed protein. Alberto says the men face physical and verbal abuse at the hands of guards, especially Latinx ones. "*Hasta nos tienen acá encerrados con criminales,*" he laments, creating distance between himself and migrants warehoused here as a result of criminal charges, affirming a binary that separates the innocent from the guilty. In December, he filed a formal grievance with human rights investigators because guards left fluorescent ceiling lights on at night, despite migrants reporting migraines and lack of sleep. And, for months, his wife did not receive his letters. After the grievance was filed, she received all twelve at once.

I ask Alberto about his daily routine in the prison. He works the breakfast shift in the kitchen, waking up at 2:00 a.m. and returning to his cell at 9:00 a.m. He laughs when I ask if he was hired as a cook. "*¿Crees que nos dejarían tocar los cuchillos aquí?*" He says migrants are not allowed to handle any sharp objects or any tools that could provoke violence for that matter. Alberto makes three dollars a day, well below minimum wage, but it is enough for phone calls to his sister, which are effectively phone calls to Eva. His conversations with her are life-giving, and he points out his Venezuelan friends in the visitation room, telling me that they keep him alive, too. The couple does not want me to share he was slashing his wrists. He says they are the only ones who understand what he escaped.

Alberto is concerned about Eva's quiet and reserved tone over the phone. He checked the status of her asylum case using the prison's computers and noticed she has been assigned a new judge. I am unsure whether to disclose that Eva is devastated, to tell him I saw her cry for the first time. Instead, I say she is confident and hopeful. I assure him that his wife's faith keeps her grounded. He smiles knowingly, "*Esa es la Eva con quien me casé.*" When a guard gives the crowd a fifteen-minute warning, Alberto shares his sister's phone number so that she can pass along character witness statements and other documents for his asylum case. I agree to translate these files, deeply aware that my own citizenship application required the labor and support of an entire community.

When I leave La Palma, I drive aimlessly for ten minutes, hoping to clear my head. Suddenly, I find myself at Skydive Arizona, the world's largest skydive drop zone. I park and watch skydivers release their multicolored parachutes as they freefall toward the ground. I wonder if the prisons are visible from the drop zone. I wonder if skydivers refer to their view as scenic and if Eva and her cellmate can see people soaring as they pray together. Skydive Arizona's website describes its surroundings as flat and uninhabited.

○

A crowd of about fifty people is assembled in front of Joel D. Valdez Main Library in downtown Tucson when I arrive a few minutes past 6:30 p.m. Attendees at the No Pride in Detention demonstration gather around a pavilion, where they have set up an art station and a refreshment counter with blue Igloo coolers and green milk crates holding burritos wrapped in aluminum foil. "Take one, or two if you want, my work donated them," a volunteer encourages me. I compliment the volunteer's makeup. They thank me but quickly clarify that they coated their eyelids with pink and blue eyeshadow to match the transgender pride flag, but the makeup has melted into a purple over the course of the day. The sky is crowded with clouds, obstructing the summer sun, and it is surprisingly not sweltering hot outside, though it is late June in the Sonoran Desert.

2.4 and 2.5 Skydivers at the largest drop zone in the world in Eloy, Arizona.

It is the last day of Pride Month, and a banner the length of my body stretches across the brick walkway, depicting monarch butterflies flying across the transgender pride flag. The message reads "NO HAY ORGULLO EN DETENCIÓN #END TRANS DETENTION." Several people in attendance wear pride flags around their necks, like capes. One flag is embroidered with a brown fist and the phrase "resist." Most people wear Familia: Trans

Queer Liberation Movement (TQLM) T-shirts, featuring a design by Lucy Sandoval, displaying two pairs of legs walking away from a burning police car—one wears strappy platform heels and has ACAB tattooed on their calf, the other one sports a knee-high pair of boots, and a message on their sole reads "*chinga la migra.*" TQLM not only organizes against migrant detention but also supports LGBTQ asylum seekers with humanitarian, legal, and medical support, and it coordinates healing programs for trans and queer *familia* who have survived displacement and incarceration. They center *jotería* in their movement spaces, refusing propriety and respectability in favor of what Chávez calls a "queer politics of fugitivity." While the sanctuary city works to repair relationships between migrants and the police, TQLM practices an abolitionist politics of intimacy and care, affirming that the police have not and will not keep communities safe. Their message is clear: *chinga la migra.*

Karolina López, director of Mariposas Sin Fronteras—an organization that supports trans and queer migrants detained in Eloy and Florence—reaches for a megaphone and hops onto a bench to address the crowd. A transgender woman from Guerrero, Karolina was incarcerated in the men's unit at Eloy for three years while awaiting asylum. The wind makes her curly, purple hair dance in every direction, almost as if mimicking the pride flags undulating in the air. "ICE *no tiene la capacidad de detener a ninguna de nuestras hermanas—a nadie—dentro de sus centros de detención. Entonces estamos aquí para exigir los cierres y la liberación de nuestras compañeras dentro los centros de detención. Seguimos esta lucha hasta que seamos escuchadas—perdónenme, escuchadxs. Muchas gracias por estar aquí. Exigimos justicia.*" Her brief remarks are clear and to the point. ICE does not have the authority to detain *anyone* in their detention centers. Karolina does not draw distinctions the way the sanctuary city does; she demands the liberation of all migrants. Hers is a different practice of sanctuary, not an ordinance or a policy but a movement or a procession.

Jennicet Gutiérrez takes the megaphone. Her hair is pulled back in a loose ponytail, and she wears oversized black sunglasses that cover the top half of her face. Jennicet is the coexecutive director of TQLM, and she is perhaps most well known for interrupting President Obama's celebratory speech in honor of the repeal of the Defense of Marriage Act. While the president considered the legalization of gay marriage a victory, Jennicet condemned his administration for detaining and deporting queer and transgender migrants. "President Obama," she yelled at the White House, "release all LGBTQ immigrants from detention and stop all deportations!"

Years later, at the rally, she continues: "*Esta campaña, No Hay Orgullo en Detención, está mandando un mensaje bien claro a la administración de Biden, al departamento de inmigración, a la agencia fronteriza que está tratando mal a nuestra comunidad.*" Jennicet turns her torso back and forth, from left to right, to make sure everyone gathered can see her. "We are seeking justice. Some of the posters that we have feature Victoria Arellano, Johanna Medina, and Roxsana Hernandez—trans undocumented women who died in ICE custody. And that is unacceptable." When she translates this last sentence to Spanish, Gutiérrez places more blame on ICE and the US government. "*Ellas fueron asesinadas por el Departamento de Inmigración.*" In Spanish, she says these women were murdered. "They lived with HIV and the agency neglected to provide care for them. We're honoring their lives, and we will continue to fight until we end trans detention. *Estamos luchando y diciendo, ¡ya basta!*" The crowd repeats forcefully, "*¡ya basta!*" clapping, whistling, and snapping their fingers. *Basta* is not reform and it does not ask for inclusion. *Basta* is a refusal of the everyday.

Before we take to the streets, Jennicet invites a member from the security team to share protocol for engaging with the police. They tell us to look for people wearing tie-dye, neon headbands in case of an emergency: "Remember, we keep each other safe." The crowd begins marching south on Stone Avenue, taking up the entire width of the road, toward Congress Street. Jennicet leads us in chanting "trans power" over and over again. We were all given 4×4 slips of paper listing official chants, but they emerge more spontaneously as we continue down the cement streets. "*No hay orgullo,*" someone shouts, and the rest of us follow with "*en detención.*" As the sun goes down and the sky grows more dim, the glimmering lights of police cars blocking the roads become more pronounced, more menacing. Our voices vibrate and send waves of sound down the two-lane street. Servers walk out of restaurants, and customers lift their eyes from menus to watch our boisterous parade. Some cheer as we walk, and a few join the procession. "Tucson, *escucha,*" an organizer screams, and the crowd responds, "*La jotería está en la lucha.*"

At one point, Jennicet reclaims the megaphone and shouts the names of transgender women who died in detention centers. "Victoria Arellano," she bellows at the top of her voice and the crowd testifies that she is *presente!* Jennicet repeats each name a handful of times. "Johanna Medina," she cries out, and we respond, *Presente!* "Roxsana Hernandez" is last, and we again insist on her presence. *Presente!* When the crowd reaches the federal courthouse, we once again say the names of the dead. We once again declare they are with us, part of our movement. We pledge our allegiance to the dead, vow to not only remember but summon their presence. This time, we also say the names of Sylvia Rivera and Marsha P. Johnson. They, too, are *presente*. Rivera and Johnson are perhaps most well known for their involvement in the Stonewall Riots, when local residents and patrons of the Stonewall Inn—a gay bar and nightclub—fought back against a police raid. The two cofounded Street Transvestite Action Revolutionaries (STAR), a mutual aid organization that offered housing, food, and community to unhoused queer young people. Johnson also established bail funds for trans and gender-nonconforming folks, practicing sanctuary as abolitionist care work.

The parade float arrives and stations itself in front of the courthouse, carrying snacks and bottled water for protesters. On the back sits a watercolor painting of Victoria Arellano, Johanna Medina, and Roxsana Hernandez, with roses and butterflies framing their heads—all looking to the sides. In the painting, none of the women look directly at the viewer. None of them smile.

While incarcerated, Arellano was held with over one hundred men in a cell designed for forty. Arellano had been diagnosed with AIDS prior to her detention and the cramped and unsanitary environment inside the prison exacerbated her condition. She became ill when ICE officials withheld her medication and she developed a pulmonary infection. Karma Chávez writes about Arellano's death in ICE custody in Southern California. Chávez describes the curative touch practiced by her cellmates. Incarcerated migrants used bath towels soaked in cold water to alleviate her fever and cleaned up her blood and vomit. "Even those who did not engage in the daily, *hands-on* caretaking of Arellano when she was at her worst, stockpiled their own rations of pain relievers in order to alleviate her immense physical pain."[49] When ICE continued to deny Arellano medical care, fellow detainees staged a strike and refused to line up for the nightly head count. Chávez insists that "the detention cell is a space of survival where the precariousness of one's own life is reflected in the lives of other detainees."[50] The condition of being smuggled inspires a contraband touch, one that is contagious and ecstatic—sacred.

○

The Hebrew Bible describes practices of sanctuary that existed before cities of refuge were established. People who had committed crimes could gain temporary safety by fleeing to a sanctuary and grasping the horns of the

2.6 A festive protest makes its way through downtown Tucson, shouting "*No hay orgullo en detención.*"

2.7 Protesters assemble against trans detention as police cars idle in the background.

altar. For example, in 1 Kings 1, Adonijah—one of David's sons—sacrifices great numbers of cattle and declares himself king. After his father anoints Solomon as his successor instead, Adonijah seeks refuge by clinging to the altar in Jerusalem—fearful of his brother's wrath. Similarly, in medieval Europe, people on the run from the law could claim sanctuary by reaching out and touching the iron or metal ring attached to the door of a church, known as a sanctuary knocker. Theologian Leo Guardado tells me over email correspondence that, in antiquity, fugitives could also enter sanctuary by grasping a bishop's robe. What matters here is the activity—the motion, the impulse—to reach out, to transgress the taboo.

In the days leading up to her asylum hearing, Eva fasted—sneaking food to her cellmate to avoid being punished or interrogated by guards. She also began exercising at night. By the morning of her hearing, she was lightheaded and shaking from fear of facing the judge. When a guard entered her cell and called her name, Eva requested to be taken to the medic on call, hoping a visit to the clinic could delay the hearing. But, seeing that Eva had no fever, the nurse immediately sent her away. As she made her way to face the judge, the narrow prison hallway feeling like it was caving in with every step, a man standing outside the courtroom whispered, "Do you want to end up like the others who are denied asylum?" Eva kept moving forward, but she heard the stranger again: "Don't walk in there." Eva says she fainted. Everything afterward is hazy. According to her, the collapse was divine intervention, her David and Goliath moment. The following month, her hearing was rescheduled with a different judge and she was granted asylum. Eva tells me the judge's words are sealed in her memory: "*Bienvenida a los Estados Unidos de América. Suerte en su nueva vida.*"

Eva calls me to pick her up from Eloy upon her release, but I am back in North Carolina—quarantining after a last-minute flight from Tucson, days before a stay-at-home order is issued across the state. We talk over the phone and I ask her questions about life in detention. I tell her that, mostly, I'm interested in the relationships between women and the ways they shelter and nurture one another. I mail her a letter with a series of questions, and she texts back:

> *¿De qué se habla en el centro de detención? Hablamos del pasado, de lo que fuimos y porque estamos aquí. Se habla de sueños, se habla de cómo será afuera y si las montañas de Arizona tienen carreteras para poderlas recorrer enteras. Se habla de la libertad y nos preguntamos por qué si hay tanta libertad afuera, los pájaros vienen en manada a pararse dentro de*

un centro de detención. Aprovechamos cada segundo en que nos sacaban a almorzar para ver el sol, ver a la calle, y decir pronto estaré afuera. Se desea la bandera estadounidense, la vemos moverse y nos preguntamos, ¿valdrá la pena? Nos sentimos por momentos que estamos en México, tanto que decimos, cuando gane y pase a los estados unidos haré esto y esto. Como si no estuviésemos en tierras americanas. Decimos, esto es como una película y literalmente así lo es. Todo esperamos con ansias el tiempo de Dios.

Eva and her cellmates dream and speak of flight—of roads that wind around Arizona's mountains and of birds that wander into and out of the detention center, indifferent to and uninterested in guidelines and protocols. When she describes the American flag, she notices its movement in the air—poetic, weightless, wavering. In those moments, she says, the women ask themselves if this country is even worth their suffering. They look forward to every second spent outdoors to see the sun, the road, and wonder what exists beyond the wire and fences. Eva's words express a restless mobility, a desire to get out, a care that organizes against policy and politics. Sacred beings and forces are desperate "*para pronto estar afuera.*"

Ultimately, the word *carceral* derives from the early Indo-European *(s) ker,* meaning something like "to bend, turn, in the sense of an enclosure." The strategy of Prevention through Deterrence bends, turns, and reroutes migrants into the most remote areas of the desert, where agents police and restrict their movements. Yet, here, I show how migrants bend and turn, not in the sense of an enclosure but rather in the sense of a meander. To recall chapter 1, to meander is to refuse utility and usefulness. It is to reject order in favor of movement. To meander is to disrupt linear paths to citizenship; it is to embrace a politics of touch that is not productive, not rational, not consistent. Contraband touch accompanies migrants as they cross borders, navigate deserts, and plot their escape from cages. Through touch, migrants practice movement even while incarcerated. Theirs is a sacred maneuver that seeks proximity and intimacy—despite the taboos placed on touch by the carceral state. Their aspirations and mobilities undermine the stability of the profane, animating other worlds that disrupt the everyday and its enforcement operations. In chapter 3, I follow how this fugitive tradition accompanies migrants after they are deported, suggesting that sanctuary neither begins nor ends in the United States.

Chapter Three

The Deported

Lines of Flight through Nogales, Sonora

No hay más que cambiar.

—GLORIA ANZALDÚA

Francisco Olachea—endearingly known as Panchito—greets me and fellow volunteers at the Nogales port of entry. He sports a custom-made, navy polo shirt, embroidered with the serpent-entwined Rod of Asclepius and "Panchito y Su Cristina" in bold letters. Samaritans volunteers Elisa and Joel Hauptman carry paisley duffel bags brimming with used clothing and medical supplies. It takes the four of us to load these donations into Panchito's makeshift ambulance, a repurposed four-by-four van. On the way to his apartment to drop off excess donations, Panchito suggests driving up a short hill and past a shrine to José Antonio Elena Rodríguez, a sixteen-year-old murdered by a Border Patrol agent in 2012. Stray dogs swarm the white van as we climb up the wrought-iron staircase to Panchito's studio apartment, furnished modestly with a futon, coffee table, and a kitchen table that seats two. Elisa scrambles to wash Panchito's dishes before his American girlfriend, Kathi, visits this weekend. I stand on my tiptoes and peer over Elisa as she scrubs coffee-stained mugs. Through the window above the sink, the rusted border wall slithers over the land.

When Panchito left his hometown of Ensenada in Baja California and crossed the US-Mexico border at the age of sixteen, only a chain-link fence separated the twin cities of Nogales, Sonora, and Nogales, Arizona. When he was deported from the United States thirty-two years later after being arrested on charges of driving under the influence, the fence had been

3.1 Panchito on the move in his sanctuary on wheels.

3.2 A view of the border wall snaking up a hillside from Panchito's apartment.

replaced by the steel bollard wall now visible from his kitchen sink. The wall has since been reinforced with six rows of razor wire—covering nearly the entire surface.

A *khata*—or Tibetan Buddhist ceremonial scarf—stamped with the eight auspicious signs of good fortune drapes over Panchito's coffee table. Devotional objects crowd the surface: white conch shells, a silver Christian cross, Mexican coins, and a pair of Elisa's red dot earrings, which she makes out of tin cans found on migrant trails to honor the dead in the desert. An unfinished wooden box holds a Buddha and Ganesha. Tibetan prayer flags hang next to selfies of Panchito and his girlfriend posing gleefully in front of the border wall: arms wrapped around each other, grinning from ear to ear. Postcards from Phoenix, Arizona, bear traces of the life Panchito led in the United States. When I text my friend Israel a picture of the eclectic altar, he insists it is very Mexican to combine religious traditions. "We pray to everything and anything."

Panchito once compared deportation to a death. Suddenly homeless, he spent his nights at the Panteón Nacional Graveyard in Nogales—one of the living among the dead, though at times he was not so sure. Panchito says he lost "everything" when he was deported, not only his material belongings but also his social relations—his kin. Deportation marked a complete and total rupture, an irrecoverable loss. Over time, he felt a deep urge to pursue change, to remake his life in the border town. At the age of forty-eight, Panchito enrolled in a local college and earned his nursing license. When I tell him that my degree is in religious studies, Panchito shares that he was studying to become a minister but abandoned that path when those courses conflicted with nursing school. Panchito credits Christianity with resurrecting him from the dead, and he once scolded me for visiting a local temple to Santísima Muerte. The nurse insists there is only one God and He is the one who defeated death, not the skeletal woman who personifies death itself. Soon after graduating and inspired by his conversion, Panchito began to walk the streets of the border town with medical supplies in his backpack—earning the reputation of "*la ambulancia caminante*." In 2013, Panchito bought a fifteen-year-old van to use as an ambulance and named it Panchito y Su Cristina, after his daughter who lives in the United States. Fittingly, today he lives on Calle Reforma.

Elisa, Joel, and I squeeze into the bench seat next to Panchito and make our way to Grupos Beta, a Mexican agency founded in 1990 with the stated purpose of defending migrants' human rights. Dressed in bright orange to be differentiated from other police officers, Grupos Beta brands itself as the humanitarian wing of federal immigration enforcement. Yet Central American migrants in Tapachula once told me that Grupos Beta officers had stalled them with food and water while waiting for *la migra* to arrive and arrest those without authorization. Migrants are allowed to sleep at the Grupos Beta office in Nogales for up to three nights; after that they must find alternative housing while they wait to cross—typically between two to three months. When we arrive, the striped Grupos Beta ambulance sits unattended in the parking lot. Panchito complains that the agency takes credit for his labor, promoting their "humanitarian" mission though he is largely responsible for aiding migrants staying at the Grupos Beta premises. "That ambulance hasn't moved in days," the nurse mutters resentfully as he parks his Suzuki van. The four of us sign in at the main office and walk around the building and past an asphalt basketball court to a modest shelter with turmeric walls.

Ricardo, a fifty-five-year-old local with impeccable English, greets us and offers to help set up the room. Unable to find steady work in Nogales, Ricardo spends his days at Grupos Beta, assisting American volunteers in exchange for gourmet chocolates and prescription drugs from the United States. He and Joel push together three folding tables branded with the Coca-Cola logo and unpack crayons and coloring books for migrant children, who slowly start trickling in with their parents. A three-year-old girl named Carolina, deliriously sick with a fever, climbs onto my lap and falls asleep, occasionally waking up to cough and blow her nose. She does not speak, but I am finally able to make her smile with images of puppies on my phone. Carolina is traveling with her *abuelita*, having been left behind by her mother who crossed the border with a man she had recently met in Nogales. Carolina's *abuelita* does not mention her daughter's flight, but she does complain about living in migrant shelters as a diabetic elderly person. She speaks with the gravelly voice of a chainsmoker, but Panchito guesses it is likely a result of living in cold and dusty conditions. Ricardo jokes that I should take Carolina across the border. "You're from North *Carolina*. It's meant to be!" he shouts, pleased with his observation. Joel asks Ricardo where he learned to speak English and the lumbering man responds that American missionaries lived in his hometown and taught him to speak their language. A few hours later, as we pick up crumpled pieces of paper and clean up glitter spills, Ricardo leans in and surreptitiously confesses to me: "There was no missionary. The truth is, I lived in the United States for fifteen years before I was caught during a workplace raid. I didn't want anyone to judge me."

Panchito takes us to dinner, where he orders *mole* and I ask for a *torta de milanesa*. While waiting for our food, I tell Panchito I want to write about his work. I remind him of the concept I proposed the previous summer—that his ministry is a sanctuary on wheels—and he responds enthusiastically, but under one condition. I cannot use a pseudonym. He wants recognition. Panchito y Su Cristina is funded largely by donors in the United States, and the nurse needs exposure. As we discuss how my fieldwork might take shape, Panchito advises me to get used to the feeling of "walking on air"—which I read as his take on the miracle of walking on water, his own defiance of the laws of gravity. He elaborates, "*Mi'ja*, I started with only a backpack full of Band-Aids and rubbing alcohol. They called me the walking ambulance. Now, I bring doctors to shelters. The doctors come to *me*. Can you believe it?" Panchito was deported from Arizona, smuggled to Nogales, strategically abandoned by both the US and Mexican governments. But, as he likes to remind me, deportation was not an end for Panchito. Rather, his deportation was a line of flight—a break in what Gilles Deleuze and Félix Guattari call molar and molecular lines, which Matt Fournier interprets as "an infinitesimal possibility of escape."[1]

Activists often frame sanctuary as a defense against deportation, "sacred resistance" that defies Immigration and Customs Enforcement (ICE) and its operations.[2] Contemporary movements like Sanctuary Not Deportation—a coalition of faith groups committed to providing refuge to "neighbors who face a deportation order"—differentiate their work from the Sanctuary Movement of the 1980s.[3] Rather than defending recently arrived migrants, the coalition focuses their work on people who have "settled" in the United States. They give priority to the experiences of migrants who own homes, have strong community ties, and form part of mixed-status families. In other words, Sanctuary Not Deportation centers their efforts on "long term members of our communities—our neighbors."[4] Given the Trump administration's promise to deport millions and to revoke President Obama's prosecutorial discretion guidelines—which offered some relief to select migrants without criminal records—the coalition worked to expand sanctuary beyond congregations. Sanctuary Not Deportation takes to the streets in defense of sanctuary cities and against local detainer policies. They put their bodies on the line to protect people subject to state-sponsored kidnapping and disappearance. The coalition hosts know-your-rights trainings. Their congregations provide legal aid, housing assistance, and bail support funds to undocumented people—understanding sanctuary not as a place of protection but, rather, a set of practices that defend people at risk of deportation.

Yet framing sanctuary as the antithesis to deportation suggests that practices of care are limited to one side of the border. While affirming efforts to defend migrants from deportation, this chapter proposes that sanctuary does not end at a port of entry. Rather, these practices travel with migrants across borders. Rather than advocating Sanctuary Not Deportation, these pages study sanctuary *in the wake* of deportation. The impulse to protect "our neighbors" and to emphasize their settled, stable lives in the United States also fixes people in time and place. It limits their possibilities of becoming, in favor of a single being or an essential self. Migrants' lives are open-ended, not immutable: full of possibilities, not closures. In the end, as César Miguel R. Vega Magallón observes, "Deportees have long been treated as permanent casualties, as if they are meant to vanish over the border. But their lives continue."[5]

Too frequently, these lives or afterlives are shaped by the violence of forced removal. Deported migrants are vulnerable to exploitation; they are often separated from their loved ones, banished from their communities, and stigmatized as criminals in their home countries. Most arrive without Mexican identifying documents and 34 percent report having their belongings confiscated by immigration officials.[6] According to Vega Magallón, after deportation, many people lack health care, jobs, and housing. They write that, although governments depend on remittances and return tourism from citizens living abroad, deported migrants are structurally abandoned and blamed for their own failures. Jeremy Slack studies forms of confinement after removal, showing how cartels and state agents surveil and entice deported migrants into organized crime. Cartels monitor ports of entry and target deportees wearing prison-issue clothing, who can be recruited to transport drugs in exchange for passage into the United States.

Panchito y Su Cristina offers sanctuary to a community that is—often forcibly—on the move and on the run. While conducting research in Nogales, I rarely saw the same person twice. Most shelters in Nogales permit overnight stays only, meaning that migrants are left to wander the streets during the day—seeking sustenance, chasing entertainment. Deportees are endlessly migrating and meandering; they relocate from one shelter to another, pack their belongings and try their luck in Reynosa or Hermosillo when they tire of waiting for asylum, sell merchandise at the port of entry, and sell their labor outside church courtyards. After being deported, they rest in local graveyards for a few nights before attempting the crossing once again. Maybe, this time, they will transit the desert with a friend they met at the basketball court adjacent to Grupos Beta. Maybe they will carry a backpack full of drugs as *burros* for a cartel. Maybe they will cross multiple times before reaching the United States or turning around and remaking life elsewhere.

Nogales is often referred to as the "city of the deported." And it is precisely the experience of deportation that authorizes Panchito's ministry in the eyes of migrants; that loss prompted his transformation. Transformation derives from the Latin verb *trare*, meaning "to cross," which is a variant of the root *tere*, or to "cross over, pass through, or overcome." *Tere* is a Proto-Indo-European root and it forms all or part of the words *attorn*, *contour*, *detour*, *return*, *thread*, *threshold*. *Tere* implies change, motion, activity. It twists and turns. One might say it meanders; one might say it is transgressive. The root word is also related to the Sanskrit *turah*, meaning "wounded" or "hurt." Transformation involves a crack or interruption, unsettling the profane. It is uncomfortable, painful even. Also from the Old French *fourmer* meaning to "formulate, express; draft, create, shape, mold," transformation is a creative and improvisational act. Deportation severs social relationships, captures and smuggles people into precarious routes, with no place to call home. Undocumented life is marked by this threat of deportability, the possibility of being stolen from everyday life. But, here, I show how migrants like Panchito embrace this impossibility of home—the awareness that stability is not guaranteed, that permanence is a fiction. I suggest that—despite deportation's attempt to foreclose possibilities for mobility—Panchito's practice of sanctuary pursues fugitive exits and transformations. His is an ongoing errantry, what Édouard Glissant calls a sacred wandering, always searching for relation and motion.[7] With sacred movements, there is no end, arrival, or resolution.

o

Perched atop a hill buttressed by concrete, La Roca Albergue Cristiano overlooks the steel wall that divides Ambos Nogales. I notice migrants hanging their laundry from clotheslines, which my friend Dora once joked would make for a great zipline across the border. "Performance art," I half-jokingly offered in response. When Panchito parks his van on the steep hill leading to the cinder-block shelter, a volunteer excitedly shouts "*¡Llego Santa Claus!*" and children rush to the ambulance. Panchito is well known in the area, and no matter where I accompany the nurse, his presence tends to elicit a similar response. Panchito instructs me to take two plastic bags filled with clothing and a handful of stuffed animals to distribute among the children. We walk up several flights of stairs, past dormitories with mattresses stacked on the unfinished floor, and to the recreation room—empty save for a rectangular folding table and two posters that read *Mas Alla* and *Regiones* alongside images of the sun rising over the earth. These remind me of the motivational posters that graced the walls of my elementary school—stock images over a black background, overlaid with vague inspirational words like "Change," "Perseverance," "Integrity," or "Attitude."

The director of the shelter assembles a group and soon the room is packed with mothers and children eagerly waiting to receive clothing and other supplies from Panchito. Women frenziedly extend their arms, reaching for bras in their sizes, graphic T-shirts that will fit their children, and socks with playful designs. There is no call to order, no procedure for receiving donations. The crowd continues to grow as more families arrive and press their way into the room. Panchito offers a size DD bra to a woman with a larger bust, which prompts laughter from others and embarrasses "*la morenita*," who snatches the bra from his hand and walks away. Panchito pauses and turns to address me, "*Toma fotos. El mundo necesita ver esto.*"

Though Panchito is convinced that others need to see the consequences of US immigration policy, I have been conditioned by Susan Sontag to distrust photography as a way to witness or access other people's pain.[8] Images of atrocities do not necessarily inspire action as much as they dull and desensitize audiences. Even worse, the images can reproduce the violence they are seeking to end. In fact, only a few weeks earlier, an image showing the limp bodies of a migrant father and toddler face down on the banks of the Río Bravo went viral—an icon of martyrdom for an American public desperate to make meaning out of tragedy, or an omen to potential migrants. Social media users feverishly reposted the image, inviting followers to gaze at suffering from the distance and comfort of their computer screens. "Photographs objectify: they turn an event or a person into something that can be possessed," Sontag suggests.[9] I hesitantly obey Panchito's command, aware that these forms of documentation are crucial for soliciting donations. With his brochures and listservs, Panchito has learned how to take advantage of photography's desire to know and possess. He has become skilled at capturing the moment.

The shelter director approaches Panchito and whispers in his ear audibly enough for me to overhear. "*Recuérdales a las mujeres que los juguetes donados son para todos los niños. Tienen que compartir.*" La Roca is run by a young couple and sponsored by a local Pentecostal church. The couple encourages migrants to embrace Christian values and, in this case, to share with one another. Panchito, in his circuitous way of speaking, begins by explaining the difficulties of seeking asylum. "*No van de vacaciones a los Estados Unidos. Van a pedir asilo político. Las van a detener. No van a dejar que pasen con maletas como si fueran de vacaciones. Sólo pueden llevar una bolsa. Por eso es importante que compartan.*" "You're seeking asylum," he reminds the crowd. "They will detain you. They will not let you bring luggage as if you're going on vacation." Families should share because their belongings will be confiscated when they cross, because people in their position cannot claim ownership. Because it is about time they learn nothing is permanent and nothing stays still.

"*Piensen en los niños,*" stresses Panchito. As always, his concern is for the children. "*Ellos son los que más me preocupan. Ustedes no me preocupan, por ambiciosas pues.*" According to Panchito, the women are too ambitious, corrupted by their stubborn attachment to some imaginary life in the United States. He invites the women to renounce the desires of the flesh and display the fruits of the spirit: patience, kindness, self-control. He reminds the crowd that the president *en el otro lado* demonizes Latin American migrants and calls them "bad *hombres.*" I tell myself that this sermon must be Panchito's way of preparing migrants for what comes next, for the violences of US immigration, which he's suffered firsthand. He also refuses liberal narratives that idealize the United States as a safe haven, a "nation of immigrants." Panchito exalts the shelter's manager, setting her apart as an example of someone who found Christ and became a servant of the people. He asks the mothers gathered in the small room, "*¿Saben porque la señora no se quiere ir al otro lado? Encontró a Cristo. Ahora su misión es dar para recibir.*" Panchito honors the manager for staying in Mexico after finding Christ. Now that she knows God, her mission is to give in order to receive. Rather than seeking wealth in the United States, she has chosen to serve migrants at La Roca. Panchito's message is martyrological. There is redemption in giving to receive, and even more so in giving without receiving. Implicitly, Panchito is celebrating himself for staying in Mexico after his deportation, for not turning back—both literally and figuratively—for the conversion that made him into a hometown hero.

The crowd appears distracted at this point; while some nod attentively, others nurse their children or try on their new clothes. Their restlessness makes it difficult for Panchito to proselytize. Out of the corner of my eye, I notice Elisa and Joel stealthily leave the room and I follow them downstairs, where we serve ourselves filtered water and rest under tents adjoining the shelter. Elisa apologizes for leaving, but she grew tired of listening to Panchito's homily. "I know he's religious, but he's not usually *that* preachy," she complains as I energetically jot down field notes. When I return to the meeting room, Panchito is offering his *testimonio*—"*Llegue a Nogales descalzo y borracho.*"[10] He tells the group he arrived in Nogales barefoot and drunk. Now, he is here, guided by a divine purpose, distributing socks and shoes. Speaking to a migrant crowd—people undergoing immeasurable loss and transformation—Panchito relates his own experiences of being undone and remade. And yet, despite his message of redemption, Panchito's own religious practice is unruly and unsettled. He accepted Christ into his life, but his home altar tells a different story. There is multiplicity even as Panchito insists on singularity. There are fugitive openings even where he points to closures.

Conversion is a common experience for people involved in sanctuary movements. In her study of activism in the 1980s, Susan Bibler Coutin argues that North Americans in particular narrated their work as a form of religious conversion. "The conversions . . . began when affluent, white, middle-class Americans crossed borders by trying to identify with the Central American poor, to act in solidarity with them, and in some sense, to *become* them."[11] North Americans, longing to identify with the oppressed, traveled to Central America to "witness" the lives of the poor and persecuted. Coutin explains that this experience of "accompaniment" made sanctuary practitioners more conscious of the violent consequences of US foreign policy. They became convinced that state violence made Central Americans closer to God and that Central American culture was superior to their own because it promoted collectivity over individualism and religion over secularism.[12] During their travels to El Salvador and Guatemala, white, middle-class Christians converted to liberation theology. Writing about the New Sanctuary Movement, Grace Yukich describes how US citizens also experienced conversion when they encountered migrants at risk of deportation. By opening their churches and becoming closely involved with undocumented migrants—seeing their struggles firsthand—they experienced a "shift in religious identity and practice that was so profound that it is best described as conversion."[13] Coutin and Yukich both characterize conversion as a linear process—a departure from the past, an encounter with the migrant poor, and a transformative shift. There are clear beginnings and endings.

In the borderlands, and especially for Panchito, there is no such arrival or resolution. Families at La Roca, for instance, are caught in a state of *nepantla*—a Nahuatl word meaning an "in between space," or *lugar entre medio*. Gloria Anzaldúa theorizes the term to mean a dismembered state and a generative space; for her, *nepantla* represents both fragmentation and transformation.[14] *Nepantla* is a *rajadura*, crack between worlds, psychic rupture. It follows an *arrebato*, a *susto* or shock that disrupts the everyday. Suspended in a state of waiting—unable to go back or move forward—migrants are caught in *nepantla*, which Anzaldúa suggests can function as moments of becoming. Not a singular moment or event of conversion, *nepantla* refuses to accept resolution. Even in moments when we think we've reached a destination, we are once again thrust into *nepantla*, which Anzaldúa visualizes as a *remolino* or whirlwind, not a path but a vortex, a current. There is no resolution and no reconstruction, only errantry and ongoing transformation. Anzaldúa reminds her reader that "every increment of consciousness, every step forward, is a *travesía*, a crossing. I am again an alien in a new territory. And I am, again and again."[15]

Panchito's transformations are more a practice of *nepantla* than a conversion. While both the 1980s Sanctuary Movement and the New Sanctuary Movement of the early 2000s stressed conversion as a linear process, as a singular encounter with migrants that leads to a more radical understanding of Christianity, Panchito's transformations are multiple and unfinished. In earlier sanctuary movements, North Americans described conversion as a result of having abandoned their comfort zones and accompanied migrants at risk of capture and deportation. But, in the end, these activists returned home, to the everyday, albeit transformed. But, for Panchito and other deported migrants, there is no possibility of return. Even if they are able to reenter the United States, they cannot escape the threat of deportability, which forecloses any possibility of permanence or stability. Rather than seeking closure, *nepantla* lingers in the space of rupture. And Panchito the *nepantlero* constantly reinvents himself. Even when he speaks to migrants, as he delivers his characteristically loquacious sermons, Panchito talks in circles, his sentences creating loops and mazes. His style is off-the-cuff and improvisational, an experiment. "*Llegue a Nogales descalzo y borracho.*"

○

While waiting for Panchito at the port of entry, I stop to speak with a man named Oscar, who shares with me that he lived in Atlanta, Georgia, for thirty years before being deported following his third DUI charge. "*¿Porque te voy a mentir?*" he shrugs, unrepentant. Oscar lost contact with his family after being deported, his children and wife disowning him "*después que tire mi green card en la basura.*" Deported to Tamaulipas, Oscar immediately boarded a bus to Nogales, determined to once again cross the Sonoran Desert. He abandoned that plan after seeing the rows of concertina wire lining the border wall and realizing how much the migratory route had changed since the 1980s. After being smuggled to Nogales in a deportation bus, Oscar spent his days sleeping on a bench near the port of entry. That is, until Panchito noticed the elderly man and offered him food and money for insulin. "*También me llevo a un albergue donde recibí ayuda médica.*" When Panchito arrives ten minutes later, clumsily parking his ambulance parallel to the border wall, Oscar greets him like an old friend. Panchito slides five hundred pesos into the man's pocket—no questions asked.

Oscar, like Panchito, was deported because of a transgression—a criminal migrant who violated a taboo and so became ineligible for inclusion in the nation-state. Deportation, in the end, works to discipline workers into conformity or docility. As Alicia Schmidt Camacho explains, in the United States, deportation has long targeted Mexicans seen as "a tractable workforce that could be recruited for employment and disposed of when no longer useful."[16] Schmidt Camacho writes that the figure of the Mexican migrant has been constructed as the perpetual outsider, "indelibly alien," excluded from the national community.[17] Adam Goodman similarly explains that racialized migrants, historically Chinese and Mexican, "represented nothing more than a source of disposable labor."[18] In the early twentieth century, as the US government began to partner with private companies to expedite and expand deportation, expulsion became a tool to discourage migrants from returning to the United States. Goodman observes that this strategy was a precursor to Prevention through Deterrence (PTD). And, like PTD, it "did not stop future immigration. But it did deliberately cause substantial, often overwhelming, physical and psychological suffering and material hardship. Not only was deportation punishment; frequently, punishment became the point."[19] Since at least the early twentieth century, Mexican migrants have been seen as disposable labor, criminalized for their mobility, and denied the status of citizen. But I follow Schmidt Camacho in arguing that this denial—the impossibility of being included—presents an opening. Schmidt Camacho's *Migrant Imaginaries* studies how Mexican artists, intellectuals, and laborers responded to deportation in the twentieth century. Writing about Américo Paredes, she observes that he located "an insurrectionary desire that might not simply oppose discrimination but release Mexican subalterns from state repression and the limited forms of subjectivity that the state could authorize."[20] In short, Mexicans often understood the condition of being denied citizenship as an opportunity to reimagine belonging. Unauthorized migrants like Panchito and Oscar who violated the taboo are prevented from entirely arriving, exiled from the profane world of law, order, citizenship, legality. But, in refusing what has been refused, to cite Fred Moten, migrants nurture other worlds.[21]

Moten is referring to a different history—the hold of the ship, meaning both the literal hold of slave ships and the condition of capture that marks contemporary Black life. In an essay on Blackness, damnation, and the present as a burial ground, he suggests that being deprived of the world, among those who cannot own, grants "poetic access to what it is of the other world that remains unheard, unnoted, unrecognized in this one."[22] Take, for instance, the women living at a schoolhouse-turned-migrant-shelter for women and girls. Here, another world emerges in the wake of the present one. Nine families are living at the shelter when I first visit with Panchito, including a *Venezolana* fleeing Maduro's regime, a *Cubana* grieving the failed promises of Castro's revolution, and a *Guatemalteca* who escaped her home in the middle of the night, without warning or goodbyes. The women flock to my friend Elisa when Panchito unlocks the back door to the shelter, complimenting her permed hair and grabbing her hands for an impromptu dance. Elisa pulls me into the dance circle, her handmade rings digging into my skin. The women have just finished eating lunch and a few of the mothers clear the long, solid wood table to make room for crafts.

La Cubana, traveling alone after leaving her daughters behind with their grandparents, orders the children to sit down before distributing puzzles, math workbooks, and coloring sheets. She is stern but protective. Meanwhile, mothers gather at the opposite side of the table to create jewelry with Elisa; today, they're using beads, crosses, and pendant icons to make rosaries and necklaces. *La Cubana* shows me a green and silver rosary she is making for the woman who saved her life on the journey through Guatemala. She does not elaborate any further, but assures me, "*Sin ella, no estaría aquí. Desde que huí mi país, las mujeres han sido mi santuario.*" I observe the women share responsibility for the well-being of the children and engage in a collective vision of mothering. When an American volunteer arrives to take the children to a birthday party, I watch the women clothe and braid their hair and offer words of advice to all children, regardless of parentage. "*No les hablen a extranjeros.*" "*Cuida a tu hermanita.*" "*No me hagan quedar mal. Pórtense bien.*"

Writing about another borderlands—Jimaní, one of the two major border-crossing points between the Dominican Republic and Haiti— Lorgia García-Peña describes the practice of women nursing and rearing each other's babies, which she claims is unthinkable in the Global North. García-Peña writes, "Women of color have been taking care of one another for centuries. It is through our communal care that we have managed to survive the atrocities of slavery, colonialism, capitalism, and migration."[23] In her first book, *The Borders of Dominicanidad*, García-Peña expands on these practices in *rayano*—or border—villages.[24] She invites readers to see these communities as a vision of a possible future, to read them as presenting an alternative narrative in which "the borderline dividing the two nations of Hispaniola can serve as a metaphor for understanding the multiplicity of experiences that make up dominicanidad rather than as a place of constant conflict and political struggle."[25] To return to Moten, being deprived of this world opens up a multitude of other ones. It births otherwise modes of relation, capacious practices of making kin that are based on mutuality rather than biological sameness or shared "roots," what Glissant terms the "hidden violence of filiation."[26]

○

Panchito acknowledges that his life has never been settled. At the age of sixteen, he crossed an international border, looking for work in the United States. For several years, he regularly traveled back and forth between Mexico and the United States—not entirely satisfied in either country, driven by a boundless energy, an urge to keep moving. In 1977, his daughter Estrella was born in Baja California. For a while, Panchito lived in Portland, Oregon, taking English-language courses and working several jobs to provide for his child. Then, in 1980, he moved to Phoenix—where he lived and worked and formed another family, until he was deported to Nogales. Panchito has reinvented himself over and over again, rejecting the idea of a single being. He has worked as a welder, an air-conditioning repairman, a mechanic—all forms of bringing disparate parts together, of diagnosing and healing a problem. His reinventions are not unlike Deleuze and Guattari's theories of the rhizome, or ways of visualizing relations. Whereas "the tree or root . . . plots a point, fixes an order," the rhizome—also called a creeping rootstalk—grows and spreads horizontally, almost erratically in many directions. There is no starting or ending point; the rhizome is "always in the middle, between things, interbeing, intermezzo. . . . The tree imposes the verb 'to be,' but the fabric of the rhizome is the conjunction, 'and . . . and . . . and. . . .'"[27] Though Panchito narrates his life after deportation as a conversion, his work paints a different picture—one of entangled and erratic transformations. Deleuze and Guattari pose a challenge to the language of conversion, suggesting that "making a clean slate, starting or beginning again from ground zero, seeking a beginning or a foundation—all imply a false conception of voyage and movement."[28] They propose instead "proceeding from the middle, through the middle, coming and going rather than starting and finishing."[29] Put differently, they propose dwelling in *nepantla*, where there is no stable or essential self. The rhizome suggests multiplicities and middles. "And . . . and . . . and. . . ."

The rhizome is made up of lines. According to Deleuze and Guattari, these include break lines, crack lines, and rupture lines, or "the line of rigid segmentarity with molar breaks; the line of supple segmentation with molecular cracks; the line of flight or rupture, abstract, deadly and alive, nonsegmentary."[30] Molar lines attempt to regulate and order society, to create binary organizations and classes, or borders. They are assumed to be rigid and fixed. Molecular lines, or crack lines, are supple and more inventive, allowing for difference and improvisation.[31] The third line, the line of flight, causes runoffs and leakages in the molar and molecular, "as when you drill a hole in a pipe."[32] The line of flight is "there from the beginning, even if it awaits its hour, and waits for the others to explode. . . . [T]here is always something that flows or flees, that escapes the binary organizations." Deleuze and Guattari use the example of the Roman Empire, with its rigid segmentarity, to elaborate on the molar. They write, "On the horizon, there is an entirely different kind of line, the line of the nomads who come in off the steppes, venture a fluid and active escape, sow deterritorialization everywhere." They describe the lines of flight of "migrant barbarians" who "come and go, cross and recross frontiers." These unruly migrants first wreak chaos and eventually some become part of the rhizome of Roman society. "They integrate themselves and reterritorialize."[33] After all, Deleuze and Guattari insist that the three lines coexist and intertwine. Nomads, like deported migrants, pursue lines of flight and eventually—inevitably—cross paths with the molar and molecular. In that contact, there is always potential for rupture.

The profane is imagined to be stable and settled, rational and orderly. In chapter 1, I described the ways the profane attempts to tame and operationalize the land, to render the Sonoran Desert sealed, secured, and productive. Chapter 2 detailed how the profane distances itself from the negative sacred, enforcing prohibitions and implementing rituals to protect the everyday from chaotic sacred forces. Here, I suggest that deportation likewise aims to discipline or contain the fugitive sacred, the tireless impulse to make and remake life. Deportation hopes to expel those sacred beings who disturb the nation's imagined purity and order. As Goodman writes in the passage cited above, deportation has become more punitive over time, its carceral and authoritarian molarity a reaction to the inability of states to control human mobility. Indeed, the sacred is always part of the assemblage or rhizome, lingering under the surface, an energetic motion ready and desperate to escape. "Taking my life back in Mexico after being gone for over thirty-four years was not easy," Panchito shares over a WhatsApp message. "It took a lot of crying and sacrifice . . . turning the negative into a positive." As he has always done, Panchito saw in deportation an opportunity to continue moving and pursuing transformations. He saw in deportation a gift—the gift of exile, which as Glissant claims, is beneficial when experienced as a search for relation and not as the desire for settlement elsewhere.[34]

Deportation smuggles people who are restlessly and energetically on the move. As Nicholas De Genova proposes, the "deportation regime" is always already a failed project, "its rigid and convulsive movements doomed to always present but a tawdry caricature of the human freedom that always precedes it and ever surpasses it."[35] Moving away from ideas of freedom as a "right" in the juridical ("and decidedly modern") sense, De Genova theorizes freedom instead as an ontological condition. Drawing on Karl Marx's understanding of labor as "life activity" or as "energy," "unrest," "motion," and "movement," De Genova insists that labor necessarily involves the freedom to move, to "purposefully transform our objective circumstances."[36] Freedom of movement, for De Genova, is the freedom of life in its most elementary, biological, "bare" sense. And, so, the deportation regime is destined to be disobeyed and exceeded by migrants' indomitable will to move. "The freedom of movement, as an inherently unpredictable and definitively open-ended precondition for human self-determination, can only ever be a perpetual and troublesome affront to the self-anointed sovereignty of state power. It manifests a restless and inassimilable alterity busily working both within and against state power's most cherished ideal: social order."[37] Migrant itineraries are frenzied, desperate, restless—against order, against the tree or root. They are rhizomatic—traveling in many directions at once, forming unruly entanglements, never able to be fully captured.

○

"*¿Tienes guantes para mí?*" asks a graying man wearing an Abercrombie polo and faded jeans as Panchito distributes business cards to people sleeping on benches near the port of entry. Panchito growls at the man to follow him to the ambulance. As he rummages through cardboard boxes for a pair of thick cable-knit gloves, a young mother approaches Panchito asking for cough syrup. Her toddler has not adjusted well to northern Mexico's wintry climate. Although he is anxious to return to the port of entry and continue about his day, Panchito begrudgingly walks to a convenience store down the street and returns with a plastic bag full of off-brand medicine. Panchito moves quickly and does not like to be sidetracked at the last minute. He hands the young woman a bottle of cold medicine and sends her away.

The Panchito who takes me around is leaner than the man visible in photos from the early years of his ministry. These days, he wakes up at the crack of dawn to run or swim at the local gym, a training regimen that forms an extension of Panchito's transformations. Wearing a North Face puffer jacket and a stethoscope around his neck, Panchito walks energetically along the port of entry delivering his business cards. "*Estamos en coordinación con varios institutos y con el gobierno. Somos una asociación civil registrada en el estado de Sonora, y me pueden llamar si es emergencia,*" he announces to migrants huddled together for warmth underneath the customs building. He looks at me and elaborates—"*Nada puede hacer uno solo.*" Panchito collaborates with Grupos Beta and other government agencies, as well as shelters, churches, and—most closely with—Voices from the Border. Based in Patagonia, Arizona, the organization partners with Panchito to provide medical care, humanitarian aid, and housing to migrants stranded in Nogales. Most recently, their work focused on Title 42, a provision of US health law that the Trump administration invoked during the COVID-19 pandemic to expel asylum seekers at the border.

Tom, a retired lawyer who was born in Spain but grew up in southern Arizona, meets us promptly at 10:00 a.m., carrying two Styrofoam cups of black coffee. One is for Panchito. Tom is immediately friendly. His tone reminds me of a sports broadcaster: animated, accelerated, crisp.

As the three of us squeeze into the front seat of Panchito's van—me in the middle with my knees pressed against my chest—the criminal defense attorney tells me that Panchito invited him to offer legal counsel to asylum seekers. The three of us travel through Bella Vista's winding roads and to a shelter for Tom's first round of consultations. On the way, we stop at a local print shop so that Tom can make photocopies of several handouts from the United States Citizenship and Immigration Services website.

When we arrive at the shelter, the children sit quietly in front of the television, seemingly bored by Spanish-language cartoons, while their moms curl up on their beds, scrolling on their phones or staring off into space. Panchito directs the women to gather at the dining tables, announcing that Tom is going to offer them important advice. The women comply immediately; my impression is that they are grateful for a distraction, an activity to give some sort of structure to their day. *El abogado* asks a series of questions—What is asylum? What percentage of people are granted asylum?—as Panchito makes the rounds of the shelter, offering each child a prenatal vitamin. Noticing two pale-faced teenage girls glistening with sweat, Panchito leans down and cusps one of their fevered heads in his hands, "*¿Qué pasa, mija? ¿Hace cuánto te sientes así?*" I cannot make out her mumbled response. Panchito takes both of their temperatures and offers the girls cough medicine. He explains that many migrants come from warmer climates and their bodies are thrown into disarray in northern Mexico, where they develop various infectious and inflammatory illnesses. "It doesn't help," he continues, "that they have to live in a single room with thirty other people." I follow closely behind as Panchito diagnoses patients and parcels out over-the-counter medicine. I am caught off guard when he turns around and reprimands me for not taking pictures. "I can't help you if you don't help yourself. You're here to research," he mutters, tired of trying to teach the same lesson to a stubborn student.

Tom holds five-minute sessions with individual women, an asylum speed-dating of sorts. When Tom asks their reason for seeking asylum, some of the women are hesitant to share details about their experience and speak in vague terms—"*la cosa se puso fea*" or "*no había trabajo en mi pueblo*"—but he urges them to be more specific. Assuming the role of an immigration officer, he asks each woman why she deserves asylum. One responds, "*No se,*" and he throws up his hands in frustration. "*Si sabes,*" he replies, urging her to take this exercise seriously or, perhaps, encouraging her to be more self-assured. He counsels each family on their responses to his questions, and he encourages single women with children to cite gender-based violence in Mexico. "It's not lying if it's true," he tells me. "Many people *are* fleeing because of femicide." Panchito paces up and down the halls of the small shelter, eager to make it to his next destination, as Tom urges the women to try and build lives in Nogales. "*Tu vida es ahora, no empieza cuando llegas a los Estados Unidos,*" he insists as they sit in silence processing their conversations. "Your life starts now," he blurts out in a desperate tone, frustrated with the women's eagerness to make it to the United States. He wants them to focus on the present, to see potential in the here and now and not wait for salvation in the future. Tom's advice strikes me as a Protestant directive, similar to sermons I heard my dad deliver to his undocumented congregation time and time again. "Your future is now. The power to change or improve your life rests squarely in your own hands." Later, when we are back in Panchito's ambulance, Tom complains that none of the women had a game plan. Few knew what asylum meant, and almost no one had strategized how to advocate for their case or convince an agent of their credible fear. He is frustrated that the women spend their days idling in the shelter and passively waiting for their numbers to be called by immigration officials. They could be settling down in Nogales, looking for work, building a life for their families. Instead, they spend their days daydreaming about an imaginary life in the United States.

"Maybe next week, I can bring a friend of mine to recruit for the *maquiladoras*?" Tom eagerly asks Panchito. "Maybe they will realize there's work here," he continues, hoping to disincentivize the women from crossing and tame their unrealistic expectations. Tom points out that after a few years working for *maquiladoras*, employees can apply for border-crossing cards and enter the United States on temporary authorization. "It's honestly their best chance for entering into the United States, legally at least." The retired lawyer is pessimistic about the likelihood that any of the women at the shelter will be granted asylum. Immigration law, Tom observes, is very similar to criminal law. "Your client doesn't have a prayer and your job is to deal with the sentence." But the women imagine lives elsewhere. They tell me about the places they hope to visit, and the cities where their family members have relocated. One says she has family in Winston-Salem, North Carolina, a small city with a population of 250,000 where I grew up after migrating to the United States. That's where she'll go when her number is called. These women dream of escape, even if it is not rational or likely. They are unsatisfied staying put in Mexico and working for *maquiladoras*—manufacturing plants run by foreign companies, where the goods produced can freely move and cross the same borders that police people. Panchito drives back through the Bella Vista neighborhood—past the sewage tumbling down its hillside and houses made of wood pallets and scrap metal. At a stoplight, he rolls down a window and offers a man some coins *"para que te compres una soda."* In the distance, he shows us rows of new tin roofs jutting into the skyline, noting that these belong to *maquiladora* employees, their reward for years of loyal service.

Panchito parks his ambulance next to the rundown basketball court at Grupos Beta, and the three of us walk toward the center of the court. Panchito assembles those within hearing distance: *"Vengan, necesitan escuchar esto."* Soon, a crowd begins to gather: a middle-aged man sporting a San Antonio Spurs ball cap holding a toddler dressed in a Spider-Man costume. Two women are wrapped in American Red Cross blankets; they both wear socks with flip flops. *"Levante su mano si están buscando asilo,"* Tom asks. Everyone raises their hand. *"Levanten la mano si han recibido asesoría legal,"* he continues. But this time, the crowd is still. Though everyone gathered is seeking asylum, no one has received legal counsel. Most cannot define the term. Tom explains that there are two requisites for asylum: a credible fear of persecution or torture, and membership in a targeted social group such as race, religion, or nationality. As he points out the differences between asylum and migration for economic reasons, he realizes that the crowd might benefit from more personalized attention. So, the lawyer moves to the metal benches next to the court and speaks to migrants one at a time.

Noticing a line forming next to his ambulance, Panchito walks over to begin his daily round of consultations. I follow and take pictures as the nurse greets his patients. *"Que pasa?"* Panchito asks a petite, dark-skinned woman as he swings open the double doors on the right side of his van, revealing a small bookshelf that he has repurposed into a medical cabinet. Here, Panchito keeps an inventory of medications and ointments in clear plastic bins, labeled "first aid," "random meds," "creams," "pain," "stomach," "children's various," "antibiotics," "cold/flu/allergy," and "vitamins." Panchito also stores boxes of latex gloves and surgical masks and a separate compartment with stuffed animals for sick children. He is swift with his parking-lot consultations. When migrants complain of dry skin, he scoops out Vaseline and portions it into dipping-sauce cups he collected from a local restaurant. He tells them to come back for more when their supply runs out. When they describe their dry eye discomfort, Panchito asks migrants to tilt their heads back so he can apply lubricating eye drops. He offers sugary vitamins to children as a treat. Everyone walks away with a twin-sized foam sleeping pad, donations Panchito received from the Mexican government.

Panchito checks a Honduran migrant's blood pressure, whispering to me that the man suffered a heart attack a few days prior. "*Tienes muy alta la presión todavía,*" he tells the migrant, who is stubbornly not taking his medicine. "*Dios no te va a salvar de todo. Hay que hacer tu parte,*" Panchito scolds him. "*Te quiero ver mañana. Aquí, a esta misma hora.*" Panchito's message is one of personal responsibility and initiative. The man has to do his part to heal; God helps those who help themselves. A woman approaches Panchito to ask for clothing, but he instantly turns her away. "*No me pidan más ropa porque la encuentro por ahí tirada,*" he says curtly before turning his back to her and returning to the Honduran patient. She demurs, protesting that he should not blame her for the actions of other women. But the nurse has neither the patience nor time. He dismisses her—insisting that it's her responsibility to intervene when other women are ungrateful. No one in the border town is in a position to "throw away blessings." She reluctantly leaves, and Panchito treats a series of patients—one with diabetes, another with low blood pressure, several with colds. The last one is a woman clinging to her child's hand and begging Panchito to cure a rash covering the entire left side of his face. Panchito is different around children—softer, more playful. He smiles tenderly at the boy, comparing the rash to a coloring book. He oohs and ahhs at the different shades of red and purple. "*Es el clima, mija,*" Panchito tells the mom. All he can do is give the boy a tube of hydrocortisone to reduce itching and swelling. Before the two leave, Panchito reaches for a toy penguin and offers it to the boy, who hugs it close to his chest and jumps on his mother's back.

When he locks up the van, Panchito suggests we go for a walk in the cemetery across the street from Grupos Beta. Rows of stone altars honor the deceased, many adorned with images and statues of Our Lady of Guadalupe and *el niño Jesús.* Panchito is at home among the dead, reminding me that he spent many nights here after being deported. When he overstayed his visit at local shelters, Panchito learned how to unlock the fenced-in gravestones and rest atop the granite surfaces overnight. The dead offered Panchito sanctuary—their graves a shelter and refuge during his darkest nights. "People get forgotten when they die," he tells me soberingly. Panchito imagines himself as one of the living dead, someone whose life ended abruptly. But the nurse seems comfortable and relaxed here. He prefers to live in the wake of a rupture, prefers to live as if the rupture is ongoing. As we pause in front of a gravestone honoring a young man who died in a shooting in 2015, Panchito continues: "Every city I visit, I like to go to the graveyards because they're like museums."

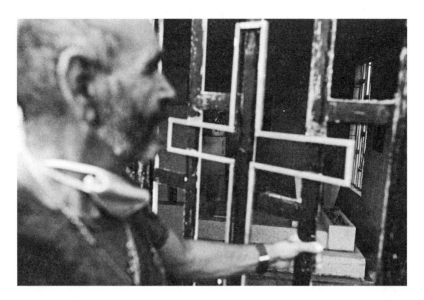

3.3 Panchito opening the door to the mausoleum where he spent his nights among the dead at Panteón Nacional in Nogales.

3.4 Panchito poses at Panteón Nacional in Nogales.

○

Panchito is getting his shoes shined when I arrive at the port of entry, his left foot resting on a wooden stool as he sips black coffee from a disposable cup. Dozens of asylum seekers wait in line for Mexican federal police officers to put their name on a list and send them away to await an asylum appointment—the metering process I described in the last chapter. COVID-19 has not yet arrived in Mexico, yet immigration officers still wear surgical masks. Machine guns hang from their necks as casually as scarves. I spot an asylum seeker scribbling notes on a Juan and Romanos devotional booklet while waiting for her turn. Two elderly women join the line. Although most migrants appear tired and disheveled, they wear stilettos and gold jewelry and their faces glow from a generous application of rouge blush. Migrant children play a game of soccer with deflated balloons; one of them begs his mother for a De la Rosa Mazapan candy, while another cries uncontrollably as Panchito tries to lighten the situation with cartoonish faces. We wait for twenty minutes for families to be processed so that we can escort them to the shelters where they'll wait for their names to reach the top of the list—a process that could take weeks or months.

The two of us accompany a family from Guerrero to the Grupos Beta office. I notice the grandmother struggling to walk and offer to help carry her Strawberry Shortcake tote bag—packed with clothes and scrapbooks. The family fled their home with two bags of belongings and a few loaves of bread. The granddaughter carefully sips from a gallon-sized carton of orange juice. When I ask how she's doing, she instinctually responds "*bien*," but her grandmother intervenes and tells her to be honest. "*Dile más o menos porque tan bien no estamos.*" The woman teaches her granddaughter to be direct and straightforward, to not sugarcoat the violence of displacement. "Tell her we are so-so because we are not doing so well." I would like to imagine that she saw me scribbling notes and insisted on leaving a record of her suffering. Or maybe she saw me scribbling notes and refused to engage as an ethnographic subject. The answer itself might be more direct, and she was just too tired for pleasantries. The children all wear pajamas and I wonder if they left in the middle of the night, an all-too-common experience for people in that region fleeing cartel violence. We drive to Grupos Beta in silence.

Panchito and I return to the port of entry to pick up a second group—three single mothers with toddlers, also from Guerrero—and take them to La Roca. The women hope to reunite with family in New York and Arkansas. "*Nos espantaron en el albergue,*" one of them confesses while we wait for Panchito to hop in the driver's seat. "*Nos dijeron que ya no estaban dando números.*" I share this information with Panchito during the short drive, explaining that someone at a shelter in southern Mexico told the women that the United States is no longer accepting asylum applicants. He responds in English, so the women do not overhear, observing that the person at the shelter wasn't entirely misguided. He continues: "But I'm not going to be the one to tell them that they'll be detained for months in Arizona and afterwards be deported back to Mexico." Panchito is often inconsistent in his approach. Sometimes he is brutally honest with migrants, even trying to dissuade them from crossing, saying that they may be separated from their children at the border. At other times, Panchito insists that his role is simply to spread love, to provide a moment of respite—not to damper a person's spirit with the brutal truth. He calls himself a "delivery boy" for God.

La Roca is abuzz with activity, and families crowd around Panchito's ambulance with questions and requests for medical attention. Panchito tells folks to gather at the rough-hewn picnic tables near the shelter's entrance, just fifteen yards from the steel border wall. I start up a conversation with a man and his wife. He lived in Chicago for many years but was deported after a workplace raid. The two of them met when he returned to Guadalajara. I cannot help but stare at the woman's eyes—one honey brown and another jade green—as he tells me the reason he's attempting to cross the border once again. "*Ya cumplí dos de los tres sueños de mi esposa—ver el mar e ir en avión. Solo me falta que vea la nieve,*" he explains. He is traveling to fulfill one of his wife's dreams, to see the snow, which is extremely rare in the central highlands of Mexico. He has a fourth dream of his own—to give his wife and child a better life. Though many people I meet in the border town have been deported from the United States, they remain eager to migrate and restless for opportunity. Many are looking for adventure; others are running away from violence and persecution. Some, like the man at La Roca, want to make it possible for their families to see snow. They are chasing possibility—thrill, transformation, prosperity, luxury. Deportation does not deter these longings.

I stay with Panchito for the rest of the day. While stopped at a red light, he motions for me to roll down my window and extend my hand to give a street vendor twenty *pesos* for a bag of clementines. A quarter mile down the two-lane road, he parks his ambulance on the side of the road and we stop at a *tienda* for two cartons of eggs and six pounds of potatoes. Panchito is always on the move, and it is difficult for me to keep up with his itinerary. He next tells me that we're going to the "railroad track barrio," formally known as Colonia de Reyes—home to some of Nogales's poorest residents. He frequently visits these struggling families with excess donations he cannot store. Panchito tells me the surplus is the product of Americans who feel guilty about the Trump administration's immigration policies. The nurse is frustrated that Americans are only *now* paying attention to the border and, even still, they offer aid to asylum seekers while completely overlooking impoverished Mexicans. In doing so, they reaffirm a criminal/innocent binary in which migrants are victims of Trump's agenda and worthy of aid while Mexico's poor are to blame for their condition. This impulse is quick to recognize the violence of Trump's immigration policies, but it fails to acknowledge what Elizabeth Povinelli calls late liberalism's "economies of abandonment," or "forms of suffering and dying, enduring and expiring, that are ordinary, chronic, and cruddy rather than catastrophic, crisis-laden, and sublime."[38] Unlike Trump's executive orders and extremist rhetoric, the forms of suffering that Povinelli calls quasi-events do not register as crises or catastrophes that demand reflection and action. So, Panchito takes it upon himself to address the quasi-event, because unlike humanitarians *en el otro lado*, he cannot unsee or ignore those living in extreme poverty in Nogales. His is an underground or covert maneuvering—a spreading that exceeds charitable intentions.

When we arrive at Colonia de Reyes, neighborhood children climb aboard the ambulance and mischievously turn on the siren and honk the horn. I am surprised when he doesn't chastise them, but rather seems amused by their pranks. He sits two children on his lap and asks if they remember the song he taught them last week. "*Que canten los niños,*" he begins to sing jovially. "*Que alaben a Dios, su voz infantil es gloria al Señor,*" they respond in unison. Panchito praises the children and offers them clementines and multivitamins as a reward. The song is one he wrote himself and performs for children living at shelters and in local *barrios*. Alongside his role as a healer, Panchito is also a teacher and an evangelist— spreading the good news wherever he travels. His gospel, though, is one of transformation. His own life is the message, the parable that authorizes his ministry. When the children's mothers approach the van, Panchito parcels out clothing and pours *frijoles* into their plastic bags. "*Así como comparto contigo, comparte con otros.*"

Back in the ambulance, I check in with Panchito about his personal life. He shares that he recently became engaged to Kathi—she proposed to him, in fact. He tells me that the wedding will happen within the next couple of years. He's in no rush, aware that his work as a first responder will change significantly when his fiancée moves in permanently. "Priorities change, you know?" In fact, he has already adjusted his work schedule while dating her, taking off weekends and putting an end to twenty-four-hour house visits. *"Ahorita, los migrantes tienen a su angelito Panchito cuando me necesiten. Pero no se cuánto tiempo voy a poder ser ese angelito para ellos,"* he tells me, suggesting that he will not always be around to offer care, that his role as a patron saint for migrants has limits. That he is human. Panchito idles through a squatters' neighborhood, periodically rolling down his window and offering multivitamins to children riding bicycles and to families picking through piles of trash. I've only ever known Panchito the nurse, Panchito the Santa Claus who delivers presents to migrant children, Panchito the *angelito*. And, so, when he confesses that he is unsure how much longer he will be able to be this iteration of himself, I worry about what this means for residents of the border town. I also wonder how this will impact my project and the protagonist I feature in my writing. But I know this period of collaboration is precarious, that Panchito's entire life has been a series of transformations, that permanence has been denied to him. So, I celebrate his next transformation, thrilled that he has fallen in love. I take it as a reminder that getting to know Panchito—that the task of ethnographic representation—will always remain incomplete, unfinished.

We visit men living at the Church of the Street, deportees with histories of addiction and drug abuse. When Panchito parks his van in the gravelly lot, the group swarms to meet us and instinctively forms a single-file line to receive consultations. Some tell Panchito they have a headache; others say they're having trouble sleeping. A few have chronic medical conditions, and Panchito knows exactly what to offer to relieve their pain. The nurse demands that some of the men ingest their pills in front of him—worried that they might be stashing or exchanging prescriptions. He knows these men and, to Panchito, his hypervigilance is a practice of care. As a nurse, he wants to help them redeem their lives the way he redeemed his own. A young, scrawny Salvadoran man is disappointed to learn I'm not a *paisana* although I'm wearing a SalvaVision T-shirt gifted to me by Dora. He plans to cross the border again soon as a *mula* for the cartels. That is how he crossed in 2012. I ask how he finds the cartels and he guffaws at my remark—likely amused by my inexperience. "No, no, they find you."

On our way back to the port of entry, the last time I see him before COVID-19 makes my visits impossible, Panchito shows me the church that sponsors the rehabilitation center and migrant shelter, a modest building with the name "Dream Center" spelled in block letters. Panchito calls it a "prosperity church," but "not in the way you think. It helps migrants *become somebody*." Prosperity churches are known for spreading an interpretation of the Bible that sees financial success as a sign of God's favor and that encourages tithing as a way to increase material wealth. But Panchito refers to prosperity churches as those that facilitate becomings, that nurture transformations. Becoming somebody is what conversion accomplished for Panchito—he became a healer and a hero in the border town. For Panchito, prosperity does not necessarily require wealth or material possessions. To become prosperous does not demand chasing success in the United States—though that is the hope of many migrants in the border town. Panchito might describe prosperity as recognition or self-actualization. What he asks of migrants is to become somebody—to share as he has shared, to abandon their addictions and vices, to nurture their bodies, to do their part in healing from dis/ease. Sometimes people listen, and at other times they disregard Panchito's words of advice. Migrants are always becoming—our ambitions cannot be constrained by policy, law, and order.

Sacred forces are endlessly undergoing transformations; Roger Caillois calls this the ambiguity of the sacred—dangerous in its potentiality, its volatility. Sacred forces are unpredictable, frenetically energetic, on the move. They are not fixed but, rather, transform with every itinerary, every passage. As I observed in chapter 1, the sacred can be both pure and impure, negative and positive. Caillois adds to this dialectic, proposing that the pure and impure sacred are reversible; they are in an ongoing process of exchange and transition. M. Jacqui Alexander writes about the transatlantic slave trade and the aftermath of the crossing, insisting that enslaved Africans transformed the sacred, spread it "everywhere;" they deposited it in "*otanes*, stones, in the mossy underground of treacherous caves; in the caress of elegant waterfalls; in forests imposing enough to assume the name Mountain; in water salt and sweet to taste the opposite in things."[39] Alexander affirms the sacred's power to shape-shift, to migrate. The crossing was not the first or the only transformation, however; sacred forces are constantly undergoing change—on African soil and in the Americas. "Crossings are never undertaken all at once, and never once and for all."[40] In Christianity, ritual practice transforms wine into blood, bread into flesh. God becomes human, and the human is remade—or reborn—after death. If anything about the sacred can be said to be certain, it is an affinity for change.

Sanctuary—a sacred tradition and practice—also demands transformations, endless searches for exits out of the everyday and the expected. Activists in the 1980s described how witnessing suffering radically transformed their religious and political convictions. They claim to have undergone an irreversible conversion. During the New Sanctuary Movement and the Expanded Sanctuary Movement, church buildings themselves were converted into temporary living quarters. Closets were transformed into bathrooms; chapels became bedrooms. Panchito's sanctuary on wheels, even, involved transforming a worn-out van into a mobile medical clinic. According to sanctuary practitioners, ritual can transform any place—even used vehicles—into a space of refuge. This is why the American Friends Service Committee launched their "sanctuary everywhere" initiative in 2017, which proposes that schools, hospitals, cities, gardens, and restaurants can become sanctuaries, too. Sacred spaces are not fixed in place, sui generis set apart from the profane. If anything, spaces become sacred through ritual, through transgressive action and motion that interrupts the everyday—in this case, actions of defiance against immigration policy and enforcement protocols. Sacred, in the end, comes from the Latin *sacrare*, or "to make sacred, consecrate; hold sacred; immortalize; set apart, dedicate." The sacred is constantly in the making, not static or fixed in place. Always in the process of becoming set apart, consecrated, dedicated, anointed. Elaine Peña teaches that space is made sacred by "devotional labor," or the performances of religious practitioners, whose prayers, sweat, touch, and movements transform physical environments.[41] The point is that the sacred is endlessly undergoing and prompting transformations. This is precisely why prohibitions are in place, to protect the routine or the profane.

o

"*Ahí entramos a México*," I text Panchito over WhatsApp as my partner collects our backpacks from the x-ray machine at the port of entry. "*Amén*," he messages almost instantly. Panchito says he's on his way and the two of us should stay where we are and wait for him.

My back is turned to him when Panchito nears the port of entry. I have not seen him or visited Nogales for over two years, since the COVID-19 pandemic interrupted my fieldwork. When he calls out my name and I turn around, I see a noticeably shaggier and more muscular Panchito wearing a blue Panchito y Su Cristina T-shirt and gray cargo shorts. A surgical mask, rosary, and red dot necklace drape around his neck. The nurse greets me with a warm hug—"*¿Qué onda, mi niña, como estas?*"—and signals for us to follow him. "Tell me, what do you want to see today?" he asks as we speedily make our way through a courtyard lined with dental clinics and pharmacies offering discounted Valium and Viagra for elderly Americans. I introduce him to Alex, my partner, who is accompanying me to take photographs for the book. Panchito nods his head and repeats, "Okay, so what do you want to do today?" I ask if we can shadow him as he visits migrant shelters. Panchito agrees and leads us to his ambulance, which is parked in front of an Oxxo and across the street from train tracks. "I don't have a schedule," he explains as we near the van. "Let's see what's happening in Nogales today."

This ambulance is a recent purchase and has more seating than his other vehicles. I climb into the back, and Alex takes a seat next to Panchito so he can document the ride. Panchito takes us along the winding streets of Colonia Del Rosario and makes several stops on the way to the apartment complex where he used to live before moving to San Carlos with his now wife. The two are remaking life together, going for early morning swims and posting sunset pictures at the Sea of Cortez to their social media, always accompanied by a pack of street dogs they've adopted. Panchito reminds me that he once told me he could not keep up the pace of his work forever. Now, he visits Nogales about once a month—his ministry always undergoing transformations, conversions.

When we arrive at the complex, Panchito explains that he is currently renting three of the apartments for migrant families. We spend several hours there with women and their children, distributing diapers and baby wipes, discussing the border crossing and life in Nogales. Panchito offers medical care to these families—tending to a woman with diabetes, a baby with a bloated belly, a toddler who won't stop coughing. But, mostly, this house call is a spiritual one.

"*No más, vénganse, tráiganse a los chamacos, ¿eh?*" Panchito gathers the women sharing this apartment, three single mothers with their children. He encourages them to sit on the leather couch and begins to discuss the asylum process, calling into question the women's claims that their lives are in danger. "*A mí me pueden decir, yo vengo porque estoy en peligro. ¿Pero cuál peligro? Por ejemplo, tú,*" he says, pointing at the youngest woman, who found work at the local elementary school. "*Ya tienes trabajo. Nadie te anda correteando.*" Panchito turns his attention to another woman: "*Tú estas aquí con la puerta abierta. Ya no estás en peligro.*" Though they may have been in danger in their home countries, Panchito is sure they are safe here, in Mexico. He tells them that their migration was a voluntary one and that they are not eligible for political asylum. Panchito goes on, dissuading the women from petitioning for asylum, saying that if their cases were truly about persecution, they would have proof: police records, newspaper clippings, photographs or witness statements. But one of the women, a

Salvadoreña, pushes back in an assertive yet polite tone. She *did* go to the police when *pandillas* began threatening her. But officers refused to act. "This is cartel territory," the police said, wiping their hands clean of any responsibility. That's why she doesn't have any tangible proof or documentation for her asylum application. Panchito cuts her off, apologizing for what has happened but encouraging her to look toward the future. "*Están para rehacer sus vidas.*"

Some days, I find Panchito's messages full of fugitive desire, proposals for escape from the present. At other times, I read them as neoliberal progress narratives, encouraging people to settle down, to choose stability over the *remolino* of *nepantla*—the uncertainty of the *lugar entre medio*. In previous versions of this chapter, I focused on his tendency to discipline migrants and attempts to tame their unrealistic longings. I faulted him for trying to make sense of their dreams, of trying to impose order on their unruly migrations. But, in the process of revision, I began to question myself and to see my own desires to settle Panchito into one identity or mode of relation. It feels foolish and even selfish to try and fit Panchito into a framework of fugitivity. After all, his ministry is as ambiguous, unpredictable and unstable, as the sacred itself. Moten observes that fugitivity escapes even the fugitive, and this appears to be the case in Nogales. The fugitive sacred escapes all of us. In the end, Caillois was right when he wrote that human beings cannot mix with sacred forces for too long.

Panchito drives in meandering motions, circling streets several times to try to catch up to a person in need, abruptly jolting the ambulance to make an unexpected U-turn. He parks in the middle of the street as cars pile up behind him to shake someone's hand, or he rolls down his window and stops traffic to deliver messages to his patients. "*Ahorita en unas horas vengo para tu mama.*" He pulls over on a side street facing an auto-body shop that had turned into a migrant encampment. He points out a homeless person resting close by, underneath a tent made of woven blankets, his broken-down wheelchair locked in place so it doesn't roll down the hill. Panchito tells us he's going to ask if the man needs help.

Panchito then turns to face my partner, Alex. "When I say the most needy, I don't only mean the poor. I mean Barbara, too." He locks eyes with me in the rearview mirror. "She needs me and this interview. People ask me all the time, 'Why are you helping her? She's writing an academic book; it's not like she's going to write about you in the *Washington Post*. What can she do for you?' But I know she's in need. And that's why I'm here." Before stepping out of the vehicle, Panchito tells Alex that he can document the

3.5 Schoolchildren in Nogales sprint home in the rain.

3.6 A rainbow frames Calle Reforma, where Panchito is renting out apartments to migrant families.

interaction, but only from a distance. "The best photographer in the world is the one who is not seen." The nurse walks toward the man, but Alex and I stay behind—far enough to not interfere with Panchito's work but close enough to be within earshot. "*¿De dónde eres?*" he asks first. The man speaks too softly for me to hear his responses, but I am able to piece together their conversation based on Panchito's questions. "*¿De Veracruz? ¿Y hace cuánto tiempo has estado en Nogales? ¿Dos años? ¿Y no tienes mujer? ¿Estás solo? ¿Y te enfermaste?*" Panchito assures the man he will be back the next morning to perform a medical examination. This is the nurse's typical routine—driving along the streets of Nogales, looking for people in need. Me included.

We stop briefly at the migrant encampment, which is buzzing with activity. Children play soccer on a makeshift concrete field. Panchito gestures to the two of us to follow him into a dimly lit room, where a group of women greet us and present bundles of embroidered *mantas* to Panchito. Because most women are from Central America and the Caribbean, they cannot find work in Mexico. Panchito sells their *mantas* to Americans like me and is able to provide stipends to these artisans—ways around prohibitions limiting their employment. Panchito often has to perform the role of a salesman—showcasing his work to empathetic Americans with disposable income. Since I haven't seen him in a long time, he falls back into that role even with me. "*Mi'ja,*" he calls out to a young woman standing idly nearby. "*Muéstrale una de tus mantas a la profesora Barbara.*" The girl delicately unfolds a square *manta*. Etched into the cloth, a young woman with long, black locks holds bundles of corn as she gazes up and into the distance. I tell her the girl in the manta resembles her, and the young woman giggles sheepishly. Panchito adds this one to his stack, gathered precariously under his left arm, and tells Alex and me to wait by the ambulance as he follows up with patients. When he finds us, Panchito says he knows the money these women make from the embroideries is not much, certainly not enough to sustain a family. "But, my catchphrase is, I'm here to change your moment, not your life."

In the car, Panchito shows us images of prosthetic legs he's made for migrants out of inexpensive household goods. He explains in detail how he uses industrial glue, rubber, pvc pipes, and fiberglass to create legs for people who have had theirs maimed by *la Bestia*, and he explains the care and precision that goes into custom-fitting each one. He adds a neoprene garter to each leg, so migrants can strap it around their upper thigh and adjust depending on their level of comfort. Panchito shows us a video that makes him tear up, of a man wearing the prostheses he made, dancing to a *bachata* at a party. The man holds a beer in one hand and takes his mother with the other, moving forward and backward to the eight-beat dance. "You give people back joy, too, Panchito," I tell him, moved by the laughter and cheerful movement in the video. Soberingly, he replies, "I'm doing a transformation."

Before he takes us back to the port of entry, I ask Panchito if he will let us take his portrait at Panteón Nacional, the graveyard where he spent nights after being deported. He agrees and, when we arrive, Panchito poses next to gravestones, shows us the mausoleum he called home. We discuss his decision to enroll in nursing school and he reminds me that he had to abandon seminary when those courses conflicted with his medical training. "God told me I had to make a choice," he observes. This, however, does not mean he had to choose one "identity" over another. Rather, Panchito embraced multiplicity. "Now I'm a nurse, a minister, a social worker, a psychiatrist, a teacher, all in one." He chuckles. "People think I'm crazy." Panchito understands healing as his divine calling and as an ancestral inheritance. His mother was also a nurse practitioner. I tell him I admire his desire to embrace many roles and to chase many lives, that he reminds me of my dad. "*Él perdió todo, tuvo que irse de su país con las manos vacías, sin saber Inglés, sin planes para el futuro. Ahora es pastor en una iglesia en Carolina del Norte—pero en realidad sigue persiguiendo más. Está pensando en convertirse en capellán de un hospital.*" Panchito nods his head. "*Amén,*" he repeats every time there's a pause.

Cecilia Vicuña writes about the etymology of "migrant." She proposes that the term likely comes from the Latin *mei*, to change or move, and *gra*, or heart, from the Germanic *kerd*. Vicuña continues, theorizing "migrant" as "'changed heart,' a heart in pain, changing the heart of the earth. The word 'immigrant' really says: 'grant me life.'"[43] This is a book about sanctuary and, so, it is a book about the sacred. And the sacred seeks transformation. It disrupts the everyday: negative and positive, contagious and restless, eager to spread regardless of the dangers it poses to the profane. Sacred forces—Panchito's sanctuary on wheels included—pursue routes, or lines of flight. Not out or around, but through and into, they seek transformation, potential, disruption. Panchito's is a migrant heart, a heart in pain but also a changed heart—an always changing heart. More than a cure, Panchito offers a series of consultations—proposals or possibilities for change, for making life. His series of conversions push him deeper and deeper into *nepantla*, or *lugar entre medio*. In the next and final chapter, I continue considering the fugitivity of the sacred, pointing to the ways the migrant dead in the Sonoran Desert resist redemption and *reposo*—choosing instead to haunt the living.

Chapter Four

The Dead

Scenes of Disturbance and Disarticulation

Do you mean that she will continue here . . . speaking aloud,
dead, speaking at the top of her voice for all of us to hear?
—SARA URIBE

Álvaro Enciso is a haunted man. When I travel with the seventy-eight-year-old to plant a cross for a migrant who died going through Ironwood Forest National Monument, I notice Álvaro has aged significantly since I met him in 2015. His curly white hair is thinner than I remember. He says he wants to die in the desert, eaten by vultures and surrounded by ghosts. Álvaro rarely speaks; when he does, it is either in mumbled quips or to make brief, though poetic, observations. "Please, no more talking," he grumbles to the volunteers as we stretch our limbs and gather supplies from the Samaritans truck. "This is sacred ground." Surrounded by expanses of desert ironwood in full lavender bloom, Álvaro reminds us we are standing in a graveyard. Later, I learn that Seri people have used uncooked ironwood seeds as food for centuries. The tree's "ghost-like bark" is so dense that it will not float. Dead trees can remain standing for millennia.[1]

We collect a wooden cross, bucket of cement, and rusted shovel from the Samaritans' red Toyota 4Runner. Alicia Baucom, a volunteer who walks with a handheld GPS unit, leads us to the precise location where an unidentified migrant's skeletal remains were recovered on January 17, 2019. Our group slithers underneath chain-link fences and pushes through thorny mesquite trees. After performing a sort of choreographed dance—two steps to the left, four steps forward, another step backward—Alicia excitedly announces, "We're here!" The data she uses comes from the Arizona OpenGIS Initiative for Deceased Migrants, a collaboration between Humane Borders and the Pima County medical examiner's office. The database lists a person's name and gender, date and cause of death, country of origin, and the coordinates where their remains were found. Álvaro trails behind the group and, when he arrives, the artist plunges his shovel into the ground and digs a hole for the four-feet-tall by two-feet-wide cross. I pour concrete into the earth and another volunteer adds water as Álvaro mixes the substances together with the kickplate of his shovel.

Later, Álvaro confesses that the moment of pouring is critical for the ritual. "Someone pours the water for me because I want to witness the moment the water touches the ground. That spot is where a migrant died and it contains some kind of physical element of that person. They stepped on it or something, *¿sabes?*" Álvaro says slowly, as if he is still formulating the thought himself. He continues: "When I'm digging a hole, *I'm disturbing the dirt*, okay, the dirt that may contain some oils and tissue of the person who died." I follow up: "So you're nurturing those remains, those traces?" He nods pensively, still lost in thought. Because many migrants die of dehydration in the desert, pouring water is a gesture of care. It hydrates remains that linger in the landscape, disturbing not only the dirt but also border enforcement policies that deliberately disappear lives. In the dictionary, to *disturb* can mean to "interfere with the normal arrangement or functioning of, to cause to feel anxious, and to interrupt sleep, relaxation, or privacy." Disturbance is a mode of sacred haunting, a refusal of the ordinary and the settled, an interruption of the profane's "normal arrangement." To disturb is to wake the dead, to rouse them from an imagined slumber.

Álvaro invites the group to scan the area for rocks to place around the cross, which is decorated with slivers of tin cans the artist finds on migrant trails. At the center of each cross—where the vertical line meets the horizontal—Álvaro places a red dot made out of metal, a reference to the dots on the Migrant Death Map that spread over the terrain like a blood splatter. As I observe the age spots forming on Álvaro's leathered face, he mentions that he likes "*que las cruces se pongan viejitas.*" He enjoys witnessing the paint chip and the dots fade. His aging crosses are a stark contrast to the lives he's mourning, young people who were not allowed to grow old. "*Aquí terminan los sueños,*" Álvaro reflects wistfully. "*Aquí terminan las vidas.*" Indeed, his project is titled "Donde Mueren Los Sueños / Where Dreams Die," and he has placed approximately one thousand six hundred

4.1 and 4.2
Álvaro disturbs the land
with his shovel.

crosses in the desert to commemorate those who died searching for what he calls the American Dream.

When I interview Álvaro at his studio in southeastern Tucson—covered from floor to ceiling with his own modernist abstract paintings—the conceptual artist disavows the American Dream, alleging it's all "bullshit." "What is it? Is it a good job? A good education? Is it a house? A picket fence? All of that can crumble at any time. A few times in my life I thought I had it." After migrating from Villavicencio, in Colombia, to New York City in the 1960s, Álvaro struggled to find purpose. He was lonely and impatient, at the end of his rope working part-time, temporary jobs: washing cars, delivering groceries, mopping floors in a peep show. When his aunt's husband kicked him out of their home, frustrated with Álvaro's lack of drive, he meandered into a Catholic church and prayed for a miracle. "Everything looked bleak and I said, 'God, I know I don't go to church and shit like that. But you gotta cut me a break. You have to do something for me because otherwise I'm not going to survive here." Days later, Álvaro received a letter drafting him to Vietnam. He considers it his salvation. Some Samaritans speculate that his time in the military is the reason why Álvaro is so familiar—comfortable, even—with the presence of the dead. After the war, he said, "I had the good job and I bought the house, and I had my doggies and my American woman, you know, my blonde woman, my trophy woman. But then we got divorced and everything crumbled. Now I have to start all over again." Like his project, Donde Mueren Los Sueños, Álvaro's American Dream has died time and time again. His elusive search for purpose and meaning is unfinished, an endless becoming. He is forever stuck in *nepantla, lugar entre medio*, a world of fragmentation and transformation.

"Do I need to move it to the left? To the right a little?" asks Álvaro as he repositions the tangerine cross. The artist then places rocks around the cross to protect it from curious animals and fluctuating weather. After the cross is firmly set, Tom, a volunteer from Flagstaff, Arizona, retrieves an acoustic guitar from his backpack. A few weeks prior, he heard Álvaro give a talk and felt inspired to memorialize the dead through his own creative practice. As volunteers form a circle around the cross, Tom repurposes Bob Dylan's "Forever Young" into a funeral hymn. His rendition moves all of us to tears. I have not heard the song before today and when I get home, I replay the lullaby on YouTube. The most-liked comments are dedicated to the dead: "My father passed last Friday and this was his last song"; "this was played at my brothers funeral he commited [*sic*] suicide 14 years ago";

"My only son has been gone four months. He was one of the kindest souls in this world. Keep him forever young oh Great Spirit. My heart is on the ground."

Noting that the sheriff's office fails to conduct a thorough sweep when they collect remains, Álvaro asks the group to look for objects that could identify this person—an item of clothing, backpack, or travel accessory. Almost immediately, a volunteer announces that he found remains near the site of the cross. He leads us to the area where a femur sits atop a pair of weathered jeans and holds the thigh bone up to his own leg to confirm that it could belong to a human being. It fits perfectly. Álvaro instructs Alicia to photograph the site and send the GPS coordinates to the medical examiner. Within hours, they will tell us the bones are indeed human. For Álvaro, finding remains makes "for a very, very special day. Some people hate the idea of finding remains. It's the American mentality. Keeping the dead out of sight, out of mind. But it makes my day because this may help a family have some answers. So, for me, that's a moment almost like communion, you know?" While scouring the area for more clues, we find a torn ball cap, frayed backpack strap, and ragged pieces of fabric. Álvaro offers a possible explanation for the unruly scene. Dehydrated people often become delusional. "Maybe this person was nearing the end when they stripped their clothes off, piece by piece, swimming in the sand thinking they were in a water hole in Chiapas or something." These desperate gestures make it difficult to identify a person and to piece together a story of their final moments.

Álvaro understands sanctuary as both "a place of refuge and [the impulse to] *darle reposo a los que han muerto*." From the Latin *pausō, reposo* means both to replace or restore and to rest or to cease from action. Without being properly mourned, the dead can neither rest nor cease from action. Donde Mueren Los Sueños attempts to lay the dead to rest so that they can stop haunting the desert. Yet the dead do not always cooperate. Largely unidentified and anonymous, the crowd of the dead is restless and wayward. They pose a problem for forensic scientists and humanitarian workers because they refuse closure, forming a crowd that continues to grow—their records overwhelming databases and their bodies filling coolers in government buildings. Their excess makes it impossible for Álvaro to ever finish his project or to offer *reposo*. This chapter is situated between two worlds—one inhabited by the living, who travel to the Sonoran Desert weekly in an effort to offer the dead *reposo*, and another, where the dead restlessly escape and resist closure. These worlds are incompatible and often at odds with each other. But, here, I present scenes where they come into contact and where sacred forces disturb the profane. The dead restlessly linger in the borderlands. On occasion, we can sense their movements.

After death, many migrant bodies undergo a process known as disarticulation, meaning the separation of two bones at their joints. Animals dig into corpses, carrying away disarticulated bones. This means that remains belonging to the same person could be found miles apart, and they may likely be labeled as separate cases. Disarticulated corpses often lie undiscovered for weeks, months, years—until there is nothing left. Robin Reineke, cofounder of Colibrí Center for Human Rights, an organization that collaborates with forensic scientists and families of missing migrants, cites a study which estimates that corpses in the desert typically remain undiscovered for six to eleven months.[2] The Pima County medical examiner's office has a formal system to classify the condition levels of corpses, measured on a scale of one to eight. Level one means the body is "fully fleshed" and just recently recovered, according to the office's annual report. Level seven is a body that is six to eight months postmortem, a condition where the corpse has reached full skeletonization. According to forensic anthropologists, if a body is found more than two months after death, the cranium and dentition—the skeletal regions most crucial for identification—are unlikely to be well preserved. In cases where a body has been skeletonized and disarticulated, experts recommend surveying a one-hundred-square-meter area to locate additional bones and personal effects, such as photographs and clothing, that could lead to information about a person's identity.[3] The task of forensic pathologists and medical examiners is to identify remains or to put a fragmented body back together. They, too, seek *reposo* or closure.

In her discussion of the postmortem "lives" of the migrant dead along the US-Mexico border, Reineke suggests that forensic scientists in Pima County counter the strategy of Prevention through Deterrence through care and touch. She writes, "This is restorative work, moving in the opposite direction from the dominant forces of violence and erasure that occur along the U.S.-México border."[4] Even still, Reineke warns that families of the dead often experience forensic care as violence. They resent forensic workers who cut their loved ones' bodies open, who scrape away at their bones and further disturb their corpses. Indeed, there must be simultaneous attraction and repulsion for the sacred to multiply its power. Forensic scientists and humanitarian workers use dental comparisons to match the dead with missing persons reports, inspect human remains for identifying marks, make incisions with their surgical knives to extract DNA. And yet, time and time again, the dead resist redemption and closure. Disarticulation extends flight beyond what the living care to imagine. Migrants rip the clothing off their bodies in their final moments of breath. These fabrics are later carried away or blown by the wind and sand. Their bones spread out over the land and their hair is plucked from their scalps by birds for building nests. Their documents and belongings are bleached by the sun. Their disarticulated, decomposed, and skeletonized bodies make it difficult for scientists to identify their bodies and to mark their cases as closed.

Disarticulation interrupts the process of mourning, which Jacques Derrida teaches "consists always in attempting to ontologize remains, to make them present, in the first place by *identifying* the bodily remains and by *localizing* the dead."[5] In *Specters of Marx*, a collection of lectures on communism as a specter haunting Europe, Derrida insists that the person mourning is troubled by not knowing, disturbed by the dead who refuse to cease from action. "Nothing could be worse for the work of mourning," Derrida writes, "than confusion or doubt: one *has to know* who is buried where—and it is *necessary* (to know—to make certain) that, in what remains of him, *he remain there*. Let him stay there and move no more!"[6] Perhaps the reason that disarticulation causes us such unease, and by us I mean the volunteers who accompany Álvaro, is that this process suggests the dead quite literally move and, in moving, multiply and become anonymous at the same time. It becomes impossible for the living to *know* and therefore to move on with our lives as (undisturbed) as before. Derrida, borrowing from Shakespeare's *Hamlet*, refers to this unease as "time out of joint," or time that is "*disarticulated*, dislocated, dislodged, time is run down, on the run and run down [*traqué et détraqué*], *deranged*, both out of order and mad. Time is off its hinges, time is off course, beside itself, disadjusted."[7] The specter's mobility is unrestrained and unlimited, posing a problem for the living and creating a rupture in time—that is, in our histories and our worlds. Derrida is careful to note that such ruptures are not destructive or debilitating. He asks, "What if disadjustment were on the contrary the condition of justice?"[8] Time that is "out of joint" rebels against the present, the ordinary, the settled, or the profane. Time that is "out of joint" is sacred, off its hinges, fugitive and energetic. The ghost tears the present open at its seams, forcing open holes and gaps in the everyday. The deranged ghost opens up otherwise possibilities for sanctuary and care. They stare directly into the present—the world of closure, stasis, *reposo*—and effusively say *no*.

Ghosts linger in the Sonoran Desert, as they do in my home country of Argentina. During the military junta in the late 1970s and early 1980s, *desaparecidos* were tortured in clandestine detention centers and later thrown from helicopters into Río de la Plata or the Atlantic Ocean. Others were abandoned in the jungles of Tucuman by armed forces, and some bodies were disappeared with dynamite or buried in anonymous mass graves. Being nowhere, they are everywhere. Their remains linger in deep seas and humid foothills; they might have fled the country or they may be buried behind auto-repair garages that were turned into detention centers in the capital. Their anonymity overwhelms the country's imagination. Their ghostly matter exceeds our grasp. Without bodies to mourn—that is, to put to rest—the disappeared become specters. To this day, mothers and grandmothers of *desaparecidos* haunt the streets of Buenos Aires, images of their children strung from their necks. They chant *aparición con vida*, refusing government exhumations and reparations, which—as Adam Rosenblatt suggests—they understand as "tools of false closure."[9] Avery Gordon echoes Rosenblatt's analysis, suggesting that these women keep the disappeared alive to counter state attempts to bury the past and erase violence that is ongoing. "*Aparición con vida* meant that the haunting ground remained and that the reckoning with the ghosts had yet to take place."[10] There is no closure when the disappeared insist on haunting the living, their restlessness and their excess reanimating the not-so-distant past, the not-yet-passed past. For instance, grieving the ghosts moves Álvaro to come face-to-face with his open wounds and unresolved losses. When he travels to the desert, the artist reflects on "my grandmother and my parents who are dead. My romantic disgraces over the years. It's part of my grieving, because grieving doesn't go away. Grieving is always there in some way. In South America, we carry our dead with us. In the back." For Álvaro, the desert's dead merge with his own dead—forming a crowd that grows endlessly. The dead behave in ways that reanimate and enliven the past, which never really passes. Their restless haunting moves us to confront trauma and absence in our own lives.

○

My *tía* Adriana died on an ordinary Tuesday in October during the second year of my doctoral program. My sister shook my shoulders in the middle of the night. "Barby, wake up. Wake up, Barby." As I struggled to open my eyes, Daniela said, "Adri was hit by a train," in between tears. All I could respond was "no," emphatically, over and over again. That word was the only one I could muster for the next twenty-four hours. My mom called my condition *susto*. Two days later, she and I were on a nonstop flight to Buenos Aires, both of us too broken and haunted to make it there on our own.

My *tía* Adriana died, but I was the one who felt like a ghost in Argentina—haunting the streets I would have called home, the places where I would have created memories, the people I would have known as family, had we not migrated. In developing his poetics of relation, Édouard Glissant writes about the impossibility of return. Glissant throws into question our preoccupation with stability, the longing to return to an untainted origin, the "trap of citizenship."[11] He favors errantry over rootedness, abandoning the idea of fixed being in favor of a rhizomatic theory of entanglement.[12] "The tale of errantry is the tale of Relation," he writes, emphasizing our vulnerability and attachment to the other.[13] I arrived to meet relatives while lacking relation. A specter in my homeland, I was absent from the photo albums on display at my aunt's house, unsure of whether or not to embrace the countless people who introduced themselves as family. Gordon writes that haunting is when the concealed makes itself visible or "when the over-and-done-with comes alive."[14] Our leaving came alive in the moment of return. I appeared as a ghost in Buenos Aires when my absence from the place of my birth could no longer be concealed, when the trauma that I assumed was "over-and-done-with" returned without warning. Haunting is a sacred maneuver, an interruption of the everyday—a refusal to stay in place.

Sitting with extended family around a kitchen table, not knowing how (or if I wanted) to drink yerba mate from the collective stainless steel *bombilla*, I was no longer able to suppress feelings of loss and absence. For Gordon, haunting indicates "when the people who are meant to be invisible show up without any sign of leaving, when disturbed feelings won't go away."[15] I left my assigned place—or the profane, the routine—by returning to Argentina, and, in doing so, I became the haunted one and the one who haunts. I was haunted not only by my *tía's* death—but by what my presence in Buenos Aires represented: fragmentation, ambiguity, contradiction. In turn, I ended up haunting my family, who did not know how to relate to me in the present when, for twenty years, I was frozen in the past—a seven-year-old with pigtails and baby teeth. Like Bob Dylan's "Forever Young," written as a lullaby for his son Jesse and sung to honor those who die young, I, too, was not allowed to grow old—like the ghost, unable to move forward. I haunted my childhood home in Boedo, across

4.3
On her fourth birthday,
the author sits on her
tía Adriana's lap.

the street from my dad's mechanic shop on Avenida Aguirre. His old co-workers were so stunned to see my mom that they could not speak. They did not even recognize her ghostly presence, so disfigured by loss and so changed by time.

I, the haunted one and the one who haunts, disrupted the profane world and its limits: origins and destinations, departures and arrivals, here and there. I haunted those boundaries, resurrected what was assumed to be resolved. My mom was unable to say goodbye to her sister. The medical examiner recommended a closed casket, given that the train left my aunt's body in parts and made her unrecognizable. In the borderlands, Colibrí staff also typically caution families against opening caskets upon receiving remains. Reineke suggests it can heighten someone's trauma to see remains that "bear no resemblance to the person they knew and loved."[16] Even when they are recovered, the dead remain unidentifiable or unknowable. The dead immediately begin the process of becoming anonymous, and the closed casket closes off opportunities for closure. At the wake, my mom stood for hours, her back rounded, hair draped over a sleek black casket—apologizing to her sister for leaving, desperate to see her one last time. Her remains haunt our family, our disturbed feelings refusing to fade, her disturbed body a reminder of the ongoing ruptures in relation.

I asked my mom to take me to Plaza de Mayo in downtown Buenos Aires the day after my aunt's burial. I wanted to see the square where las Abuelas hosted an insurgent ritual every Thursday during the dictatorship. I wanted to participate in the haunting.

o

Álvaro is a notoriously reckless driver. He speeds down rutted roads and across washes, throwing up rocks and debris. During the almost two-hour drive to Ironwood Forest National Monument, Álvaro mentions his upcoming trip to Colombia—the first time he's visiting since migrating to the United States over fifty years ago. I ask about his reasons for returning, hoping to bond over our disturbed feelings about our countries of birth. But Álvaro is largely uninterested in discussing personal matters. Alicia breaks the silence by asking if Álvaro's considered planting a cross for Gurupreet Kaur, the six-year-old Indian girl who recently died of heat stroke crossing Organ Pipe Cactus National Monument. "Is it legal?" asks a journalist on his first trip, eagerly opening his spiral notebook. Álvaro shrugs, explaining that it would be a disastrous public relations strategy to arrest an elderly man for planting crosses. "Anyways, the law outlaws leaving *permanent* structures on public lands." His crosses are not designed to last more than five years. Memorializations disappear, re-anonymizing the dead.

There is a lull in the conversation as Alicia steps out of the truck to unlock a chain-link fence so that we can drive through private lands. I take the opportunity and ask Álvaro to elaborate on his comments about impermanence. "For me, the crosses themselves are not what's interesting about my project. It's the *doing* that matters," Álvaro responds as he looks into the rearview mirror to make eye contact with me briefly. "The performance of the piece!" I excitedly chime in. He nods his head in agreement. "The crosses are eaten by termites. They get knocked down by cows. They are shot to pieces by hunters, and they get dragged away. About a year and a half ago, I went to the Tohono Flea Market and I saw one for sale," he explains, a bit amused but mostly begrudging. A trained cultural anthropologist, Álvaro insists that ritual activity invokes the sacred. Sanctuary, which comes from the past participle of the Latin *sancire*—meaning to consecrate—is, after all, an activity, a doing, a becoming. Michael

Taussig suggests that transgression, the act of disrupting taboos, activates sacred forces.

Álvaro activates sacred forces when he travels to the interior of the desert to dig a hole, pour concrete, and "disturb the dirt." Sacred forces, after all, transgress the limits of the profane world: militarized checkpoints, border walls, surveillance technologies. To return to chapter 1, states attempt to repurpose the desert's sacred energies for profane ends, wounding and deforming the land, transforming the border into what Gloria Anzaldúa calls "*una herida abierta*."[17] Steel bollards driven deep into the earth, barbed wire cutting into animal flesh, natural spring water depleted to pump for concrete: the border itself defaces and deforms land. Álvaro's performance, the weekly activity that disturbs the land, is then a "defacement of the defacement," what Taussig might call a mimetic counter-reaction that culminates in a "magico-religious moment."[18] According to Taussig, to deface is to negate or undo something. But in the moment of undoing there are a series of unintended consequences, one of which is the reification of that object: in this case, the land's unruly sacred energies. According to Taussig, disfiguring the copy acts on what it is a copy of, and the defaced copy "emits a charge which seems . . . to enter the body of the observer and extend to physically fill, overflow, and therewith create an effusion of proliferating defacements."[19] He goes on: defacement issues "forth a *hemorrhage* of sacred force."[20] This hemorrhage cannot be contained; it is a fugitive moment, uncontrollable. Taussig draws inspiration from Georges Bataille to argue that transgression "*suspends* the taboo without suppressing it," or violates the prohibition while exaggerating it.[21]

We visit a cross that Álvaro planted years ago for an unidentified woman, which has since been repurposed into a shrine. Over time, migrants have left behind coins, votive candles, and rosaries hoping for safe passage. Some offer garlic, which is believed to protect against snake bites. Álvaro taps me on the shoulder and explains how his technique has evolved over time: "Notice how the red dots are missing from the earlier crosses? That's because I used to paint them. Now I use metal." Paint fades and chips away when exposed to the sun, but metal is designed to endure these volatile conditions. Though he insists the crosses are meant to disappear, Álvaro also seems intent on preserving these red dots. When I visit Álvaro a year later, I notice red duct tape wrapped around the bottom of a cross. A volunteer confirms this is a new practice, designed to protect crosses from termites and extend their life span. Álvaro claims the crosses are not meant to last. He tells me the doing is what matters. At the same time, he and his team insist on the crosses' longevity.

Sacred and profane worlds are incompatible, at odds. They often collide and coincide, but—to return to Roger Caillois—these moments of contact cannot last. Álvaro straddles both worlds, most comfortable in *el lugar entre medio*. Often, it is apparent that he is being pulled in competing directions—the artist pursues the fugitivity of the sacred and longs for the stability of the profane.

o

We usually plant three crosses every Tuesday, but today is an exception. We travel to a site in the Altar Valley where four men's bodies were recovered off a paved road in April 2002. The cause of death is listed in official records as "multiple injuries due to a motor vehicle accident." But Álvaro expands the archive, imagining the group was fleeing the Border Patrol when the driver lost control of the vehicle. It is unusual to commemorate people who died together, and a volunteer says they find comfort in seeing the dead assembled "like a real cemetery."

Álvaro digs a hole while volunteers collect rocks to place around the cross. After ensuring the cross is standing straight, the artist fills the hole with dirt and compresses it with his shoe. Meanwhile, the rest of us wander the area to look underneath mesquite branches for abandoned objects, shredded clothing, any item that could identify the dead. Like Todd Ramón Ochoa writes about Palo rituals in Cuba, volunteers in the Sonoran Desert similarly gather materials—including dirt—and engage with them to create the sacred. Here, too, "the dead spread through matter."[22] The dead travel through the dirt that Álvaro taps with the sole of his shoe and the rocks that volunteers arrange in a circle. The dead spread through our touch and labor. Ochoa explains that, in Palo, "other than bones and blood, [earth] is the privileged matter of the dead. . . . It is porous, plastic, and generic. Each anonymous grain lends itself to transformation. . . . Dirt underwrites the contagious in unique ways, being a workable, receptive surface, permeable and penetrable."[23]

Brother Andrés, a Puerto Rican priest affiliated with San Siervos Misioneros de la Santísima Trinidad, often officiates impromptu memorial services after the crosses are in place. The soft-spoken clergyman drapes a rosary over each cross and reads a prayer from a thin booklet titled *The Migrant's Way of the Cross*. Our heads lower as Brother Andrés speaks:

Dios misericordioso, que ama a tantos inmigrantes, despojados de su digni-
dad humana, con el mismo amor con que amaste a tu Hijo Jesús, humil-
lado en la pasión y muerte en la cruz. Sana las heridas de los inmigrantes
con el mismo poder con que resucitaste a Jesús de la tumba. Que amemos
y difundamos tu justicia, para tener frente a las fuerzas que siguen despo-
jando a Jesús de nuestros hermanos inmigrantes por el trato inhumano que
reciben. Que nuestro horror al ver a Jesús despojado de sus vestiduras, nos
mueva a luchar por los inmigrantes. Amén.

The prayer compares migrants to Jesus Christ, who was also denied human dignity, humiliated in the passion and death on the cross. The priest prays that our horror at seeing Jesus stripped of his garments and exposed to the elements moves us to fight for migrants, who are similarly disavowed by the state. He asks God to heal the wounds of migrants with the same power with which he raised Jesus from the grave. Death, in Christianity, is a world or realm that Jesus overcame—one that he defeated. And the prayer offered up by Brother Andrés likens healing to this miracle over death, to stitching the wound closed. As much as the fugitive dead will allow.

Álvaro, too, draws on a Catholic vocabulary to describe his work, even if ambivalently. Initially, the artist was reluctant to take up the cross because he feared audiences would interpret his project as a Christian one. Yet, after learning that the cross was used by the Roman Empire to murder dissident prophets and enemies of the state, he embraced it. "The people on these crosses, they'd hang there without any water in the sun until they died, you know? That's how they killed Jesus Christ." Like Brother Andrés, he compares migrant deaths to the crucifixion of Jesus, pointing out that border crossers also succumb to dehydration and exposure. For Álvaro, the crosses also represent a geometric formula. He notes, "If you deconstruct the cross, it's nothing more than a vertical line and a horizontal line, and those two lines have to meet somewhere in order to have some kind of action. When we are alive, we are vertical and when we are dead, we are horizontal. So, the cross shows the moment between life and death." Though Álvaro's equation imagines the dead as lying down, a horizontal stasis, it nonetheless accounts for exchange and communion between worlds. The cross is a threshold, not a *reposo*. It is a crossing and a crossroads, an intersection that marks where worlds meet and clash, where the sacred and profane come into contact—if only briefly.

Álvaro's ritual draws from elements of Catholicism. Trips to the desert resemble pilgrimage and the artist's elaborate speeches seem like his way of administering last rites. Volunteers often pray and others—like Brother Andrés—read from Catholic texts. They bless crosses with holy water or wrap rosaries around the memorials. In the Altar Valley, following Brother Andrés's prayer, Álvaro drapes an Ichthys medallion over one of the crosses. The gold pendant was a gift from a migrant who believes it kept him safe during the border crossing. The man asked Álvaro to leave it in the desert, hoping it would also protect the dead in their next lives. Today's ceremony concludes when Alicia reads the names and ages of the deceased—Jaime Arteaga Alba, age twenty-two; Juan Gabriel Solis Castellanos, age twenty; Jorge Yin Cervantes, age twenty-eight; and Adalberto Lopez Zunija, age thirty-seven. She takes a deep inhale and wipes her face, admitting she's not sure if she's rubbing off tears or sweat.

On the way to the next site, Alicia instructs the group to pay attention to signs of migrant activity—especially voices or objects. I point out a threadbare blanket draped over a palo verde, and she responds that it may have been placed there by a migrant seeking respite from the desert sun. Álvaro draws our attention to an ATV tire slumped over in a distant *arroyo*, explaining that Border Patrol agents use these to smooth the ground and check for footprints. But, in an example of what Álvaro calls the "triumph of third world creativity," *coyotes* train sweepers to walk behind migrants and clean prints. Some even carry horseshoes and layer them over human footprints to deceive enforcement agents. As they cross the desert, migrants become imperceptible as a mode of survival. They wear camouflage and cover their tracks, traveling at night and seeking shelter during the day. They rip up their passport photos and destroy evidence of transoceanic plane tickets before climbing the border wall. Many carry black water bottles to avoid reflecting light at night. Years ago, migrants were known to coat their gallon-sized bottles with dark nail polish but companies in border towns like Altar, Sonora, now manufacture these black bottles especially for migrants. A political economy caters to the imperceptible crowd and facilitates their migrations. Even in life, migrants are trained to disappear in the desert, to enter into vanishing time, to embrace the power of the crowd.

Indeed, Greg Hess—the Pima County chief medical examiner—tells me that finding objects near a body, even a name stitched into a pair of jeans or an identification card, does not guarantee a positive identification. Migrants travel under aliases and with fake documents. In his office, a stone-faced Hess answers my questions carefully. If working for decades with the dead has affected him in any way, he has learned not to show it. He says the number one cause of death over almost twenty years is "undetermined" due to a lack of information. Without a body, it is nearly impossible to determine the cause. Even when Hess and his team identify a person, many families refuse to participate in repatriation. Hess attributes this refusal to mistrust of the US government, hope that their loved ones are still alive, or *coyotes* who extort family members by convincing them a migrant is being held captive. Hess and his team store unidentified remains and bodies that go unclaimed "almost like a museum would. So, we're kind of curating a skeletal collection of unidentified individuals." Museums exist to contain and classify objects, storing and preserving them in archives and sealed vaults. But the dead exceed the medical examiner's office—they refuse to be contained and instead spread out over the terrain. They form a crowd that is desperate to grow.

Elias Canetti is clear about the powers of the crowd: anonymity, intimacy, the ecstasy of destruction. Canetti teaches that crowds are dissatisfied with the status quo; they gather as a revolt against the limits of the profane world.[24] In the borderlands, the crowd keeps people alive largely by offering protection from detection. Migrants who are typically found dead are those who have been abandoned by their companions, those who have been severed from the crowd. The Border Patrol is known to employ a technique called chase and scatter, which disintegrates the crowd, disorients border crossers, and makes people easier to catch. To capture migrants, enforcement agents know they must disrupt the fugitive assembly. The crowd presses together as it crosses—huddling as one under mesquite trees, squeezing into the backseat of a car across the border. And there is a level of equality in the migrant crowd—the slow crowd moves toward a common, remote direction; it walks in sync, with a shared rhythm and shared urgency. Migrant caravans have become incredibly popular (and troubling for the nation-state) precisely because of the allure of the crowd, its sacred powers. Yet, while Canetti romanticizes the potential of the crowd to eliminate difference, those typically left behind or targeted for abuse by *coyotes* and fellow crossers are women, children, and the elderly. For Canetti, the crowd launches an attack on boundaries—between self and other, inside and outside. The crowd of the living courses through the desert, disrupting prohibitions and subverting taboos.

Álvaro pauses at a well-known migrant pickup location adjacent to a Border Patrol compound. This is the final part of the journey, far enough away from checkpoints, where migrants can wait for a vehicle that will take them to a safehouse. Here, we find booties (often wrapped around shoes to avoid leaving behind any footprints), backpacks, clothing, and water bottles. The booties are but one example of their strategies for survival, which depend on making themselves invisible and unintelligible, on escaping the profane world of individuation and identity. Álvaro observes that it is becoming increasingly rare to find objects on the migrant trail. Drug cartels control migratory routes and they typically limit what migrants can carry on the journey. As they prohibit migrants from traveling with certain objects, *coyotes* further anonymize the living and facilitate the fugitivity of the dead. Without personal objects such as photographs and notebooks, it is nearly impossible for forensic scientists to discover their identities and for Álvaro's team of volunteers to utter their names.

"Álvaro, stop the car," shrieks Alicia as she draws our attention to a pink cross splintered in half, disarticulated right where the vertical line meets the horizontal. A few miles north of the site where we planted the four crosses, this cross marks the spot where Esteban Salazar Hernandez's remains were found in 2005. Álvaro seems unbothered, insisting that he will come back and plant another one—"*así los chingo.*" But Alicia has several pairs of shoelaces in her purse and she insists that we put the cross back together. "Stop the car," she repeats, more forcefully this time. "This will only take a few minutes." With the help of volunteers, Alicia wraps the fibers around the wood; the repetitive movements and the knot they create form a connection between the crowd of the dead and the living. Álvaro and Alicia are committed to preserving these sites and healing what is fragmented—vandalized crosses and disarticulated bodies. Even as I help place rocks around the base of the repaired cross, I know someone could just as easily undo our work. And, as long as borders impede movement, there will always be another cross to plant, another person to memorialize. On our way out, I absentmindedly step on brittle bone fragments strewn along a wash. Álvaro picks up what resembles a femur—"It can't belong to Esteban, this was more recent"—and asks Alicia to document the scene and send the images to the medical examiner. If they are human remains, the medical examiner will contact the sheriff's office.

○

Located southwest of Phoenix, about eighty miles north of the Mexico border, the Sonoran Desert National Monument is controlled by cartels. At least that's what Álvaro tells me as we continue west on Interstate 8. He points out Tabletop Mountain and Antelope Peak in the distance— well-known points of reference for migrants and their *coyotes*. After about an hour and a half on the road, we exit the interstate and head south on Vekol Road. Álvaro tells us to "hang tight" as he abruptly shifts gears and we continue along roads lined with mesquite and ironwood. Our windows are down and, as he speeds up, desert brush erupts through the windows. Milk crates containing canned food and gallon jugs rattle in the trunk, and water sloshes back and forth each time Álvaro speeds over *arroyos*. When we hop out of the red SUVs and prepare to hike to the spot where an unidentified person died in 2002, Álvaro cautions us that "they" know we're here. He is referring to *halcones*, the eyes and ears of smuggling routes.

We walk about a mile to the site of death, keeping our eyes peeled to the ground to avoid jumping cholla, its barbed spines known to latch onto skin and clothing. Everything moves in the desert, even the cacti. As volunteers disperse to collect rocks, Álvaro takes a swig from the gallon water bottle intended to mix with the concrete, satiating his thirst and linking his body to that of the person he's memorializing. Concrete rustles as it pours out of the paper bag. Powdery dust fills the air as the contents are emptied into the hole dug by Álvaro, and water splatters as it is mixed with the concrete. After planting the cross, Álvaro insists that "this person needs for us to be here, at least once." But, as the ceremony continues, I begin to realize that we might need the dead more than they need us. Álvaro organizes these weekly pilgrimages in an effort to care for the migrant dead. But the crowd of the dead acts on the artist, too. They stir him to action. After a volunteer visiting from Connecticut offers to recite *El Maleh Rachamim*, the Jewish prayer for the dead, Álvaro invites the group to reflect on hauntings in our own lives. Just as this person's spirit is still in torment, their burial rituals interrupted, we should take a moment of silence to consider unsettled or unfinished mourning in our own lives. What are we holding onto? Instantly, I think of Adriana and her disfigured body. I think of my mom, hunched over the closed casket, tears streaming down her face just as water trickles into the desert's holes.

As we continue on the now-sandy road, our group peers left and then right, looking for signs of human activity. The land is alive with unruly amaranth, fluorescent palo verdes, and greenish purple brittlebush. A green Travel Caution sign on our left warns that "smuggling and illegal immigration may be encountered in this area" and I tell the group that I've seen this sign before. It was October and I was with Álvaro planting crosses near this site. Someone had spray-painted "Stolen Land" over the placard, defacing the state's announcement. The second cross we plant is also for an unidentified migrant who died underneath a mesquite tree, next to the dirt road. Álvaro decorated this cross with a Jumex wrapper and the red cross at the center—where the vertical and horizontal lines meet—sits inside an

Altoids can found on the migrant trail. There is no name etched onto the cross, no marker that identifies who this site is intended to honor. Instead, Álvaro embellishes each wooden cross with items carried by anonymous border crossers.

"Wait," Álvaro says when Alicia tells us we have reached the site of death. "It's too visible, we can't put the cross here." He is concerned the cross will be vandalized this close to the road, so we hike about a quarter mile to protect the cross from defacement. It's a tribute to this migrant, in a way. "They hide in life, and I hide the cross in death," Álvaro proposes. To return to Taussig, concealing the cross is "intertwined with taboo, and hence with transgression, so as to create a powerful yet invisible presence; indeed, the presence of presence itself, essential to religion."[25]

Before leaving, we pause to share food. Most volunteers carry snacks in small plastic bags, and we take turns reaching for an assortment of home-made brownies, individually wrapped cheeses, roasted nuts, and baby carrots. Álvaro turns down the latter, insisting they are "too healthy" for his diet and reaches for a brownie. Elisa slaps his hand away and nags Álvaro for not showing up to their double date the previous night. "It's not personal. I'm introverted and I don't like to socialize. You know that, Lisa." I notice another productive tension: time and time again, Álvaro insists he is an introvert. He is typically quiet during ceremonies. When the elderly man speaks, it is to chastise folks for being loud or to deliver eulogies in the wilderness. And, yet, he also craves an audience for his desert theater. Álvaro is thrilled when journalists and researchers document his project. He invited Maria Hinojosa to join him in the Sonoran Desert. Countless documentaries feature his work. Recently, Álvaro admitted to me that he has become "one of the go-tos" for people studying the militarized border. For him, there is both the safety of concealment and the thrill of exposure.

Alicia and Álvaro tell me about last week's cross trip at Ironwood Forest National Monument, during which they found human remains—a jawbone, femur, and ribcage hidden underneath creosote bushes. They typically stumble onto skeletal remains every time they visit the area, which tends to irritate the local sheriff—who is tasked with collecting the bones and delivering them to the medical examiner. Last week, the duo found two crosses plucked from the ground. Álvaro insists that only human hands can do that because "a cow is not going to pull the concrete out of the ground." They both suspect the sheriff's office is responsible, that it's their way of expressing their frustration with the project, their way of asking Álvaro to leave the dead alone. Yet Álvaro refuses to walk away from the project. "I'm always there," he tells me while sharing a plate of tacos. "I forget the name of this character in mythology who is the caretaker of the dead. This is what I am." I wonder if he's referring to Hermes, who conducts the dead to the realm of Hades in the underworld, or Charon, who ferries the dead between the world of the living and the underworld, over the river Styx. In some depictions, Charon is an old man with a disheveled look and unkempt hair. He bears an eerie resemblance to Álvaro. Like Charon, the Colombian artist ensures the dead are prepared for the next life and that the proper funerary rites have been conducted.

But Álvaro is not alone in drawing inspiration from Greek mythology. Mexican poet Sara Uribe repurposes Sophocles's play *Antigone* to eulogize the disappeared in Mexico and honor those who defy taboos to look for their bodies. *Antígona González* is an experimental documentary poem, in which Uribe compiles lines from the play, Mexican newspapers, and testimonies from family members of the disappeared. At times, the poet intervenes, but she sets apart her sources with italics: "Did you wash the body?" she asks, "*We are many.*" "Did you close both eyes? *We are many. Did you bury the body? We are many. Did you leave it abandoned? We are many.*"[26] It is unclear if the chorus of the many are living or disappeared. Uribe's long poem closes with a line from Sophocles: "*Will you join me in taking up the body?*"[27]

While acknowledging the importance of humanitarian aid work, Álvaro shares, "I wanted to deal with this thing from the point of view of the dead. The dead are terribly important here. And it is the people dying out here that get people to do something, so it's always about the dead." Álvaro refuses to see the dead only as recipients of care, insisting that the dead "get people to do something." They act on the living. Their disarticulated remains interrupt the everyday. Animal scavenging and the forces of monsoons and dust storms scatter skeletal elements, making it nearly impossible to identify a body and mark the case as closed. The dead's restlessness—the way they spread over the desert—makes it impossible to ignore their presence. They are everywhere—often moving in packs, their remains mingling and becoming indistinguishable from one another. Álvaro hopes to offer the dead *reposo*, to play the role of Charon and usher the dead to another life. Yet, like the dead, he refuses to go away, to stay still. Every Tuesday, he chases their *huellas*—generating and nurturing their hauntings. "I'm always there," he tells me, referring both to the Sonoran Desert and to the *lugar entre mundos*—where the dead and living meet, the river Styx.

○

Once again, I am ten minutes late to Borderlinks, an educational organization in downtown Tucson where the Samaritans station their vehicles overnight. Although Álvaro has already taken off, Elisa refuses to leave without me. "You are the definition of solidarity," I tell her as I squeeze into the backseat of the red SUV. After a stop at McDonalds, where volunteers get to know each other over breakfast sandwiches and iced lattes, we drive through Kino Springs and to the sector of the border scarred by Normandy fencing, named after the X-shaped barricades on Normandy beaches during D-Day. We pause while Alicia tinkers with the GPS technology, strategizing how to circumvent fences and roadblocks. Álvaro points out the bridge that the Border Patrol built over the Santa Cruz River the previous March, a result of the Trump administration's ballooning border enforcement budget. Four white-tailed deer search for water underneath the bridge, approaching our group for food. "Soon, these deer will be cut off from migration routes and unable to join herds on the other side," Álvaro laments—pointing to the ways nonhuman animals cross borders for their very survival.

The first cross is half a mile from the border wall, planted in honor of a man named Carlos Rafael Montero de Leon. According to the medical examiner, he had been dead for less than a day when his body was found in 2007. The cause of death is listed as exposure. Carlos was forty-five years old. "But, Álvaro," I complain, "exposure seems like such an insufficient explanation. It's so misleading. He didn't just die of exposure—it's not like he was a hiker who stayed out in the sun for too long." Medicalization helps to elide responsibility. He responds with a line I have heard many times before. "That's why I'm here, to point fingers." Álvaro collaborates with the dead and, together, they disturb the official cause of death, the erasures in databases and archives. They dig up the "over-and-done-with," haunting the desert. Álvaro continues: "I hate planting crosses because they don't belong here in the Sonoran Desert. I'm desecrating the beautiful landscape. But it's necessary because—like I said—I'm pointing fingers. No one else will do it." The artist emphasizes the violence of desecrating what he considers pristine land, the shovel wounding sacred ground. A new volunteer instantly chimes in: "I don't think you're desecrating land. You're honoring sacred space."

But the two are not mutually exclusive. I agree with Taussig that desecration creates the sacred, that defacement brings out an object's "inherent magic nowhere more so than when [it] has become routinized and social, like money or the nation's flag in secular societies." Or a border. For Taussig, desecration is "the closest many of us are going to get to the sacred in this modern world," or a world in which humans have replaced God as the masters of our own fates.[28] Similarly, Michel Foucault argues that the death of God restores us to "a world exposed by the experience of its limits, made and unmade by that excess which transgresses it," suggesting that human beings endlessly exceed prohibitions and taboos. "Profanation in a world which no longer recognizes any positive meanings in the sacred . . ." he says, "is this not more or less what we call transgression?"[29] Our desert troupe produces sanctuary by transgressing state-sponsored taboos and disrupting utilitarian enforcement operations. Migrants who charge through border checkpoints and force holes into militarized fences transgress the limit, activating life-transforming forces that echo the "sacred" in a world without God. So does Álvaro, with his rusted shovel and bucket of concrete.

The next cross is within sight of the border wall, an area teeming with Border Patrol agents in four-wheelers. Álvaro uses his rusted shovel as a walking stick, struggling to make his way up the rugged terrain where Yuliana Garcia Quiroz died as a result of blunt-force head trauma. She was thirty-two years old. Álvaro supposes that she jumped over the border wall and fell and broke her neck. "At night, this desert is a gauntlet," he proposes, describing how Yuliana may have sluggishly dragged her body to this creosote bush, the needles of jumping chollas puncturing her skin. Was she a mother? Alicia wonders. Did she leave children behind? What was she running from? Did she pray before she died? Was another migrant present to witness her final breath, there to console her at the moment of death? These moments when we relive the final moments of death are a way to re-create the last rites, to cleanse or save a person's soul and prepare them for their next journey. They are also a practice of critical fabulation, aimed to expand the archive. But, in the end, the story cannot be told. There is no flesh and there is no document and there is no witness.

In a 2008 essay, "Venus in Two Acts," Saidiya Hartman similarly struggles to re-create a narrative from the absences and partial traces in the historical archive. Through a method she terms "critical fabulation," Hartman seeks to exhume the life of Venus, who was murdered alongside another enslaved girl on a cargo ship. At their moment of death, Hartman imagines the girls cradling each other—"two world-less girls [finding] a country in each other's arms."[30] She yearns to uncover the care and sanctuary that persists despite the violence and terror of the slave ship, not in an effort to

4.4 and 4.5 Elements of a fugitive ritual.

give voice to the enslaved but out of a desire to "create a space for mourning where it is prohibited. To fabricate a witness to a death not much noticed."[31] Yet, in the end, Hartman questions her impulse to rewrite the story and to recover what is missing in the archive. "My account replicates the very order of violence that it writes against by placing yet another demand upon the girl, by requiring that her life be made useful or instructive, by finding in it a lesson for our future or a hope for history. We all know better."[32] Like Hartman's project, Donde Mueren Los Sueños attempts to witness deaths that the state strategically produced and then invisibilized. In performing critical fabulation, we play the role of alchemist and magician. Yet, as Hartman suggests, we also try to control the narrative or redeem a migrant's value—imagining their children, their religion, their aspirations. We try to rescue this migrant from anonymity and redeem the person deemed disposable by the state. Álvaro and his co-performers want to know the dead—to recover a story, to make meaning—but the dead resist these impulses. They meander in ways that resist our control and that refuse our narratives.

While approaching the water treatment plant where an unidentified man was found dead in 2005, we notice that the Border Patrol and the railroad police have just stopped a cargo train to apprehend a group of border crossers. Within minutes, a private contractor van used to transport migrants to detention centers zooms past our group as we unload supplies from the SUVs. As Álvaro digs a hole for the cross, his Apple Watch sliding down his wrist, Alicia explains this man was found floating in a tank, "killed by the water that he hoped would save him." After we pray, Alicia opens the YouTube app on her phone and plays Alison Krauss's rendition of "Down to the River to Pray," an African American spiritual popularized by the film *O Brother, Where Art Thou?*—where the hymn provides the soundtrack to a baptism scene. It is thought that the song contained coded messages for enslaved Africans fleeing north. When enslaved people fled captivity, they would walk in the river because water would cover their scent from bounty hunters' dogs. "Good Lord, show me the way" is often interpreted as a prayer for God's guidance to find the escape route.

As volunteers turn to walk back to the Samaritans vehicles, Elisa stops us in our tracks. "Wait!" she screams out. "I want to read a poem." She reaches for a crumpled piece of paper tucked into her pant pocket and begins to recite Langston Hughes's "Harlem." The poem opens with a famous question: "What happens to a dream deferred?" Hughes's poem spills off the page. He describes foul meat that overpowers the senses; a withered grape, leathery after being overexposed to the sun; a sore that festers, and then, possibly—like the fugitive—runs. The last line of the poem is italicized, an unfinished thought. "*Or does it explode?*"

o

"Okay, so you said you wanted to talk about the dead's agency," Álvaro reminds me as the two of us sit together in the back seat of a Samaritans vehicle. These days, he splits the driving with volunteers. He says he no longer has the energy to drive such long stretches. "I hear a lot of people using that word—agency—but I don't know what it means," he confesses. "Well, it's complicated," I respond, "but when I say agency, I mean activity. I want to know how you've seen the dead act, if they intervene in your work." "Well, the dead leave *huellas*," Álvaro tells me, launching into a speech he has probably recited many times before. *Huellas* translates to footprints or traces. *Huellas* hint that someone is present, or has been present, and they point toward a possible direction. They invite the spectator to follow in their path. "The dead are tormented, you know, because they are unidentified," Álvaro continues. "In Latin America, we say that people who don't have a proper burial stick around; they haunt the living." I ask Álvaro about decomposition in the desert. Do the oils from a person's body seep into the dirt? He uses this same dirt to plant crosses: Is this a practice of communion? A way to involve the dead in the ceremony? He seems irritated by this question. "*Como te he dicho antes*, yes, the dead are present anytime there is unfinished business. The dead are performers in my theater."

Álvaro insists that the dead "get the living to do something," that they exert a forceful and turbulent presence in the borderlands—through disarticulation, their bodies travel; their power multiplies. This is not a metaphor, but rather a reconfiguration of the ontological distinction between the living and the dead. Álvaro approaches the dead as actors, rather than as inert corpses or the casualties of Prevention through Deterrence. Here, I am inspired by Marisol de la Cadena, who writes about Ausangate—which I may call a mountain but her interlocutors engage with as an earth-being, whose presence cannot be reduced to metaphor or belief. De la Cadena insists that the notion of metaphor or belief transports or translates earth-beings "to a field (that of culture)," to something that can be believed in rather than a presence that simply is, "that is enacted through everyday practices."[33] Ausangate is present and active in the lives of *runakuna*, participating in the war against Spaniards in the nineteenth century and more contemporary struggles against the Cuzco elite who owned and managed *haciendas*. De la Cadena proposes cosmopolitics, or a pluriversal politics of "partial connections," that accounts for the coexistence of distinct but connected worlds. To return to Álvaro, the artist does not simply "believe" the dead are active in the Sonoran Desert. When he says the dead perform in his theater, he is not employing a metaphor. The dead simply are. Throughout this book, I have proposed that sanctuary is a sacred practice, one that interrupts and threatens the workings of the profane world. All along, I have been speaking of diverging and competing worlds—they meet on occasion, including here, as Álvaro generates the presence of the dead to point fingers at the profane. The dead are fully sacred—negative and positive, too unstable for the everyday, surrounded by taboos. Álvaro transgresses the limits of the profane by conspiring with the dead. In the scenes I share, he translates between worlds, using tools from each, on the borders of both.

A team of documentary filmmakers trails behind us in their rental car. I ask Álvaro to say more about their project, but he struggles to remember: "There are about ten movies about me in the works and I can't keep them straight." Everyone in the car laughs, teasing Álvaro about his newfound celebrity. I tell him I remember the early days, when he thought no one would ever see his crosses and that volunteers and the dead were his only audience members. "Oh, yes, yes," he recalls and sits a little straighter. "I used to say that maybe a rancher would stumble onto my crosses or that a lost migrant would see one on their journeys." I interrupt him, "And now you're everywhere." Álvaro nods his head, a little proud of himself, noting that the crosses have become another element in the desert, that they have become part of the landscape. Friends and acquaintances will send him articles about the borderlands and—almost always—the crosses are there, haunting the page.

Clouds of smoke bubble from a wildfire on Baboquivari Mountain. From a distance, the group watches in anticipation as helicopters drop fire retardant onto the blaze. Peter and David, Álvaro's most devoted companions, who accompany him every Tuesday without fail, tell me the wildfire was sparked by lightning. Baboquivari has been burning for at least a week—plumes of smoke covering the sky—and even though it's mostly contained, the early summer's dry heat and blustery winds could further the spread.

Álvaro takes over the wheel at Three Points, a gas station and convenience store advertising the QAnon-sponsored Border Walla-Palooza taking place during the Fourth of July weekend. During a lull in the conversation, I ask Álvaro if he heard that Gustavo Petro won the election in Colombia. "Is that good?" he asks, unaware or perhaps uninterested in the politics of his home country. I tell him I think it is, and David says that he read Petro was involved with guerrillas in his youth. "At least the guerrillas were fighting for change," counters Álvaro. I take the opportunity to ask if he plans to visit Colombia again, but it seems whatever attachment he had to that place belongs to the past. "I had an idea of what I left behind in Colombia. But it's changed so much." Álvaro no longer recognizes the place where he grew up. He says he no longer belongs there, but he doesn't belong here either. He haunts both homes, more comfortable in the desert—in between "the first world and the third."

The drive to the first site of death is bumpy as usual. Our side-view mirrors fold in as rows of palo verdes slam into the Samaritans car. The trees screech against the car as we make our way down the rocky path. Predictably, Álvaro tells us to hold tight every time we reach a wash or make an abrupt turn. Peter and David are incredibly knowledgeable about the desert's wildlife, occasionally pointing out a caracara perched on top of a saguaro—a yellow ring around its head—or a jackrabbit sprinting across the road, almost too fast to be seen. Some saguaros appear decapitated, missing their top half, and others are scarred by nesting holes. This happens when Gila woodpeckers and gilded flickers hollow out a home for their nests, and saguaros react by forming a shell or callus over the wound. Made of resinous sap, this shell known as the "saguaro boot" prevents the cactus from losing fluid and makes the nest hole waterproof. Other birds looking for cooler temperatures also seek shelter in the saguaro boot.

We are near Tohono O'odham land. "See those power lines?" asks David. "They go all the way to the reservation." The first cross we plant is for an unidentified person whose skeletal remains were found in 2020. Álvaro explains the ritual to the filmmakers. "After we put up the cross, we look for objects near the site that might help us to identify remains." He tells the two how quickly bodies deteriorate in the desert, how the elements disappear human remains, how dry washes become rivers and bury remains under the sand or wash away bones. As we return to the car, I point out what seems to be the petrified carcass of a plant, and Peter explains it is the skeleton of a cholla cactus. "Sometimes, when their arms are stretched out, they look like a cross."

With two cameras pointed in his direction, Álvaro is in his element. He does what he does best—delivers a critical fabulation. "Edgar was found fully fleshed, which means a Tohono rancher likely came looking for a stray cow and found the body. But we don't really know. What we do is invent a story." Álvaro continues talking to the filmmakers, offering his well-rehearsed speeches about the American Dream and how it was never intended for Black, Asian, and Indigenous people. He goes on about the families of the dead and how they are the invisible casualties of border militarization. I've heard all of this before, but when I catch him alluding to his project as one that will always be unfinished, I tune back in. "You know, the medical examiner calls cases like Edgar's finished. They were able to identify him and establish a cause of death. The family received the body. But it's not finished. People are still dying," he reminds them—embracing what Christina Sharpe calls "wake work."[34] By *wake*, Sharpe refers to the path behind a ship, the practice of keeping vigil over the dead, and the experience of coming to consciousness. Sharpe's writing is grounded in the wake of slavery, and also living in the wake of ongoing forced migration across the "Black Mediterranean" and more globally, including the Américas. Sharpe theorizes the wake from "the forced movements of the enslaved to the forced movements of the migrant and the refugee . . . to those ongoing crossings of and drownings in the Mediterranean Sea . . . to the reappearances of the slave ship in everyday life in the form of the prison, the camp, and the school."[35] Sharpe proposes wake work as a way to "defend the dead," to keep watch and linger with the body.[36] Realizing that it is impossible to bury the past when violence is ongoing, wake work refuses to rest, to cease from action.

o

We park the car almost immediately after taking a left turn onto Silverbell Road. Peter wonders out loud if Álvaro stopped to take a leak, but he waves at us to follow. "We're going to check on a cross; it's right around the corner here." Álvaro moves slowly and methodically, using his shovel as a cane. The olive drab cross is still intact, though the rocks holding it in place have begun to loosen. Peter readjusts them, one by one, and then looks for a few more to secure the cross more firmly. I notice a palo verde branch has wrapped itself around Peter's left foot, clinging to his hiking boot. Two single-engine fighter jets scream overhead.

Álvaro explains that this cross tells "a very sad story." The man it honors was waiting for a *coyote* to pick him and his son up on Pump Station Road, a few miles south of this site. While waiting, his son died of dehydration. When the *coyote* finally arrived, he refused to transport the young boy's limp body in his truck. "Maybe he thought that would put him in more legal trouble or something," Álvaro speculates. So, this man, refusing to abandon his son in the desert, walked to this spot looking for help. He collapsed here and died alone. "How do you know this much about him?" I ask. "Well, when we went to plant a cross where the boy was found, we saw two white crosses with the man and son's pictures taped in the center.

I guess the Armadillos [a search-and-rescue group] put them there. We pieced together the evidence." Álvaro wears a Plaza del Carmen graphic T-shirt from a Mexican souvenir shop, a Union Pacific blue ball cap, and a red bandana around his neck. He does, in the end, stop to urinate before getting back in the Samaritans all-terrain vehicle.

We continue along the road, which borders the copper mine—mountains in shades of silver, purple, and bronze. The car rattles as we drive over washes, making me nauseous. There are only bright yellow open-range signs pierced by bullet holes lining the road. Cows roam, while others take shelter under trees. A pink rectangular sign alerts us that Silverbell Cemetery is on federal lands and warns visitors to leave the area undisturbed. "Enjoy, don't destroy your American heritage." The cemetery houses about a dozen scattered white crosses, and there is one grave with a tombstone. They are dilapidated and anonymous. The drive to our own site of death lasts about an hour—fifteen miles or so—past the deserted mining camp and through Ironwood Forest National Monument. We follow parallel power lines that form a cross when they intersect. The terrain changes suddenly along Silverbell Road. In the blink of an eye the saguaro forest is replaced by rows of pencil cholla—shrubby cacti that can grow to fifteen feet tall.

"Ooh, this is good soil," Álvaro calls out delightedly as he plunges his shovel into the desert floor. The only cross we plant today is for Cesar Gabriel Velazquez, age twenty-one, whose fully fleshed body was recovered in 2020. The ritual is the same as always, except today there is no prayer or song or speech that Álvaro delivers to journalists and filmmakers looking for a good story. Because it's just the four of us, the performance is more efficient than usual. Combs, clothing, and other personal items are buried in the sand around us, bleached by the sun to resemble rocks. I walk in circles looking for stones, dropping them into my backpack almost instantly so they don't burn my hands. When I return, I see Peter walking toward the cross, a plastic water bottle tucked into his back pocket, on the verge of falling out. He anoints the cross with holy water and a neon green rosary before walking away. Under his breath, he mutters a short prayer: "Rest in peace, my friend."

"How did they find him, one day after he died, in such remote land?" asks David. Álvaro responds instantly. "It's obvious, no? His travel companions must have alerted someone that they left him behind. They must have sent Border Patrol or someone to look for him." Then, the artist turns to address me: "But we don't really know for sure. We are amateur detectives, always piecing together information." I silently pray for Cesar, until David breaks the silence by sinking into a hole dug by desert critters, maybe squirrels or javelinas. "Sorry I'm disturbing your home," he apologizes half-jokingly. I think to myself that this is precisely our contribution to the desert—disturbance, defacing the defacement.

When I write of the dead, I refer to the dead from this year and the dead from the next and the dead from the last and the dead that have gathered over centuries of colonization. The dead are present and future and past, all at once. Like Todd Ramón Ochoa's description of Kalunga, or the sea, the Sonoran Desert's dead "exceed plurality and become instead a dense and indistinguishable mass."[37] The dead form a crowd that grows and expands endlessly. They are, as Ochoa writes, the ambient dead who are not always felt but nevertheless make themselves known like an atmosphere or climate.

In this chapter, I described how Álvaro facilitates contacts between worlds—those of the living and the dead, the profane and the sacred. Álvaro is himself a specter, haunting the desert and refusing to go away. He returns over and over again, every week with a shovel and bucket of cement in hand. While devising ways to preserve his crosses, Álvaro insists that the performance is what matters: transgressing taboos, defacing the "pristine desert," and communing with the crowd of the dead. But, with no remains

4.6 Álvaro's cross in the shadow of the border wall or, alternatively, *wake work*.

and no documents, the dead are difficult to find and even more difficult to identify. Their disarticulated bodies haunt the desert and force us to consider, paraphrasing Derrida, what if disarticulation is the very condition of justice? After all, as Reineke suggests in her discussion of forensic care, if migrant remains are discovered fully fleshed, forensic scientists must remove and clean the head completely in order to take a bone sample from the tibia or cranium. She writes, "The effects of immigration policy, desert conditions, and the lived experience of structural vulnerability of the migrants themselves have taken such a toll on the remains that the forensic scientists often start with so little that *they must disarticulate in order to reconstitute*."[38] Disarticulation is an invitation and an opening, to become undone as to be able to imagine otherwise.

The dead suggest that sanctuary is a time out of joint, a disruption of the profane world: the world of borders, prisons, fences, checkpoints, agents. Álvaro is most comfortable here, in the disturbance. He is Hermes, Charon, Antigone—ushering the dead to the next life, crossing borders between multiple worlds, never settling into one. He describes his sanctuary practice as a *reposo*, but the artist is never at rest. "I'm always there," he reiterates, an unrelenting presence who points fingers and defaces the defacement. In the end, sanctuary always concerns the dead. Even when the word refers to an altar or the innermost part of a temple or church, the dead are present. Catholic altars hold relics, and the earliest Christians celebrated mass in cemeteries and over the tombs of martyrs. The dead are always there. "The dead get us to do something," and they inspire us to reimagine sanctuary not as a destination but as a sacred practice: a fugitive crossing of worlds, a relentless activity.

Presente

El Tiradito's shrine is tucked away in Tucson's Barrio Viejo. According to local wisdom, the shrine is dedicated to a young man who fell in love with a married woman—in some tellings, his mother-in-law—and was murdered when her husband discovered the affair. The Catholic Diocese refused to bury the young man's body in the local cemetery, so his remains rest at the very site where he was killed. El Tiradito, after all, means the castaway or discarded one. Devotees have, over time, gathered at the wishing shrine to intercede on behalf of El Tiradito. His is allegedly the only Catholic shrine in the country dedicated to a sinner—one who transgressed a norm and was killed and refused a legitimate burial as a result. The walled grotto is carpeted with devotional candles, stuffed animals, and artificial flowers—some of which bear the Virgen of Guadalupe's silhouette on their petals. Torn pieces of papers are wedged into the cracks of the shrine's stone walls, the castaways' prayers for redemption.

I am here for a vigil honoring fifty-three migrants who died only a few days ago inside a tractor-trailer on the outskirts of San Antonio, Texas. Their bodies were found stacked atop each other in the suffocatingly hot vehicle, after *coyotes* tasked with transporting them across the border fled the scene. Survivors were suffering from heat exhaustion and dehydration. Dora Luz Rodriguez takes the microphone at the start of the vigil, sharing how she survived a similar horror. Dora says that the dead weigh on her, and that massacres like this one bring her back to 1980, when she witnessed thirteen of her fellow migrants die in Organ Pipe Cactus National Monument after their *coyotes* also abandoned them. She says moments like this resurrect the past, that the migrant dead resurrect her "over-and-done-with," to return to Avery Gordon. Dora insists that migrant deaths are not an accident and that our country's immigration policy is to blame. Justice, she continues, will only become possible when borders no longer restrict movement.

A crowd of about forty people circle Dora, holding battery-powered tealight candles, as she shares that the names of the dead have not been released. Even still, she asks that we say *presente* fifty-three times, once for every person. *Presente* is a Latin American tradition of not merely remembering, but resurrecting those disappeared and murdered by authoritarian regimes. By reciting the names of the dead, each followed by the word *presente*, the living affirm that their comrades are still active in the struggle, still engaged in the present. We not only honor the dead but awaken them. With *presente*, we welcome the dead to stir us into action. After Dora utters the first *presente*, the crowd joins her in the performance. I hear my voice grow louder and more forceful with each iteration. And with each inhale, I embrace the haunting.

Dora invites the crowd to place our candles on the ground in front of the shrine in the shape of a heart, and she gives us each a plastic daisy to lay in the center. When I bend down with my flower, I notice a piece of paper bleached by the sun out of the corner of my eye, held in place by two rocks. When I get closer, I see a printout of the faces of the nineteen children and two teachers murdered at Robb Elementary School in Uvalde, Texas. They look at me, make demands on me, invite me to be their collaborator. The crowd of the dead teaches that sanctuary can never be finished, that there is no *reposo*.

This section is meant to be read aloud. The following list contains the recorded deaths in the Tucson sector of the borderlands, the bodies and remains recovered since I began fieldwork in June 2019 and until I submitted the final manuscript of this book in September 2023. On these pages, the names of the dead crowd together, creating a fugitive chorus that continues to grow. By the time this book is published, there will be even more names and unidentified bodies. Please resist the temptation to skim the list. Please embrace the repetition; it is key to the ritual. Keep a cold glass of water nearby, to replenish your body and as an offering to those who died without water. Add *presente* after you read each name. You might also say, *no olvidadx*. Or, *descanse en poder*.

○

Kenia Garcia Gonzalez. Jesus Agramon Valdez. David Gomez Vivas. Balmore Sanchez Cartagena. Alduvin Duarte. Randy Bamaca Gomez. Gurupreet Kaur. Lucas Vi Caba. Victoria Mendez Carreto. Unidentified.

Unidentified. Unidentified. Manuel Xum Guarchaj. Unidentified. Unidentified. Nestor Vidaurre Gutierrez. Homero Labrador Corrales. Mynor Socon Canel. Unidentified. Everardo Perez Ramirez. Roderico Navarro Miranda. Oscar Gomez Sermeno. Adrian Aguilar Valdez. Benedicto Lopez Ambrocio. Unidentified. Yonatan Monterroso Morales. Unidentified. Jesus Mendoza Torres. Enedina Felipe Pineda. Dario Hernandez Lopez. Raul Mendez Villafuerte. Milton Espinoza Velecela. Jose Minchala Lema. Cristian Ventura. Unidentified. Unidentified. Natali Reyes Campos. Unidentified. Roberto Tox Saqui. Roger Valdez Roman. Roni Lopez Secaida. Unidentified. Porcario Perez Chavez. Cesar Martinez Mejia. Roberto Primero Luis. Luis Cortez Cebrero. Jaime Gaspar Rojas. Unidentified. Elmer De Leon Ortiz. Unidentified. Unidentified. Carlos Mejia Romero. Jonathan Gonzalez Cruz. Diana Guerrero Guzman. Unidentified. Axel Tinti Piotun. Jose Flores Vazquez. Juan Pina Lopez. Unidentified. Mario Hernandez Arroyo. Jesus Valdez Melendez. Jose Tagle Reynoso. Ezequiel Herrera Bretado. Unidentified. Juan Herrera Estrada. Elia Mendez Cruz. Unidentified. Gonzalo Reyes De Jesus. Araceli Algodon Jimenez. Unidentified. Unidentified. Unidentified. Luis Rojas Fernandez. Unidentified. Unidentified. Unidentified. Ronal Garcia Mazariegos. Domingo Tum Mejia. Jose Rodas Pineda. Unidentified. Unidentified. Unidentified. Unidentified. Unidentified. Unidentified. Unidentified. Jaime Garcia Gamez. Unidentified. Unidentified. Unidentified. Unidentified. Unidentified. Unidentified. Unidentified. Unidentified. Jose Balderas Bernardo. Unidentified. Unidentified. Unidentified. Unidentified. Unidentified. Adrian Garcia Lopez. Sergio Ramos Lopez. Unidentified. Unidentified. Unidentified. Unidentified. Unidentified. Unidentified. Joel Serrano Ochoa. Unidentified. John Ramos Zapata. Unidentified. Unidentified. Constantino Bautista Cruz. Efrain Medrano Morales. Unidentified. Unidentified. Gilberto Salazar Garcia. Angel Calderon Balderas. Unidentified. Unidentified. Unidentified. Unidentified. Unidentified. Unidentified. Noe Muro Hernandez. Unidentified. Unidentified. Unidentified. Unidentified. Unidentified. Unidentified. Unidentified. Unidentified. Unidentified. Unidentified. Jose Lopez Guillen. Unidentified. Benjamin Barcenas Hernandez. Unidentified. Unidentified. Unidentified. Unidentified. Unidentified. Unidentified. Unidentified. Angel Camacho Arellanes. Unidentified. Unidentified. Margarita Ortiz Zamora. Unidentified. Unidentified. Unidentified. Unidentified. Unidentified. Unidentified. Unidentified. Unidentified. Unidentified. Unidentified. Gerardo Bautista Martinez. Elbert Gonzales Dominguez. Unidentified. Unidentified. Unidentified. Unidentified. Jesus Vasquez Garcia. Unidentified. Unidentified. Unidentified. Angelica Valderrabano. Jeremias Soto Ambrocio. Unidentified. Diego Reyes Carrillo. Unidentified. Unidentified. Unidentified. Unidentified. Hilaria Gonzalez Vasquez. Rita Vasquez Garcia. Unidentified. Jose Vazquez Perez. Unidentified. Jose Villalobos Castillo. Angel Zepeda Oyuela. Jose Martinez Martinez. Ismael Bedolla Plata. Jesus Lopez Patishtan. Miguel Arce Venegas. Roberto Cruz Bautista. Raul Mauricio Gonzalez. Unidentified. Unidentified. Cesar De La Cruz Gomez. Unidentified. Unidentified. Unidentified. Jose Rebollo Torres. Juan De Jesus Garcia. Roberto Segundo Garcia. Marvi Alvarado Perez. Unidentified. Natanael Zunun Gonzalez. Felix Lopez Hernandez. Uriel Aburto Jimenez. Jose Antonio Guillermo. Sabino Sica Alvarado. Unidentified. Felipe Aguilar Gabriel. Horacio Garcia Robles. Donald Perez Lopez. Elmer Ruiz Domingo. Juan Lopez Valenzuela. Jeser Merlo Meza. Unidentified. Ferlandy Lucas Martinez. Gildardo Morales Morales. Mario Lopez Gomez. Cesar Gabriel Velazquez. Humberto Mendoza Ventura. Fernando Diaz Roblero. Jesus Penuelas Moreno. Unidentified. Jose Carrasco Popocatl. Ricardo Garcia Santana. Javier De Jesus Cortez. Unidentified. Juan Cortes Trejo. Jose Aboyte Sepulveda. Santos Alonzo Castro. Agileo Lopez Osorio. Rogelio Velazquez Lopez. Roy Del Carmen Beltran. Pedro Ruiz Gomez. Joel Hernandez Santos. Osman Aldana Sanchez. Hedilma Corona Yool. Diego Guzman Giron. Unidentified. Salvador Alfonso. Carlos Aguilar Arreola. German Peralta Hernandez. Unidentified. Jovita Garcia Ortiz. Valeriana Perez Rojas. Edilsar Matias Velasquez. Unidentified. Yorman Hernandez Hernandez. Victor Reyes Godinez. Juan Tui Tojin. Heriberto Rosales Ortuno. Unidentified. Unidentified. Unidentified. Carlos Morales Martinez. Jorge Garza Contreras. Unidentified. Unidentified. Adalberto Roblero Ventura. Unidentified. Alejandro Beltran Figueroa. Heber Aguilar Cruz. Unidentified. Edilberto Morales Valencia. Unidentified. Unidentified. Unidentified. Unidentified. Ireny Perez Escalante. Duval Zuniga Oseguera. Esteban Pedraza Mandujano. Angel Alberto Lazaro. Mario Chen Tahuico. Marcelino Diaz Gomez. Jose Caro Hernandez. Unidentified. Guadalupe Villar Romero. Unidentified. Unidentified. Victor Vives Cordero. Ricardo Roblero Agustin. Unidentified. Unidentified. Fines Valencia Santos. Miguel Orduno Arguelles. Silverio Pacheco Medina. Yuliana Zapata Corrales. Rosalinda Basurto Basurto. David Espinosa Farrera. Unidentified. Unidentified. Unidentified. Unidentified. Unidentified. Unidentified. Unidentified. Unidentified. Unidentified. Unidentified. Unidentified. Unidentified. Unidentified. Unidentified. Unidentified.

Juan Gomez Gomez. Unidentified. Unidentified. Unidentified. Unidentified. Unidentified. Unidentified. Unidentified. Elias Alvarado. Unidentified. Unidentified. Unidentified. Unidentified. Fernando Luisa Trejo. Roman Campos Velazquez. Edith Alvarez Galeana. Samuel Hernandez Perez. Unidentified. Silberio Rosales Hernandez. Unidentified. Unidentified. Unidentified. Unidentified. Pablo Flores Ramirez. Unidentified. Unidentified. Unidentified. Jose Peralta Noperi. Unidentified. Unidentified. Unidentified. Joel Rodriguez Herrera. Unidentified. Unidentified. Unidentified. Unidentified. Vicente Ramirez Lopez. Unidentified. Unidentified. Unidentified. Guillermo Navarrete Reyes. Unidentified. Unidentified. Unidentified. Victorina Velasquez Herrera. Unidentified. Unidentified. Unidentified. Javier Mendoza Mendoza. Unidentified. Maria De La Cruz Ac. Unidentified. Unidentified. Unidentified. Unidentified. Unidentified. Unidentified. Rogelino Perez Pastor. Unidentified. Unidentified. Lorenzo Bartolo Cardona. Unidentified. Unidentified. Unidentified. Blanca Lopez De Aguirre. Unidentified. Unidentified. Unidentified. Unidentified. Sergio Santiago Antonio. Otilio Serrano Garay. Unidentified. Unidentified. Manuel Yaxon Meletz. Unidentified. Juan Carrillo Gomez. Unidentified. Emmanuel Velasco Pedraza. Cristian Hernandez Antonio. Jony Tiney Ixen. Carlos Escobedo Roman. Unidentified. Erika Nuñez Estrada. Susana Gaona Santos. Adolfo Hernandez Romero. Juan Rayos Franco. Unidentified. Unidentified. Unidentified. Juan Hernandez Romero. Maria Gonzalez Nuñez. Unidentified, Unidentified. Odalys Vazquez Galvez. Filiberto Ramirez Carranza. Marcos Lopez Lopez, Byron Chocojay Umul. Juan Jimenez Godinez. Reynaldo Jimenez Fuentes. Marvin Castro Jaime. Beatriz Gomez Lopez. Leobardo Reyes Martinez. Gilberto Ruiz Toala. Zoila Barrera Cuzco. Francisco Merino Sanchez. Ruben Ramirez Hernandez. Gabino Lopez Lopez. Unidentified. Mely Calderon Reyes. Bertha Larios Perez. Octavio Garzon Brito. Unidentified. Juana Alvarez Rodriguez. Macario Melchor Ramos. Miguel Bartolon Hernandez. Arli Rochez Mendoza. Orlando Suarez Flores. Olger Herrera Lopez. Unidentified. Wilmer Peralta Sucuzhanay. Jose Montoya Suarez. Bonifacio Lopez Aguilar. Eswin Guinac Cruz. Heber Gomez Sanchez. Carlos Arevalo Gonzalez. Roberto Ramirez Matias. Heriberto Garcia Perfecto. Jaime Aguayo Malpica. Juan Martinez Zelaya. Unidentified. Lauzerico Ferreira. Felipe Vargas Preciado. Unidentified. Lorena Pablo Lopez. Fabio Pinto Ramos. Romeo Ramirez Perez. Fabiana Lopez Huinil. Unidentified. Francisco Sanchez Camarillo. Ignacio Gomez Perez. Unidentified. Unidentified. Nicolas Francisco De Jesus. Miguel Domingo Alonzo. Enrique Lopez Carrillo. Unidentified.

Unidentified. Pedro Martinez Olivarez. Jose Silvestre Cardona. Jesus Ayala Araujo. Abner Morales Lepe. Fernando Venegas Andrade. Unidentified. Victor May Tun. Fernando Sanchez Collazo. Walter Guarcas Coguach. Saul Alvarado Marroquin. Herman Reynoso Mendez. Unidentified. Mibzar Perez Roblero. Jorge Osorio Hernandez. Pedro Hernandez Marcos. Adolfo Arcos Sanchez. Misael Renderos Morales. Yoni Cornejo Vasquez. Unidentified. Unidentified. Unidentified. Unidentified. Fernando Calihua Ramos. Ronaldo Molina Roblero. Unidentified. Unidentified. Maria Xia Charuc. Unidentified. Unidentified. Unidentified. Unidentified. Jose Baltazar Mauricio. Luis Rascon Vega. Hugo Daza Martinez. Unidentified, Francisco Garcia Caballero. Ramon Juan Lucas. Raul Hernandez Martinez. Catalina Velasco Perez. Maria Nicolas Francisco. Jorge Santis Mendez. Enedina Flores Ramirez. Kevin Baca Maradiaga. Leonel Luna Hernandez. Sandy Montufar Tortola. Eduardo Cruz Garcia. Unidentified. Unidentified. Unidentified, Ernesto Garcia Cruz. Unidentified. Unidentified. Jose Velasquez Velasquez. Jesus Romero Vilchez. Unidentified. Juan Trejo Alonso. Isaias Choc Chen. Unidentified. Unidentified. Fernando Xalamihua Tzompaxtle. Unidentified. Unidentified. Jonathan De La Cruz Marcelino. Unidentified. Unidentified. Unidentified. Unidentified. Bernardo Lopez Calicio. Bonifacio Hernandez Jeronimo. Sigilfredo Lorenzo Reyes. Virginia Sanchez Luna. Efrain Garcia Morales. Unidentified. Unidentified. Unidentified. Unidentified. Unidentified. Unidentified. Unidentified. Alvaro Chim De Leon. Unidentified. Unidentified. Unidentified. Unidentified. Unidentified. Unidentified. Unidentified. Diego Domingo Lucas. Unidentified. Kevin Nelson Aguilar. Unidentified. Unidentified. Marcos Rodriguez Salgado. Unidentified. Unidentified. Unidentified. Jose Sanchez Torres. Jose Quintano Garcia. Unidentified. Unidentified. Santos Mendoza Pablo. Unidentified. Marco Lopez Alvarez. Mauricio Vasquez Gonzalez. Unidentified. Jeremias Pop Elias. Unidentified. Anderson Benavente. Juan Mendoza Perez. Unidentified. Silvestra Garcia Espinobarros. Unidentified. Unidentified. Unidentified. Cecilia Espinoza Vega. Carmelo Cruz Marcos. Unidentified. Unidentified. Mateo Salucio Domingo. Unidentified. Unidentified. Joel Vazquez Bravo. Unidentified. Unidentified. Unidentified. Susana Cornejo Cornejo. Unidentified. Francisco Cortes Altamirano. Unidentified. Jaime Tax Aguilar. Unidentified. Unidentified. Gilberto Mejia Agustin. Jesus Montes de Oca Perez. Donaciano Gonzalez Hernandez. Roberto Covarrubias Raygoza. Jose Balcazar Perera. Unidentified. Josue Cardenas Padilla. Griselda Verduzco Armenta. Martin Zamora Pastrana. Unidentified. Unidentified.

Ulises Valdovinos Zamudio. Ricardo Betancourt Avitia. Unidentified. Alexander Guinea Tale. Griselda Alvarez Lopez. Ana Esteban De Leon. José Balan Castro. Eulalio Quiquivix Garcia. Henry Ixchop Marroquin. Unidentified. Unidentified. Abigail Roman Aguilar. Unidentified. Kevin Lopez Torres. Evelin Garcia Garcia. Unidentified. Aurelio Cruz Lopez. Unidentified. Unidentified. Unidentified. Elmer Mucia Jimon. Dianer Casco. Unidentified. Unidentified. Bryant Vargas Garcia. Arturo Esteban Domingo. Unidentified. Estela Bamaca Gonzalez. Macario Tomas Miguel. Unidentified. Renata Lopez Lopez. Unidentified. Rosalina Perez Chum. Angelica Alonzo Lopez. Victoriano Hernandez Gomez. Unidentified. Unidentified. Unidentified. Valeria Gonzales Lopez. Nicolasa Cua Rosales. Luis Gutierrez Torres. Cristian Rojo Hermosillo. Orlin Rodriguez Gamez. Juan Lopez Ramirez. Carlos Garcia Avila. Unidentified. Unidentified. Yefri Guzman Barrios. Unidentified. Unidentified. Filiberto Ramirez Hernandez. Unidentified. Eleazar Urias Palma. Sebastián Toj Algua. Unidentified. Yoni Ajpuac Can. Unidentified. Guillermo Chúm Súc. Uriel Octaviano Osorio. Juan Cervantes Campos. Unidentified. Silvestre Leonardo Cuellar. Roberto Martin Ramirez. Pancho Cruz Matias. Benito Muñoz Muñoz. Nelson Godinez Lopez. Rosa Asicona Escobar. Unidentified. Diego Baltazar Ramon. Josue Mendoza Ramirez. Nicolas Sanchez Mendez. Unidentified. Iriselda Domingo Mejia. Unidentified. Unidentified. Unidentified. Luis Valenzuela Lopez. Tony Ramirez Vasquez. Unidentified. Cruz Vargas Bustillos. Marivel Linares Contreras. Esteban Rosete Diaz. Ignacio Rubio Garcia. Alexis Mendez Lopez. Unidentified. Serafin Lopez Mendez. Guillermo Bautista Lopez. Unidentified. Unidentified. Gustavo Gonzalez Torres. Israel Rodriguez Miguel. Unidentified. Unidentified. Rafael Avila Lerma. Angel Lopez Mendez. Unidentified. Alberto Hernandez Lopez. Wilmer Chamorro Tzic. Unidentified. Manuel Campusano Encarnacion. Elfido Rax Chocoj. Unidentified. Unidentified. Unidentified. Unidentified. Unidentified. Unidentified. Oscar Naranjo Tlaltecatl. Unidentified. Unidentified. Unidentified. Idali Rivera Landa. Unidentified. Unidentified. Cristian Sauceda Lopez. Noe Perez Navarro. Carlos Merida Caño. Unidentified. Unidentified. Unidentified. Unidentified. Unidentified. Benito Juarez Sanchez. Unidentified. Irwin Leon Calderon. Unidentified. Unidentified. Gabriel Cuen Buitimea. Sergio Quino Tohom. Anderson Guzman Barrientos. Melvin Lopez Gomez. Juan Martinez Moran. Unidentified. Unidentified. Unidentified. Unidentified. Unidentified. Mauricio Sanchez Bautista. Unidentified. Jose Sanchez Corona. Graciela Ortega Rodriguez.

Nicolas Velazquez Hernandez. Eduardo Alvarado Diaz. Gloria Lopez Perez. Carlos Rodas Betancourt. Unidentified. Unidentified. Unidentified. Unidentified. Juan Hernandez Lopez. Unidentified. Unidentified. Unidentified. Unidentified. Unidentified. Prakash Vaz. Unidentified. Unidentified. Unidentified. Unidentified. Unidentified. Unidentified. Unidentified. Sergio Quiroz Ayon. German Gomez Paredes. Unidentified. Unidentified. Unidentified. Humberto Marin Sanchez. Unidentified. Unidentified. Paulino Martinez Lagunas. Marcelino Sanchez Gomez. Unidentified. Unidentified. Unidentified. Alonso Tlelo Tlachino. Bartolome Coc Caal. Unidentified. Marcos Pedro y Pedro. Hortensia Oliveros Lopez. Unidentified. Unidentified. Sonia Lopez Garcia. Antonio Salinas Ocampo. Unidentified. Jose Hernandez Vasquez. Unidentified. Unidentified. Jose Ortiz Wario. Miriam Guzman Figueroa. Salomon Carcamo Guerrero. Unidentified. Virgilio Chajon Patzan. Lizbeth Sanchez Ramirez. Luz Alzate Vasquez. Unidentified. Victor Trinidad Hernandez. Unidentified. Unidentified. Josue Zapeta Pretzantzin. Aldo Xamba Morales. Pascual Diego Cristobal. Jesus Raymundo Sanchez. Unidentified. Fredi Perez Bautista. Elizabeth Santiago Valdez. Luis Romero Peraza. Unidentified. Ignacio Munoz Loza. Hilda Veliz Maas De Mijangos. Dulce Martinez Morales. Samuel Perez Morales. Jhoanna Saucedo Lara. Mayra Rosas Medina. Roberto Zarat Son. Unidentified. Yeiszon Herrera Ramos. Unidentified. Unidentified. Mayra Giron Julian. Karoll Arriaga Cruz. Unidentified. Isabel Simon Diego. Melvin Alvarado Toj. Maria Merida Morales. Cruz Ramos Chajal. Maria Hernandez De Basilio. Marco Santiz Perez. Unidentified. Juan Plascencia Jimenez. Fernando Santiz Guzman. Efrain Garcia Carrillo. Unidentified. Marco Yucute Yucute. Carlos Martinez Payan. Edgar Gonzalez Xon. Roman Gasga Guillen. Unidentified. Jorge Sierra Lainez. Yanira Pulex Castellanos De Francisco. Unidentified. Unidentified. Sarahi Gomez Martinez. Unidentified. Waldemar Rios Gutierrez. Unidentified. Unidentified. Reynaldo Cabrera Regules. Unidentified. Unidentified. Unidentified. Unidentified. Antonio Caal Tiul. Juana Andres Andres. Rudy Rodriguez Mendez. Vilma Moran Suc. Juan Gomez Lopez. Alan Castillo Gonzalez. Jose Ramos Lemus. Angel Barragan Lopez. Tereso Nuñez Carranza. Jose Figueroa Figueroa. Arturo Aguirre Garcia. Juan Aguilar Solis. Unidentified. Kevin Ramirez Lopez. Ofelia Bamaca Perez. Santos Marcos Gaspar. Unidentified. Unidentified. Unidentified. Santos Martinez Alvarado. Moises Ramirez Bautista. Unidentified. Alejandro Morales Armira. Unidentified. Scarlett Gomez Gomez. Unidentified. Unidentified. Unidentified. Edelmira Aguilar Maldonado. Unidentified.

Samuel Never Left Sanctuary

"Sanctuary is not the building. Sanctuary is the people of the church. The brothers and sisters," cries out Daniel Oliver-Perez during a vigil for his father, Samuel, who was detained without warning during a biometrics appointment after living in sanctuary for eleven months. In an address to allies and activists gathered outside the Cary, North Carolina office of Immigration and Customs Enforcement (ICE), Daniel affirms that sanctuary exceeds the bounds of a church. He leads the crowd in a chant seemingly inspired by Assata Shakur's "To My People," which she wrote while imprisoned: "I will harbor you. I will defend you. We must love each other and support each other. We have nothing to lose but our chains."[1] Practicing sanctuary in the most unlikely of places (the field office of an agency notorious for its brutal enforcement tactics) and in the most inhospitable conditions (gusts of wind so forceful that our white vigil candles could not stay lit for longer than a couple of minutes), Daniel shares how twenty-seven people were arrested for defending his father. As ICE agents dragged Samuel to an unmarked van with blackened windows, supporters formed a human wall by locking their arms around the vehicle. They remained unshaken for nearly three hours, praying and singing "Amazing Grace" and "We Shall Not Be Moved," African American spirituals that sustained activists in the Civil Rights Movement. City-Well pastor Cleve May tells reporters that the idea behind creating such a wall was to re-create the sanctuary they had offered Samuel at their church. According to the pastor, Samuel never left sanctuary. Sanctuary flees the building.

During the vigil that December, I lit a candle for Samuel. I saw a pastor perform the Eucharist under the eyes of surveillance technology, surrounded by Homeland Security vehicles. I felt the bodies of strangers pressed next to me; people crowded shoulder to shoulder to keep each other warm. A bodily communion like the one taking place among detainees in ICE facilities. I joined along as CityWell's worship leader performed an acoustic version of "*Tu Fidelidad*," a gospel song by Marcos Witt that my dad had a habit of playing during road trips and on Sunday mornings. The song's lyrics returned to me instantly: *Tu fidelidad es grande / Tu fidelidad incomparable / Nadie como tu bendito Dios / Grande es tu fidelidad.* The pastor speaking to the crowd admitted that sometimes it is difficult to praise God. That night was such a time.

Here, I return to the state where I was raised because it is also where I spent years writing this book. As I suggested in chapter 1, place matters. I write this conclusion from my bungalow in downtown Durham, North Carolina, a bike ride away from the church where Samuel lived and a short drive from where Pastor José Chicas also spent years inside Saint John's Missionary Baptist Church. This project was first and foremost inspired by the ways they, and Juana, narrated their lives in sanctuary as a gentler incarceration, by the ways they strategized to escape. To return to Daniel Oliver-Perez, sanctuary is not the building. Or, at least, sanctuary is not *only* the building.

I began conducting research for this book by considering how sanctuary is spreading beyond places of worship and why activists draw on this tradition to defy militarization. Through fieldwork, I saw how sanctuary transgresses borders and interrupts worlds. How sacred beings and practices refuse routines, boundaries, habits, traditions, conventions, rules, procedures, customs. Taboos and prohibitions are in place to limit or contain the sacred—migrants living in sanctuary churches are made to wear ankle monitors; migrants with criminal records are denied the protections of the sanctuary city. These are in place because sacred forces pose a problem for the profane world of law and order. Recall Zaira Livier and our conversation about Tucson Families Free and Together. Her team steered away from using "sanctuary" in their campaign because it is a "triggering" word for potential voters. In the end, I agree with Zaira. Sanctuary presents a danger for the routine. Sanctuary threatens to unmake everything.

Daniel Oliver-Perez faced felony charges for placing an arresting ICE officer in a chokehold and taking control of the steering wheel of the vehicle that captured his father. I often remember the young man's insistence that sanctuary is not a building, and I have lit a candle for both father and son numerous times while writing this book. Usually, I choose Santo Niño de Atocha, his shoes tattered from a long journey, his devotees turning to the infant Jesus to aid pilgrims and migrants. Following his arrest, Samuel Oliver-Bruno was smuggled to Stewart Detention Center in Georgia and almost immediately transferred to Port Isabel Detention Center in Brownsville, Texas. He was forcibly moved from one prison to another as his family tried desperately to locate him. Only days after being kidnapped by ICE agents, Samuel was taken to the International Bridge and ordered to walk to Mexico. While members of Congress denounced ICE's actions and defended Samuel, calling him a "decades-long resident of North Carolina with no significant criminal history and a loving family that includes his U.S. citizen son," ICE spokesman Bryan Cox described Samuel as a "convicted criminal" by virtue of crossing a border without authorization.[2] As A. Naomi Paik instructs in her abolitionist manifesto, "The core paradox of liberal sanctuary lies here: being a law-abiding, 'good' immigrant will not save you as long as the state can determine what it means to be a law-abiding, 'good' immigrant."[3] Samuel was deported and neither his long-term residence nor his loving family could save him. The refuge he received came from his son, who was arrested for tackling plainclothes officers when they handcuffed his father. It came from Colectivo Santuario—a coalition of people living in sanctuary and organizing to get out, among them my friend Juana Luz Tobar Ortega. And from Casa del Migrante in Reynosa—a shelter adjacent to the one where Eva and Alberto stayed while awaiting their asylum interviews. Nuns affiliated with the Daughters of Charity met him at the International Bridge and helped him call his family, practicing sanctuary as radical accompaniment. Sanctuary escaped buildings and exceeded detention centers and crossed borders.

This book studies sanctuary and the sacred, moments when the profane world is interrupted by those forces that it has desperately tried to keep out. These moments are unsustainable and even intolerable for the everyday. They cannot last. While sanctuary is often associated with a set-apart or sacred place, in these pages I show how this practice has long functioned as a "mobile strategy"—to use John Fife's words. The fugitive sacred cannot be confined to a city or a charter. It is at odds with procedure and policy. Sanctuary travels with migrants and other fugitives as they flee captivity and confinement; it emerges alongside the smuggled, who pose a perpetual threat to the settled. As Fred Moten and Stefano Harney affirm, "Never being on the right side of the Atlantic is an unsettled feeling, the feeling of a thing that unsettles with others . . . [This feeling] produces a certain distance from the settled, from those who determine themselves in space and time, who locate themselves in a determined history."[4] The sacred unsettles the profane world. Taboos are in place to prevent its spread, to contain its restless energies. In the borderlands, these take the form of checkpoints, surveillance towers, ports of entry, and detention centers, to name a few. But the sacred is contagious, eager to spread.

In this book, I refer to the sacred as fugitive, as forces that run from the everyday. In chapter 1, I wrote about the sacred as positive and negative—its excess "too much" to be managed by Prevention through Deterrence. Chapter 2 described the sacred as contagious, as radiant and restless to spread, to touch, to pursue ecstatic intimacy. Chapter 3 considered how the sacred chases lines of flight and exit routes out of the everyday and how these practices of becoming never fully arrive at any destination. Chapter 4 proposed that sacred beings, among them the migrant dead, refuse closure and *reposo*, instead choosing to disarticulate and haunt the routine. Fugitivity does not seek arrival, nor does it pursue resolution. Fugitivity is unsustainable, uncomfortable, and cannot last forever. But it does present a series of openings for undocumented people and for those crossing without authorization—those who are forbidden from entering into the ordinary, profane world. For one, fugitivity makes possible immanent relations with land—canyons, mountains, *arroyos*, monsoons, mesquite, brittlebush, palo verdes, *coyotes*, jackrabbits, javelinas, cows, ancestors, ghosts.

Migration is often narrated as loss or trauma. And while that is certainly true for many migrants, including my own family—whose leaving marked a death—migration is also creative and improvisational. It is life-giving and it is world-shattering at the same time. The characters in this book engage in vibrant, emergent practices of becoming—creating what was not thought possible, creating in excess, creating through escape, creating possibilities out of displacement. Soon after she fled Eloy, Eva's husband, Alberto, was also released from La Palma and now—years later—they continue to remake their lives, enjoying movies together once again. Though now, they watch on a thirty-two-inch flat screen while cuddled on their leather couch, no longer repurposing their cell phones as televisions. For this couple, migration represents a beginning and an opening. And over a decade after his deportation, Panchito asked me to write a letter of recommendation in support of his application for a visa to reenter the United States. He continues to transform his life. Sanctuary, in the end, cannot be put to rest. It will not settle (down).

Juana is back home, tending to her houseplants. But, she continues to report for regular check-ins with ICE, unsure if and when they will tell her that her time in this country is up and she must once again pack her bags. Juana tells me that, this time, she will not seek sanctuary. Samuel Oliver-Bruno died in 2021 due to sustained injuries from a car accident in Veracruz, Mexico. Deportation not only violently captures and disappears people from their families and communities, but also works to separate migrants from networks of care and kinship that sustain life. Deportation polices the mobility of people whose restless energies defy borders and threaten national boundaries. Human beings place prohibitions and punishments around the sacred, hoping to capture it for instrumental ends. But the sacred flees. Sanctuary cities limit who is eligible for care. Sanctuary universities prohibit ICE from entering campus, unless agents have a warrant. Sanctuary churches embrace the mother with a US citizen child but are often hesitant to welcome "criminal" or deviant migrants. The charter and the city are not enough. Sanctuary exceeds these spaces. It refuses them. It returns with deportees and facilitates intimacies inside prison cells. It pursues proximity. It is unintelligible and unsettled, everywhere.

Notes

INTRODUCTION

Epigraph: Gumbs, *Spill*, 95.

1 Felons, Not Families is part of a long history of criminalizing migrants, creating harmful binaries that ignore the ways immigration policy determines what activity counts as criminal and who is eligible for deportation. A. Naomi Paik elaborates on the narratives and laws that contribute to criminalization in "Abolitionist Futures and the US Sanctuary Movement."

2 In 2011, ICE released a memo detailing its sensitive locations policy, which prohibits certain enforcement activities at schools; hospitals; churches, synagogues, mosques, or other institutions of worship; sites of funerals, weddings, or other public religious ceremonies; and sites that are the occurrence of public demonstrations, such as marches, rallies, or parades. There are, of course, exceptions to this rule. While Juana was living in sanctuary, she told me about an Indonesian asylum seeker, Binsar Siahaan, living at a church in Maryland, who was arrested by ICE officers who knowingly violated the agency's sensitive locations policy.

3 Bagelman, *Sanctuary City*, xvii.

4 Bagelman, *Sanctuary City*, 95.

5 Bagelman, *Sanctuary City*, 68. Bagelman turns to medieval England to trace a history of "rituals of supplication," or performances that require migrants to confess their distress and desperation in exchange for welcome and hope. She shows how sanctuary seekers had to first confess their crimes to clergy (in elaborate detail), surrender their arms, pay a fee, and agree to obey the rules and customs of the religious space. She explains that the ritual was highly dramatized and that the person seeking sanctuary was often expected to wear a letter branded on the skin to publicize their criminal status (*Sanctuary City*, 79–80).

6   Orozco and Andersen, "Sanctuary in the Age of Trump."

7   Lurie, "They Built a Utopian Sanctuary."

8   Thank you to Krishni Burns who provided these definitions and helped me think through the differences between *sacer* and *sanctus*.

9   Benveniste, *Indo-European Language*.

10 Pérez writes about micropractices such as ceremonial food preparation and storytelling in the kitchen that are relegated to the sidelines of religious life, but that nevertheless are crucial in "fashioning sacred selves, spaces, and societies" (Pérez, *Religion in the Kitchen*, 11). Peña describes acts of devotional labor, including walking long distances for pilgrimage and sweeping the sidewalk in front of a shrine that sanctify space and imbue devotees' "bodies and keepsakes with a form of the sacred" (Peña, *Performing Piety*, 44).

11 Caillois, *Man and the Sacred*, 35.

12 Caillois, *Man and the Sacred*, 22.

13 Durkheim, *The Elementary Forms*, 44.

14 Durkheim, *The Elementary Forms*, 38.

15 Otto, *The Idea of the Holy*.

16 I learned to think about the sacred and excess as a teaching assistant in Todd Ramón Ochoa's "Introduction to Religion and Culture" course. These insights would not be possible without his lectures.

17 Eliade, *The Sacred and the Profane*, 11.

18 Caillois, *Man and the Sacred*, 39.

19 Durkheim, *The Elementary Forms*, 322, 327.

20 Durkheim, *The Elementary Forms*, 322.

21 Douglas, *Purity and Danger*, 2.

22 Douglas, *Purity and Danger*, 5.

23 Gandolfo, *The City at Its Limits*, xii.

24 Bataille, *Theory of Religion*, 52.

25 Bataille, *Erotism*, 67–68.

26 Gandolfo, *The City at its Limits*, 14.

27 Bataille, *Erotism*, 63.

28 Isasi-Díaz, *En La Lucha*.

29 Caillois, *Man and the Sacred*, 99.

30 Lloyd Barba, in *Sowing the Sacred*, similarly uses "the profane" to refer to forms of routinized violence faced by Mexican farmworkers from the 1920s to the 1960s. He writes about the profane as "dehumanization, biological reductionism, delousing, DDT fumigation, pesticide exposure while out at work, wage exploitation, relegation to the status of replaceable laborers, squalid housing, polluted water, denial of cultural and legal citizenship, and deportation along with its constant threats" (*Sowing the Sacred*, 7–8).

31 Through their social movements and political organizing, many do lay claim to the United States. Slogans like "Home Is Here" and "Here to Stay" show these longings for settlement and stasis. Sanctuary campaigns that

stress how long a migrant has lived in this country, how they have become beloved members of their communities, and how they cultivate social ties in their schools and workplaces are other examples of the ways migrants make claims to home and roots.

32 Anzaldúa, "La Prieta," 232. *This Bridge Called My Back.*

33 Ochoa, *Society of the Dead,* 8.

34 Caillois, *Man and the Sacred,* 34 (my emphasis).

35 Bayetti Flores, "The Pulse Nightclub Shooting."

36 Torres, "In Praise of Latin Night" (my emphasis).

37 Luiselli, *Lost Children Archive,* 141.

38 Truett, *Fugitive Landscapes,* 6.

39 Magrane and Cokines, *The Sonoran Desert.*

40 Papadopoulos, Stephenson, and Tsianos, *Escape Routes,* 43.

41 Dillon, *Fugitive Life,* 55.

42 Papadopoulos, Stephenson, and Tsianos, *Escape Routes.*

43 St. John, *Line in the Sand,* 16.

44 Zamora, "Poems," 31.

45 Halberstam in Moten and Harney, *The Undercommons,* 11.

46 "Felipe Baeza with Zoë Hopkins."

47 Moten and Harney, *The Undercommons,* 97.

48 Lethabo King, *The Black Shoals,* 122, 123.

49 Pelaez Lopez, *Intergalactic Travels,* 82.

51 Pelaez Lopez, *Intergalactic Travels,* 91.

52 Pelaez Lopez, *Intergalactic Travels,* 77.

53 See Cunningham, *God and Caesar,* for more description on the process of declaring sanctuary (32–34). *Testimonio* as a genre emerged alongside insurgent and revolutionary movements in mid-twentieth-century Latin America. Told by witnesses of state violence or colonial injustice, these narratives are expressions of struggle and survival. They challenge official narratives told by the elite and government agents and instead privilege women, the poor, illiterate, and Indigenous. Rigoberta Menchú's autobiography is among the most well-known *testimonios.*

54 Fife, "Letter to William French Smith, March 23, 1982."

55 Fife, "Letter to William French Smith, March 23, 1982."

56 Guardado, *Church as Sanctuary,* 19.

57 Robinson, *Black Marxism,* 137.

58 Roberts, *Freedom as Marronage.*

59 Purnell, *Becoming Abolitionists,* 107, 108.

60 However, as I will mention in chapter 1 by citing the work of Hazel Carby, maroons sometimes collaborated with colonial powers by surveilling formerly enslaved fugitives and suppressing rebellions.

61 Villareal, "Sanctuaryscapes in the North American Southwest," 44, 44, 47.

62 Rabben, *Sanctuary and Asylum*, 32.

63 Cunningham, *God and Caesar*, 69 (original emphasis).

64 Cunningham, *God and Caesar*, 701.

65 Chávez, "Sanctuary, Fugitivity, and Insurgent Models," 91.

66 Cunningham, *God and Caesar*, 40.

67 Coutin, *The Culture of Protest*, 110.

68 Cunningham, *God and Caesar*, 175.

69 *Basta!*, quoted in Cunningham, *God and Caesar*, 40.

70 In an interview with *Borderless*, Arellano shares: "The Puerto Rican community was one of the most important communities that helped me during that time. All of them, including young people, came to the church to protect me. There was one person always outside guarding the church entry. The most impactful moment for me was when that person held up the Puerto Rican flag as a symbol of resistance and the lucha." Arellano quoted in Hurtado, "Keeping the Faith."

71 Caminero-Santangelo, "The Voice of the Voiceless," 96.

72 Caminero-Santangelo, "The Voice of the Voiceless," 97.

73 Chávez, *Queer Migration Politics*, 61.

74 Chávez, "From Sanctuary to a Queer Politics of Fugitivity," 65.

75 Paik, "Abolitionist Futures," 16.

76 Groups like Mijente also embrace the queer, fugitive, and abolitionist visions proposed by Chávez and Paik. Tania Unzueta—the organization's political director—calls for dismantling "the current policing apparatus that acts as a funnel to mass incarceration and the deportation machine" (Unzueta, "Expanding Sanctuary"). She proposes expanding sanctuary by decriminalizing and reducing arrests, eliminating the use of local and state gang databases (which are used to exclude people from protections in sanctuary cities), ending local contracts with immigration enforcement, decreasing police funding, and reinvesting in community institutions. For years, Mijente has pointed to the limits of sanctuary cities, showing how—through contracts with data broker companies—ICE is able to bypass sanctuary protections and collect data on undocumented migrants. See Unzueta, "Expanding Sanctuary."

77 Coelho, *The Alchemist*, 147.

78 Unzueta Carrasco and Seif, "Disrupting the Dream," 283.

79 Nicholls, *The Dreamers*, 50.

80 Unzueta Carrasco and Seif, "Disrupting the Dream," 288.

81 Unzueta Carrasco and Seif, "Disrupting the Dream," 291.

82 Unzueta Carrasco and Seif, "Disrupting the Dream," 296, 297.

83 Günel, Varma, and Watanabe, "A Manifesto for Patchwork Ethnography."

84 Vogt, *Lives in Transit*, 20.

85 Zambreno, *Drifts*, 5.

86 Rosas, "The Thickening Borderlands," 336.

87 Inda and Dowling, *Governing Migration through Crime*, 10.

88 Walia, *Border and Rule*, 21.

89 Walia, *Border and Rule*, 29.

90 Brand, *A Map to the Door of No Return*, 24.

91 Schaeffer, *Unsettled Borders*, 4.

92 Shimoda, "State of Erasure."

93 Glissant, *Poetics of Relation*, 16.

94 Berry et al., "Toward a Fugitive Anthropology," 550.

95 Narayan, "How Native Is a 'Native' Anthropologist?," 677.

96 Berry et al., "Toward a Fugitive Anthropology," 547.

97 See Goldstein, "Laying the Body on the Line."

98 Horton, *They Leave Their Kidneys in the Fields*, 188.

99 Jamison, *Make It Scream, Make It Burn*, 148 (original emphasis).

100 Brand, *The Blue Clerk*, 3.

1. THE DESERT: VANISHING TIME AND SACRED LANDSCAPES

Epigraph: Gómez-Barris, *The Extractive Zone*, 3.

1 Riley, *The Bahidaj Harvest*.

2 Schermerhorn, *Walking to Magdalena*, 6.

3 Anzaldúa, *Borderlands*.

4 Underhill, *The Papago Indians*, 49.

5 Wright, *Long Ago Told*, 7.

6 Wright, *Long Ago Told*, 8.

7 For more background on PTD and its deadly consequences, see the collaborative series of reports by No More Deaths / No Más Muertes and Coalición de Derechos Humanos—*Deadly Apprehension Methods: The Consequences of Chase and Scatter in the Wilderness, Interference with Humanitarian Aid: Death and Disappearance on the US-Mexico Border*, and *Left to Die: Border Patrol, Search and Rescue, and the Crisis of Disappearance*, http://www.thedisappearedreport.org/reports.html.

8 US Border Patrol, "Border Patrol Strategic Plan 1994."

9 Samaritans hike migrant trails and leave behind water, food, and other supplies in an effort to mitigate suffering—practicing a mobile approach to aid. I met Álvaro while volunteering with the Tucson Samaritans during the summer of 2015. The group introduced me to direct aid in the borderlands, and it was by joining them on water drops that I entered into relation with the Sonoran Desert.

10 US Border Patrol, "Border Patrol Strategic Plan 1994" (my emphasis).

11 Simpson, *As We Have Always Done*, 178.

12 Though, as I mentioned in the introduction, especially after the Sanctuary trials, sanctuary participants in the Southwest were selective about

whom they transported across the desert, making sure to screen migrants and confirm they were eligible asylum seekers before embarking on the journey.

13 Corbett, *Goatwalking*, 137.

14 Corbett, *Goatwalking*, 3, 9.

15 Corbett, *Goatwalking*, 6–7.

16 Corbett, *Goatwalking*, 29.

17 Corbett, *Goatwalking*, 198.

18 Corbett, *Goatwalking*, 84.

19 This is a precedent to PTD. Newspaper clippings in the Sanctuary Trial Papers at the University of Arizona read: "Summer Was Deadly for Aliens Crossing Desert," "The Desert Heat Has Claimed More Victims," "Pitiless Sun, Lack of Water Mean Four People Perish in Desert," "4 Fleeing El Salvador Die in Arizona Desert as Water Runs Out," and "Desert Heat Kills Five Salvadorans near Tacna." And, as Timothy Dunn explains, since 1978, the borderlands have been increasingly militarized as part of efforts to control both unauthorized migration and drug trafficking. See Dunn, *The Militarization of the U.S.-Mexico Border*.

20 Corbett, *Goatwalking*, 149.

21 Bataille, *Theory of Religion*, 28.

22 Corbett, *Goatwalking*, 13.

23 Bataille, *Theory of Religion*, 24.

24 Corbett, *Goatwalking*, 71.

25 Zamora, *Solito*, 17.

26 Zamora, *Solito*, 19.

27 Liboiron differentiates between Land as "the combined living spirit of plants, animals, air, water, humans, histories, and events recognized by many Indigenous communities" and lowercased land as a "colonial world-view whereby landscapes are common, universal, and everywhere, even with great variation" (Liboiron, *Pollution Is Colonialism*, 7). They insist that Land and land are fundamentally different—what Marisol de la Cadena might call "partially connected" epistemological and ontological worlds (de la Cadena, *Earth Beings*).

28 Magrane and Cokinos, *The Sonoran Desert*, xv.

29 To be clear, purchasing a pair of pants and writing alongside a saguaro does not imply good relations. I am not claiming Indigenous land relations as my own. While conducting fieldwork, I was confronted by the ways that living undocumented had shaped my relations with land. Growing up, I learned to avoid certain routes because of driver's license checkpoints and to keep to a simple routine—school, grocery store, church—to avoid the risk of capture. I was cut off from local histories. I was taught not to get too comfortable in North Carolina because we could leave at any moment. I open with these

vignettes from my fieldwork to show how our theories are inseparable from land and the ways we enter into relation with more-than-human inhabitants. If I had accepted that land is a resource, a tool that humans can use and abuse, I would have never written this chapter. I would have accepted the theory that the desert is a weapon, that PTD has succeeded in conscripting the Sonoran Desert to do its dirty work of disposing of migrants. And I would have moved on.

30 Bataille, *Theory of Religion*, 39.
31 Bataille, *Theory of Religion*, 38.
32 Bataille, *Theory of Religion*, 35.
33 Caillois, *Man and the Sacred*, 21.
34 Caillois, *Man and the Sacred*, 25.
35 Caillois, *Man and the Sacred*, 43.
36 Caillois, *Man and the Sacred*, 45.
37 Urrea, *The Devil's Highway*, 4.
38 Fontana, *Of Earth and Little Rain*, 16.
39 Fontana, *Of Earth and Little Rain*, 12, 16.
40 Fontana, *Of Earth and Little Rain*, 34.
41 John Russell Bartlett in St. John, *Line in the Sand*, 30.
42 "Treaty of 1889."
43 St. John, *Line in the Sand*, 26.
44 Rosas, "The Managed Violences of the Borderlands"; De León, *The Land of Open Graves,* 8.
45 De León, *The Land of Open Graves,* 29–30.
46 De León, *The Land of Open Graves,* 37.
47 Thank you to Hillary Kaell for suggesting that I think more seriously about the word *conscript.*
48 Liboiron, *Pollution Is Colonialism*, 43.
49 Liboiron, *Pollution Is Colonialism*, 43.
50 Emory, *Report on the United States and Mexican Boundary Survey*, 21.
51 Antebi, "Border Landscapes."
52 National Park Service, "Chamizal."
53 Miller, "How Border Patrol Occupied the Tohono O'odham Nation."
54 Dunn defines militarization as "the use of military rhetoric and ideology, as well as military tactics, strategy, technology, equipment, and forces" (*The Militarization of the U.S.-Mexico Border*, 3).
55 Devereaux, "What's in a Name."
56 Miller, "How Border Patrol Occupied the Tohono O'odham Nation."
57 Blanchfield and Kolowratnik, "Persistent Surveillance."
58 Gilberto Rosas proposes the term *policeability* to describe how immigration policing is a form of "racialized management" that subjects both unauthorized migrants and Indigenous people to mobility controls (and,

importantly, many migrants *are* Indigenous people) (Rosas, "The Managed Violences of the Borderlands," 404).

59 *Oversight Hearing on Destroying Sacred Sites.*

60 Glissant, *Poetics of Relation.*

61 Tohono O'odham Nation, "No Wall."

62 Lethabo King, *The Black Shoals,* xi.

63 Lemons, "Tohono O'odham Chairman Ned Norris' Statement."

64 Edward Brathwaite, in *The Arrivants,* writes about "arrivants" forcibly shipped to the Américas—destabilizing the settler/native binary. Many, though not all, Latin American migrants are arrivants, forced onto stolen land due to European and Anglo-American colonialism and imperialism.

65 Urrea, *The Devil's Highway,* 5.

66 Urrea, *The Devil's Highway,* 4.

67 The video "There's No O'odham Word for Wall" includes statistics like the following: "For nearly two decades, the Nation has spent more than $3 million of its own funds annually and 60% of its time on border enforcement and security;" "From 2002 to 2016, the Tohono O'odham Police Department and US Border Patrol working together have seized on average over 313,000 pounds of illegal drugs per year." The Nation's leaders often reiterate their willingness to work with the Border Patrol to halt unauthorized migration in order to show the futility of a wall and surveillance infrastructure. See Tohono O'odham Nation, "No Wall."

68 Thus far in this chapter, I have elaborated on three ways to relate to the land: settler states that attempt to domesticate the desert; Indigenous communities that engage in deep, reciprocal relationships; and migrants, who move through the desert using fugitive strategies. There are also *coyotes,* who know the desert well enough to establish mutual relations, but who use their knowledge to turn the desert toward profane, or useful ends.

69 O'odham Anti-Border Collective (@antibordercollective), "One year ago today, September 9th, 2020, two Hia-Ced women were arrested for using their bodies . . . ," Facebook, September 9, 2021, https://fb.watch /92J2YEZsyK/.

70 Muñoz, *Cruising Utopia.*

71 Muñoz, *Cruising Utopia,* 21.

72 Though, as Hazel Carby writes of Taíno *cimarrones* on the island of Jamaica, while they offered sanctuary to fugitives and joined rebellions alongside the enslaved, maroons also entered into negotiations with "conquistador-settlers." They were eventually granted tenure over their lands and limited self-government in exchange for ceasing to harbor runaways and assisting in the suppression of Black rebellion (Carby, *Imperial Intimacies,* 274).

73 Caillois, *Man and the Sacred.*

74 Mack, *Acim O'odham (We the O'odham),* 15.

75 Nelson, *Bluets,* 1 (original emphasis).

76 Muñoz, *Cruising Utopia*, 22.

77 "Welcome to Kino Springs Golf," Kino Springs Golf Club, https://www
.kinospringsgc.com/, accessed July 30, 2020; Asmelash and Silverman,
"Hundreds of Unwelcome Vultures."

2. THE DETAINED: CONTRABAND TOUCH IN THE CARCERAL
BORDERLANDS

Epigraph: Nancy, "Rethinking Corpus," 85.

1 People's Defense Initiative, "FAQ Tucson Families Free and Together."

2 Paik, "Abolitionist Futures," 16; "Law and order" is a phrase popularized
and mobilized during Richard Nixon's 1968 presidential campaign and his
administration's declaration of the War on Drugs, which prompted the
militarization of the southern border. Throughout his presidency, Nixon
embraced law and order as a proxy for discussing race and white fears of
Black criminality. Donald Trump invoked the phrase in his presidential
acceptance speech and in response to protests following George Floyd's
murder.

3 Bataille, *On Nietzsche*, 258.

4 Bataille, *Theory of Religion*, 41.

5 Bataille, *On Nietzsche*, 258.

6 Elizabeth Pérez elaborates on the Western philosophical tradition's demon-
ization of taste and hierarchy of senses in *Religion in the Kitchen*.

7 Nancy, "Rethinking Corpus," 85.

8 Hernández, "Carceral Shadows," 70.

9 Notably, as Erica Rand explains in *The Ellis Island Snowglobe*, enforcement
agents at Ellis Island also coercively managed and policed migrants. They
forcibly disrobed, inspected, and scrutinized migrants to "create, alter,
instill, and police" raced and sexed boundaries (Rand, *The Ellis Island
Snowglobe*, 75).

10 García Hernández, *Migrating to Prison*, 27.

11 Durkheim, *The Elementary Forms*, 224.

12 Gandolfo, *The City at Its Limits*, 77.

13 Gandolfo, *The City at Its Limits*, 228.

14 Lytle Hernández, *Migra*, 142.

15 Nancy, "Rethinking Corpus," 81.

16 Chávez, "Spatializing Gender Performativity," 2, 8.

17 "About Eloy," accessed April 15, 2020, https://eloyaz.gov/280/About-Eloy.

18 Blue, "The Means and Meanings of Carceral Mobility," 103.

19 As of 2016, the latter houses the majority of Hawaii's male prison population.
Liza Keānuenueokalani Williams explains that Hawaii has transported
prison populations to the mainland since 1995 to alleviate overcrowding.

Drawing connections between land dispossession, the displacement of Indigenous Hawaiians, and the incarceration of "aliens," Williams writes that Eloy exemplifies the "binding of multiple histories of oppression to a racialized and classed commodification that rearticulates dominance through capitalism" (Williams, "Currencies of U.S. Empire," 154).

20 Bauer, *American Prison*, 16–22.

21 Caillois, *Man and the Sacred*, 38–39, 21.

22 Angela Davis and Gina Dent agree that "the prison is itself a border." They elaborate that "this analysis has come from prisoners, who name the distinction between the 'free world' and the space behind the walls of the prison" (Davis and Dent, "Prison as a Border," 1236–37).

23 Miller, *Empire of Borders*.

24 Huerta, "Migrants Trapped in the Mexican Vertical Border." And, indeed, in recent years, Mexico has surpassed the United States in the number of Central Americans the country deports per year.

25 Huerta, "Migrants Trapped in the Mexican Vertical Border." Further, as Shannon Speed argues, Indigenous migrants whose first language is not Spanish and who are racially marked as others are disproportionately vulnerable along the migrant route and in detention centers (Speed, *Incarcerated Stories*, 46).

26 Andreas, *Border Games*.

27 Not all migrants experience the vertical border crossing in the same way; Eva and Alberto benefit from class privilege that allowed them to pay bribes, rent apartments, and purchase flights. They are also a heterosexual married couple, and their light skin grants them a degree of protection. Poor and Indigenous Central Americans are uniquely vulnerable to state and cartel violence, and queer and transgender women regularly report experiencing sexual violence in the vertical borderlands.

28 Moten and Harney, *The Undercommons*, 98.

29 Moten and Harney, *The Undercommons*, 98.

30 Fanon, *Black Skin, White Masks,* 10. Many Latin American migrants are descendants of enslaved Africans, and neoliberal development projects driving forced migration disproportionately affect Black communities like Garifuna in Honduras.

31 Mezzadra, "The Right to Escape," 270 (original emphasis).

32 See Caillois, *Man and the Sacred*, for a discussion of the ambiguity of the sacred.

33 Moten, *Black and Blur*, 36.

34 Elhillo, "self-portrait with no flag," 138.

35 Elhillo, "self-portrait with no flag," 138.

36 Elhillo, "self-portrait with no flag," 139.

37 Jenkins, "Arizona to Transfer."

38 Nancy, "Rethinking Corpus," 81.

39 Morrison, *Beloved*, 103–4.

40 Spillers, "To the Bone."

41 Spillers, "To the Bone."

42 Spillers, "To the Bone."

43 Nancy, "Rethinking Corpus," 83.

44 John 20:27.

45 Guenther, *Solitary Confinement*, xiii (my emphasis).

46 Crawley, *Blackpentecostal Breath*, 36.

47 Canetti, *Crowds and Power*, 15.

48 Canetti, *Crowds and Power*, 21.

49 Chávez, "Spatializing Gender Performativity," 10 (my emphasis).

50 Chávez, "Spatializing Gender Performativity," 10.

3. THE DEPORTED: LINES OF FLIGHT THROUGH NOGALES, SONORA

Epigraph: Anzaldúa, *Borderlands / La Frontera*, 49.

1   Fournier, "Lines of Flight," 121.

2   Barba and Castillo-Ramos, "Sacred Resistance."

3   Church World Service, "Sanctuary Not Deportation."

4   Church World Service, "Sanctuary Not Deportation."

5   Vega Magallón in Vásquez, "There Is No Abolishing ICE."

6   Slack, *Deported to Death*, 112, 154.

7   Glissant, *Poetics of Relation*.

8   Sontag, *Regarding the Pain of Others*.

9   Sontag, *Regarding the Pain of Others*, 102.

10 Earlier, I outlined the history of *testimonios* and how it emerged as a revolutionary tradition in Latin America. Here, I use *testimonio* to refer to Evangelicals telling the story of how they welcomed Jesus into their lives. These *testimonios* mark a transformation from sin to salvation, showing how God redeemed a person from a former life of indecency and waywardness. Usually, *testimonios* are given publicly to show God's power and inspire others to follow suit.

11 Coutin, *The Culture of Protest*, 71 (original emphasis).

12 Coutin, *The Culture of Protest*, 155. In so doing, Coutin argues, the movement created monolithic, static, and romanticized images of Central Americans. It also excluded Central Americans who could not (or would not) narrate their displacement in ways that were legible to white, affluent laypeople.

13 Yukich, *One Family under God*, 88.

14 Anzaldúa, *Light in the Dark*, 28.

15 Anzaldúa, *Borderlands / La Frontera*, 48.

16 Schmidt Camacho, *Migrant Imaginaries*, 27.

17 Schmidt Camacho, *Migrant Imaginaries*, 215.

18   Goodman, *The Deportation Machine*, 74.

19   Goodman, *The Deportation Machine*, 74.

20   Schmidt Camacho, *Migrant Imaginaries,* 60.

21   Moten, "Blackness and Nothingness," 756.

22   Moten, "Blackness and Nothingness," 776.

23   García-Peña, *Community as Rebellion*, 27.

24   García-Peña, *The Borders of Dominicanidad*, 132.

25   García-Peña, *The Borders of Dominicanidad*, 134.

26   Glissant, *Poetics of Relation*, 143.

27   Deleuze and Guattari, *A Thousand Plateaus*, 7, 25.

28   Deleuze and Guattari, *A Thousand Plateaus*, 25.

29   Deleuze and Guattari, *A Thousand Plateaus*, 25.

30   Deleuze and Guattari, *A Thousand Plateaus*, 200.

31   Deleuze and Guattari, *A Thousand Plateaus*, 215.

32   Deleuze and Guattari, *A Thousand Plateaus*, 204.

33   Deleuze and Guattari, *A Thousand Plateaus*, 205, 216, 222.

34   Glissant, *Poetics of Relation*, 18.

35   De Genova, "The Deportation Regime," 59.

36   De Genova, "The Deportation Regime," 40.

37   De Genova, "The Deportation Regime," 58–59.

38   Povinelli, *Economies of Abandonment*, 13.

39   Alexander, *Pedagogies of Crossing*, 289.

40   Alexander, *Pedagogies of Crossing*, 290.

41   Peña, *Performing Piety*.

42   Vicuña, "Language Is Migrant."

4. THE DEAD: SCENES OF DISTURBANCE AND DISARTICULATION

Epigraph: Uribe, *Antígona González*, 35.

1   Rymer, "The Ironwood."

2   Reineke, "Necroviolence," 153.

3   Beck et al., "Animal Scavenging," 19.

4   Reineke, "Necroviolence," 160.

5   Derrida, *Specters of Marx,* 9 (original emphasis).

6   Derrida, *Specters of Marx,* 9 (original emphasis).

7   Derrida, *Specters of Marx,* 20 (original emphasis).

8   Derrida, *Specters of Marx*, 22.

9   Rosenblatt, *Digging for the Disappeared,* 95.

10   Gordon, *Ghostly Matters*, 115.

11   Glissant, *Caribbean Discourse*, 231.

12   Glissant, *Caribbean Discourse*, 14.

13   Glissant, *Poetics of Relation*, 18.

14 Gordon, *Ghostly Matters*, xvi.

15 Gordon, "Some Thoughts on Haunting and Futurity," 2.

16 Reineke, "Necroviolence," 155.

17 Anzaldúa, *Borderlands / La Frontera*, 3.

18 Taussig, *Defacement*, 30.

19 Taussig, *Defacement*, 25.

20 Taussig, *Defacement*, 52 (my emphasis).

21 Taussig, *Defacement*, 142 (original emphasis).

22 Ochoa, *Society of the Dead*, 21.

23 Ochoa, *Society of the Dead*, 172.

24 Canetti, *Crowds and Power*.

25 Taussig, *Defacement*, 209.

26 Uribe, *Antígona González*, 159, 161.

27 Uribe, *Antígona González*, 171.

28 Taussig, *Defacement*, 1, 5.

29 Foucault, "A Preface to Transgression," 32, 30.

30 Hartman, "Venus in Two Acts," 8.

31 Hartman, "Venus in Two Acts," 8.

32 Hartman, "Venus in Two Acts," 14.

33 De la Cadena, *Earth Beings*, 26.

34 Sharpe, *In the Wake*, 13.

35 Sharpe, *In the Wake*, 21.

36 Sharpe, *In the Wake*, 10.

37 Ochoa, *Society of the Dead*, 34.

38 Reineke, "Necroviolence," 160 (my emphasis).

CONCLUSION: SAMUEL NEVER LEFT SANCTUARY

1 Shakur, *Assata*, 52.

2 ABC 11, "Supporters of Detained Undocumented Immigrant;" by Perchick, "Community Holds Vigil."

3 Paik, "Abolitionist Futures," 16.

4 Moten and Harney, *The Undercommons*, 97.

Bibliography

ARCHIVAL SOURCES

Gustav Schultz Sanctuary Collection, Graduate Theological Union Archives, Berkeley, California.
Sanctuary Trial Papers, The University of Arizona, Tucson, Arizona.

SECONDARY SOURCES

ABC 11. "Supporters of Detained Undocumented Immigrant Samuel Oliver-Bruno Rally in Wake County." November 26, 2018. https://abc11.com/samuel -oliver-bruno-undocumented-immigrant-ice-detainee-wake-county -detention-center/4768116/.

Alexander, M. Jacqui. *Pedagogies of Crossing: Meditations on Feminism, Sexual Politics, Memory, and the Sacred.* Durham, NC: Duke University Press, 2005.

Andreas, Peter. *Border Games: Policing the U.S.-Mexico Divide.* Ithaca, NY: Cornell University Press, 2000.

Antebi, Nicole. "Border Landscapes: The River Is a Seam." *Labocine,* September 8, 2018. https://www.labocine.com/spotlights/border-landscapes-the-river-is -a-seam.

Anzaldúa, Gloria. *Borderlands / La Frontera: The New Mestiza.* San Francisco: Aunt Lute Books, 1987.

Anzaldúa, Gloria. *Light in the Dark / Luz en el Oscuro: Rewriting Identity, Spirituality, Reality.* Durham, NC: Duke University Press, 2015.

Anzaldúa, Gloria. "La Prieta." In *This Bridge Called My Back: Writings by Radical Women of Color,* edited by Cherríe L. Moraga and Gloria E. Anzaldúa, 220–33. Berkeley, CA: Third Woman Press, 1981.

Asmelash, Leah, and Hollie Silverman. "Hundreds of Unwelcome Vultures Are Perched on US Border Patrol's Texas Radio Towers." CNN, January 10, 2020.

https://www.cnn.com/2020/01/10/us/vulture-customs-border-protection
-trnd/index.html.

Bagelman, Jennifer. *Sanctuary City: A Suspended State*. Basingstoke, UK: Palgrave
Macmillan, 2016.

Barba, Lloyd. *Sowing the Sacred: Mexican Pentecostal Farmworkers in California*.
New York: Oxford University Press, 2022.

Barba, Lloyd, and Tatyana Castillo-Ramos. "Sacred Resistance: The Sanctuary
Movement From Reagan to Trump." *Perspectivas* 16 (2019): 11–36.

Bataille, Georges. *Erotism: Death and Sensuality*. San Francisco, CA: City Lights
Books, 1986.

Bataille, Georges. *On Nietzsche*. Albany, NY: State University of New York Press,
2015.

Bataille, Georges. *Theory of Religion*. Princeton, NJ: Zone Books, 1973.

Bauer, Shane. *American Prison: A Reporter's Undercover Journey into the Business of
Punishment*. New York: Penguin Random House, 2018.

Bayetti Flores, Veronica. "The Pulse Nightclub Shooting Robbed the Queer Latinx
Community of a Sanctuary." *Remezcla*, June 13, 2016. https://remezcla.com
/features/music/pulse-nightclub-sanctuary/.

Beck, Jess, Ian Ostericher, Gregory Sollish, and Jason De León. "Animal Scaveng-
ing and Scattering and the Implications for Documenting the Deaths of
Undocumented Border Crossers in the Sonoran Desert." *Journal of Forensic
Sciences* 60, no. 1 (2015): 11–20.

Bell Wright, Harold. *Long Ago Told (Huh-kew Ah-kah) Legends of the Papago Indians*. London: D. Appleton, 1929.

Benveniste, Émile. *Indo-European Language and Society*. Miami: University of
Miami Press, 1973. https://archive.chs.harvard.edu/CHS/article/display
/3964.book-6-religion-1-the-sacred-.

Berry, Maya J., Claudia Chávez Argüelles, Shanya Cordis, Sarah Ihmoud, and
Elizabeth Velásquez Estrada. "Toward a Fugitive Anthropology: Gender,
Race, and Violence in the Field." *Cultural Anthropology* 32, no. 4 (2017):
537–65.

Blanchfield, Caitlin, and Nina Valerie Kolowratnik. "Persistent Surveillance: Militarized Infrastructure on the Tohono O'odham Nation." *Avery Review* 40
(May 2019). https://averyreview.com/issues/40/persistent-surveillance.

Blue, Ethan. "The Means and Meanings of Carceral Mobility: U.S. Deportation
Trains and the Early Twentieth-Century Deportation Assemblage." In
*Caging Borders and Carceral States: Incarcerations, Immigration Detentions,
and Resistance*, edited by Robert Chase, 93–125. Chapel Hill: University of
North Carolina Press, 2019.

Brand, Dionne. *The Blue Clerk: Ars Poetica in 59 Verses*. Durham, NC: Duke University Press, 2018.

Brand, Dionne. *A Map to the Door of No Return: Notes on Belonging*. Toronto: Vin-
tage Canada, 2001.

Brathwaite, Edward Kamau. *The Arrivants: A New World Trilogy—Rights of Passage/ Islands/ Masks.* Oxford: Oxford University Press, 1988.

Caillois, Roger. *Man and the Sacred.* Glencoe, IL: Free Press, 1959.

Caminero-Santangelo, Marta. "The Voice of the Voiceless: Religious Rhetoric, Undocumented Immigrants, and the New Sanctuary Movement in the United States." In *Sanctuary Practices in International Perspectives: Migration, Citizenship, and Social Movements,* edited by Randy Lippert and Sean Rehaag, 92–106. New York: Routledge, 2013.

Canetti, Elias. *Crowds and Power.* New York: Farrar, Straus, and Giroux, 1984.

Carby, Hazel. *Imperial Intimacies: A Tale of Two Islands.* London: Verso, 2021.

Chávez, Karma. "From Sanctuary to a Queer Politics of Fugitivity." *QED: A Journal in GLBTQ Worldmaking* 4, no. 2 (2017): 63–70.

Chávez, Karma. *Queer Migration Politics: Activist Rhetoric and Coalitional Possibilities.* Champaign: University of Illinois Press, 2013.

Chávez, Karma. "Sanctuary, Fugitivity, and Insurgent Models of Migrant Justice." *Departures in Critical Qualitative Research* 9, no. 1 (2020): 89–94.

Chávez, Karma. "Spatializing Gender Performativity: Ecstasy and Possibilities for Livable Life in the Tragic Case of Victoria Arellano." *Women's Studies in Communication* 33 (2010): 1–15.

Church World Service. "Sanctuary Not Deportation: A Faithful Witness to Building Welcoming Communities." Last modified October 2017. https:// unitedwedream.org/wp-content/uploads/2017/10/Toolkit-Sanctuary -Movement-Updated-1.pdf.

Coelho, Paulo. *The Alchemist.* New York: HarperOne, 1993.

Corbett, Jim. *Goatwalking: A Guide to Wildland Living, a Quest for the Peaceable Kingdom.* New York: Viking Press, 1991.

Coutin, Susan Bibler. *The Culture of Protest: Religious Activism and the U.S. Sanctuary Movement.* Boulder, CO: Westview Press, 1993.

Crawley, Ashon T. *Blackpentecostal Breath: The Aesthetics of Possibility.* New York: Fordham University Press, 2016.

Cunningham, Hillary. *God and Caesar at the Rio Grande: Sanctuary and the Politics of Religion.* Minneapolis: University of Minnesota Press, 1995.

Davis, Angela, and Gina Dent. "Prison as a Border: A Conversation on Gender, Globalization, and Punishment." *Signs: Journal of Women in Culture and Society* 26, no. 4 (Summer 2000): 1235–41.

De Genova, Nicholas. "The Deportation Regime: Sovereignty, Space, and the Freedom of Movement." In *The Deportation Regime: Sovereignty, Space, and the Freedom of Movement,* edited by Nicholas De Genova and Nathalie Peutz, 33–65. Durham, NC: Duke University Press, 2010.

De la Cadena, Marisol. *Earth Beings: Ecologies of Practice across Andean Worlds.* Durham, NC: Duke University Press, 2015.

De León, Jason. *The Land of Open Graves: Living and Dying on the Migrant Trail.* Berkeley: University of California Press, 2015.

Deleuze, Gilles, and Félix Guattari. *Nomadology: The War Machine.* Los Angeles: Semiotext(e), 1986.

Deleuze, Gilles, and Félix Guattari. *A Thousand Plateaus: Capitalism and Schizophrenia.* Minneapolis: University of Minnesota Press, 1993.

Derrida, Jacques. *Of Hospitality.* Stanford, CA: Stanford University Press, 2000.

Derrida, Jacques. *Specters of Marx.* New York: Routledge, 1994.

"Desert Aid Volunteer Program." No More Deaths. Accessed September 16, 2022. https://nomoredeaths.org/volunteer/desert-aid-volunteer-program/.

Devereaux, Ryan. "What's in a Name: How Post 9/11 Visions of an Imperiled Homeland Supercharged U.S. Immigration Enforcement." *The Intercept,* September 10, 2021. https://theintercept.com/2021/09/10/immigration-enforcement-homeland-security-911/.

Dillon, Stephen. *Fugitive Life: The Queer Politics of the Prison State.* Durham, NC: Duke University Press, 2018.

Douglas, Mary. *Purity and Danger: An Analysis of Concepts of Pollution and Taboo.* New York: Routledge, 2002.

Dunn, Timothy. *The Militarization of the U.S.-Mexico Border 1978–1992: Low Intensity Conflict Doctrine Comes Home.* Austin: University of Texas Press, 1996.

Durkheim, Émile. *The Elementary Forms of Religious Life.* New York: Free Press, 1995.

Elhillo, Safia. "self-portrait with no flag." In *Ink Knows No Borders: Poems of the Immigrant and Refugee Experience,* edited by Patrice Vecchione and Alyssa Raymond, 138–39. New York: Seven Stories Press, 2019.

Eliade, Mircea. *The Sacred and the Profane: The Nature of Religion.* New York: Harcourt Books, 1959.

Emory, William H. *Report on the United States and Mexican Boundary Survey.* Washington, DC: A. O. P. Nicholson, Printer, 1857.

Fanon, Frantz. *Black Skin, White Masks.* New York: Grove Press, 1952.

"Felipe Baeza with Zoë Hopkins." *Brooklyn Rail,* September 2022. https://brooklynrail.org/2022/09/art/Felipe-Baeza-with-Zoe-Hopkins.

Fontana, Bernard. *Of Earth and Little Rain.* Tucson: University of Arizona Press, 1989.

Foucault, Michel. "A Preface to Transgression." In *Language, Counter-memory, Practice: Selected Essays and Interviews by Michel Foucault,* edited by Donald F. Bouchard, 29–53. Ithaca, NY: Cornell University Press, 1977.

Fournier, Matt. "Lines of Flight." *TSQ: Transgender Studies Quarterly* 1, no. 1–2 (May 2014): 121–22.

Gandolfo, Daniella. *The City at Its Limits: Taboo, Transgressions, and Urban Renewal in Lima.* Chicago: University of Chicago Press, 2009.

García Hernández, César Cuauhtémoc. *Migrating to Prison: America's Obsession with Locking Up Immigrants.* New York: New Press, 2019.

García-Peña, Lorgia. *The Borders of Dominicanidad: Race, Nation and Archives of Contradiction.* Durham, NC: Duke University Press, 2016.

García-Peña, Lorgia. *Community as Rebellion: A Syllabus for Surviving Academia as a Woman of Color.* Chicago: Haymarket Books, 2022.

Glissant, Édouard. *Caribbean Discourse: Selected Essays.* Charlottesville: University Press of Virginia, 1989.

Glissant, Édouard. *Poetics of Relation.* Ann Arbor: University of Michigan Press, 1997.

Goldstein, Daniel M. "Laying the Body on the Line: Activist Anthropology and the Deportation of the Undocumented." *American Anthropologist* 116, no 4 (2014): 839–42.

Gómez-Barris, Macarena. *The Extractive Zone: Social Ecologies and Decolonial Perspectives.* Durham, NC: Duke University Press, 2017.

Goodman, Adam. *The Deportation Machine.* Princeton, NJ: Princeton University Press, 2021.

Gordon, Avery. *Ghostly Matters: Haunting and the Sociological Imagination.* Minneapolis: University of Minnesota Press, 1997.

Gordon, Avery. "Some Notes on Haunting and Futurity." *Borderlands* 10, no. 2 (2011): 1–21.

Guardado, Leo. *Church as Sanctuary: Reconstructing Refuge in an Age of Forced Displacement.* Ossining, NY: Orbis Books, 2023.

Guenther, Lisa. *Solitary Confinement: Social Death and Its Afterlives.* Minneapolis: University of Minnesota Press, 2013.

Gumbs, Alexis Pauline. *Spill: Scenes of Black Feminist Fugitivity.* Durham, NC: Duke University Press, 2016.

Günel, Gökçe, Saiba Varma, and Chika Watanabe. "A Manifesto for Patchwork Ethnography." Member Voices, *Fieldsights*, June 9, 2020. https://culanth .org/fieldsights/a-manifesto-for-patchwork-ethnography.

Hartman, Saidiya. "Venus in Two Acts." *Small Axe* 12, no. 2 (June 2008): 1–14.

Hernández, David Manuel. "Carceral Shadows." In *Caging Borders and Carceral States: Incarcerations, Immigration Detentions, and Resistance,* edited by Robert Chase, 57–93. Chapel Hill: University of North Carolina Press, 2019.

Hertz, Robert. *Death and the Right Hand.* Glencoe, IL: Free Press, 1960.

Horton, Sarah Bronwen. *They Leave Their Kidneys in the Fields: Illness, Injury, and Illegality among U.S. Farmworkers.* Berkeley: University of California Press, 2016.

Huerta, Amarela Varela. "Migrants Trapped in the Mexican Vertical Border." *University of Oxford Border Criminologies Blog* (2018). https://www.law.ox.ac.uk /research-subject-groups/centre-criminology/centreborder-criminologies /blog/2018/06/migrants-trapped.

Hurtado, Leslie. "Keeping the Faith: The Woman Who Started the Sanctuary Movement." *Borderless,* February 15, 2022. https://borderlessmag.org /2022/02/15/keeping-the-faith-the-woman-who-started-the-sanctuary -movement/.

Inda, Jonathan, and Julie Dowling, eds. *Governing Migration through Crime: A Reader.* Stanford, CA: Stanford University Press, 2013.

Isasi-Día, Ada Mari. *En La Lucha / In the Struggle: Elaborating a Mujerista Theology.* Minneapolis, MN: Fortress Press, 2004.

Jamison, Leslie. *Make It Scream, Make It Burn: Essays.* New York: Penguin, 2019.

Jenkins, Jimmy. "Arizona to Transfer 2,706 Prisoners from State-Run Prison to Private CoreCivic Facility." *Arizona Republic*, January 6, 2022. https://www .azcentral.com/story/news/local/arizona/2022/01/06/arizona-transfer -2—706-prisoners-state-run-prison-private-facility/9121316002/.

Lemons, Stephen. "Tohono O'odham Chairman Ned Norris' Statement; Activist Mike Wilson Reacts in Scottsdale This Week for Q & A." *Phoenix New Times*, March 1, 2010. https://www.phoenixnewtimes.com/news/tohono -oodham-chairman-ned-norris-statement-activist-mike-wilson-reacts-in -scottsdale-this-week-for-q-and-a-6499280.

Lethabo King, Tiffany. *The Black Shoals: Offshore Formations of Black and Native Studies.* Durham, NC: Duke University Press, 2019.

Liboiron, Max. *Pollution Is Colonialism.* Durham, NC: Duke University Press, 2021.

Luiselli, Valeria. *Lost Children Archive.* New York: Knopf, 2019.

Lurie, Julia. "They Built a Utopian Sanctuary in a Minneapolis Hotel: Then They Got Evicted." *Mother Jones*, June 12, 2020. https://www.motherjones.com /crime-justice/2020/06/minneapolis-sheraton-george-floyd-protests/.

Lytle Hernández, Kelly. *Migra: A History of the U.S. Border Patrol.* Berkeley: University of California Press, 2010.

Mack, Stephen. *Acim O'odham (We the O'odham): The Himdag Ki: and the Tohono O'odham Community.* Washington, DC: Institute of Museum and Library Services, 2018.

Magrane, Eric, and Christopher Cokinos, eds. *The Sonoran Desert: A Literary Field Guide.* Tucson: University of Arizona Press, 2016.

Menchú, Rigoberta. *I, Rigoberta Menchú: An Indian Woman in Guatemala.* London: Verso, 1984.

Mezzadra, Sandro. "The Right to Escape." *Ephemera: Theory and Politics of Organization* 4, no. 3 (2004): 267–75.

Miller, Todd. *Empire of Borders: The Expansion of the US Border around the World.* London: Verso, 2019.

Miller, Todd. "How Border Patrol Occupied the Tohono O'odham Nation." *In These Times*, June 12, 2019. http://inthesetimes.com/article/21903/us-mexico -border-surveillance-tohono-oodham-nation-border-patrol.

Moraga, Cherrie, and Gloria Anzaldúa, eds. *This Bridge Called My Back: Writings by Radical Women of Color.* Berkeley, CA: Third Woman Press, 1983.

Morrison, Toni. *Beloved.* New York: Random House, 1987.

Moten, Fred. *Black and Blur.* Durham, NC: Duke University Press, 2017.

Moten, Fred. "Blackness and Nothingness: Mysticism in the Flesh." *South Atlantic Quarterly* 112, no. 4 (2013): 737–80.

Moten, Fred, and Stefano Harney. *The Undercommons: Fugitive Planning and Black Study.* New York: Minor Compositions, 2013.

Muñoz, José Esteban. *Cruising Utopia: The Then and There of Queer Futurity.* New York: New York University Press, 2009.

Nancy, Jean-Luc. "Rethinking Corpus." In *Carnal Hermeneutics: From Head to Foot,* edited by Richard Kearney and Brian Treanor, 77–91. New York: Fordham University Press, 2015.

Narayan, Kirin. "How Native Is a 'Native' Anthropologist?" *American Anthropologist* 95, no. 3 (September 1993): 671–86.

National Park Service. "Chamizal: The Flowing Border." US Department of the Interior. Last modified 2012. https://www.nps.gov/cham/learn/nature/upload/River-Movements-copier-no-bleed.pdf.

Nelson, Maggie. *Bluets.* Seattle, WA: Wave Books, 2009.

Nicholls, Walter. *The Dreamers: How the Undocumented Youth Movement Transformed the Immigrant Rights Debate.* Stanford, CA: Stanford University Press, 2013.

Ochoa, Todd Ramón. *Society of the Dead: Quita Manaquita and Palo Praise in Cuba.* Berkeley: University of California Press, 2010.

Orozco, Myrna, and Noel Andersen. "Sanctuary in the Age of Trump: The Rise of the Movement a Year into the Trump Administration." Church World Service, January 2018. https://www.sanctuarynotdeportation.org/uploads/7/6/9/1/76912017/sanctuary_in_the_age_of_trump_january_2018.pdf.

Otto, Rudolph. *The Idea of the Holy.* Oxford: Oxford University Press, 1950.

Oversight Hearing on Destroying Sacred Sites and Easing Tribal Culture: The Trump Administration's Construction of the Border Wall: Testimony before the Subcommittee for Indigenous Peoples of the United States. 116th Congress (2020). Statement of Ned Norris, chairman of the Tohono O'odham Nation.

Paik, A. Naomi. "Abolitionist Futures and the US Sanctuary Movement." *Race and Class* 59 (2017): 3–25.

Papadopoulos, Dimitris, Niamh Stephenson, and Vassilis Tsianos. *Escape Routes: Control and Subversion in the Twenty-First Century.* Ann Arbor, MI: Pluto Press, 2008.

Pelaez Lopez, Alán. *Intergalactic Travels: Poems from a Fugitive Alien.* Brooklyn: Operating System, 2020.

Peña, Elaine. *Performing Piety: Making Space Sacred with the Virgin of Guadalupe.* Berkeley: University of California Press, 2011.

People's Defense Initiative. "FAQ Tucson Families Free and Together." Accessed December 1, 2022. peoplesdefenseinitiative.org/our-campaigns/faq-tucson-families-free-and-together.

Perchick, Michael. "Community Holds Vigil for Durham Man Detained by ICE." ABC 11, November 27, 2018. https://abc11.com/man-detained-by-ice-seeking-sanctuary-samuel-oliver-bruno/4756589/.

Pérez, Elizabeth. *Religion in the Kitchen: Cooking, Talking, and the Making of Black Atlantic Traditions.* New York: New York University Press, 2016.

Povinelli, Elizabeth. *Economies of Abandonment: Social Belonging and Endurance in Late Liberalism.* Durham, NC: Duke University Press, 2011.

Purnell, Derecka. *Becoming Abolitionists: Police, Protests, and the Pursuit of Freedom.* New York: Astra House, 2021.

Rabben, Linda. *Sanctuary and Asylum: A Social and Political History.* Seattle: University of Washington Press, 2016.

Rand, Erica. *The Ellis Island Snowglobe.* Durham, NC: Duke University Press, 2005.

Reineke, Robin. "Necroviolence and Postmortem Care along the U.S.-Mexico Border." In *The Border and Its Bodies: The Embodiment of Risk along the U.S.- México Line,* edited by Thomas E. Sheridan and Randall H. McGuire, 144–73. Tucson: University of Arizona Press, 2020.

Riley, Mitch, dir. *The Bahidaj Harvest.* Tucson, AZ: Public Media, 2020. https://thinktv.pbslearningmedia.org/resource/d0046fac-ff10–40d2–8e53–6b740be0d577/the-bahidaj-harvest-native-tradition-video-the-arizona-collection/.

Roberts, Neil. *Freedom as Marronage.* Chicago: University of Chicago Press, 2015.

Robinson, Cedric J. *Black Marxism: The Making of the Black Radical Tradition.* Chapel Hill: University of North Carolina Press, 2000.

Rosas, Gilberto. "The Managed Violences of the Borderlands: Treacherous Geographies, Policeability, and the Politics of Race." *Latino Studies* 4 (2006): 401–18.

Rosas, Gilberto. "The Thickening Borderlands: Diffused Exceptionality and 'Immigrant' Social Struggles during the 'War on Terror.'" *Cultural Dynamics* 18, no. 3 (2006): 335–49.

Rosenblatt, Adam. *Digging for the Disappeared: Forensic Science after Atrocity.* Stanford, CA: Stanford University Press, 2015.

Rymer, Cathy. "The Ironwood: Stately Sanctuary in the Sonoran Desert." *Master Gardener Journal.* Last updated July 28, 2003. https://cals.arizona.edu/maricopa/garden/html/pubs/about.html.

Schaeffer, Felicity Amaya. *Unsettled Borders: The Militarized Science of Surveillance on Sacred Indigenous Land.* Durham, NC: Duke University Press, 2022.

Schermerhorn, Seth. *Walking to Magdalena: Personhood and Place in Tohono O'odham Songs, Sticks, and Stories.* Lincoln: University of Nebraska Press, 2019.

Schmidt Camacho, Alicia. *Migrant Imaginaries: Latino Cultural Politics in the US-Mexico Borderlands.* New York: New York University Press, 2008.

Shakur, Assata. *Assata: An Autobiography.* Chicago: Zed Books, 1987.

Sharpe, Christina. *In the Wake: On Blackness and Being.* Durham, NC: Duke University Press, 2016.

Shimoda, Brandon. "State of Erasure: Arizona's Place, and the Place of Arizona, in the Mass Incarceration of Japanese Americans." Asian American Writers Workshop, January 20, 2017. https://aaww.org/state-erasure-arizona/.

Simpson, Leanne Betasamosake. *As We Have Always Done: Indigenous Freedom through Radical Resistance.* Minneapolis: University of Minnesota Press, 2017.

Slack, Jeremy. *Deported to Death: How Drug Violence Is Changing Migration in the US-Mexico Border.* Berkeley: University of California Press, 2019.

Sontag, Susan. *Regarding the Pain of Others.* New York: Picador Modern Classics, 2003.

Speed, Shannon. *Incarcerated Stories: Indigenous Women Migrants and Violence in the Settler Capitalist State.* Chapel Hill: University of North Carolina Press, 2019.

Spillers, Hortense. "To the Bone: Some Speculations on Touch." YouTube, Gerrit Rietveld Academie, Stedelijk Museum Amsterdam, March 21, 2018. https://www.youtube.com/watch?time_continue=865&v=AvL4wUKIfpo&feature=emb_logo.

St. John, Rachel. *Line in the Sand: A History of the Mexico-U.S. Border.* Princeton, NJ: Princeton University Press, 2012.

Taussig, Michael. *Defacement: Public Secrecy and the Labor of the Negative.* Stanford, CA: Stanford University Press, 1999.

Tohono O'odham Nation. "No Wall." February 19, 2017. http://www.tonation-nsn.gov/nowall/.

Torres, Justin. "In Praise of Latin Night at the Queer Club." *Washington Post*, June 13, 2016. https://www.washingtonpost.com/opinions/in-praise-of-latin-night-at-the-queer-club/2016/06/13/e841867e-317b-11e6-95c0-2a6873031302_story.html.

Torres, Justin. *We the Animals.* Boston: Mariner Books, 2012.

"Treaty of 1889." In *Treaty Series, No. 241.* Washington, DC: Government Printing Office, 1914. https://web.archive.org/web/20151007014537/http://www.ibwc.state.gov/Files/TREATY_OF_1889.pdf.

Truett, Samuel. *Fugitive Landscapes: The Forgotten History of the U.S.-Mexico Borderlands.* New Haven, CT: Yale University Press, 2008.

Underhill, Ruth. *The Papago Indians of Arizona and Their Relatives the Pima.* Lawrence, KS: Haskell Institute, 1940.

Unzueta, Tania. "Expanding Sanctuary: What Makes a Sanctuary City Now?" Last updated January 2017. https://www.ctunet.com/rights-at-work/text/2017-01-30-sanctuary-expanded-final.pdf.

Unzueta Carrasco, Tania A., and Hinda Seif. "Disrupting the Dream: Undocumented Youth Reframe Citizenship and Deportability through Anti-deportation Activism." *Latino Studies* 12, no. 2 (Summer 2014): 279–99. https://doi.org/10.1057/lst.2014.21.

Uribe, Sara. *Antígona González.* Translated by John Pluecker. Los Angeles: Les Figues Press, 2016.

Urrea, Luis Alberto. *The Devil's Highway: A True Story.* New York: Little, Brown, 2004.

US Border Patrol. "Border Patrol Strategic Plan 1994 and Beyond: National Strategy." Homeland Security Digital Library. Accessed March 25, 2020. https://www.hsdl.org/?abstract&did=721845.

Vásquez, Tina. "There Is No Abolishing ICE without Restorative Justice for the Deported." *Prism*, June 29, 2021. https://prismreports.org/2021/06/29/there
-is-no-abolishing-ice-without-restorative-justice-for-the-deported/.

Vicuña, Cecilia. "Language Is Migrant." *Poetry Foundation*, April 18, 2016.
https://www.poetryfoundation.org/harriet-books/2016/04/language
-is-migrant#:~:text=Language%20is%20migrant.,Even%20galaxies%20
migrate.

Villareal, Aimee. "Sanctuaryscapes in the North American Southwest." *Radical
History Review* 135 (October 2019): 43–70.

Vogt, Wendy. *Lives in Transit: Violence and Intimacy on the Migrant Journey*. Berkeley: University of California Press, 2018.

Walia, Harsha. *Border and Rule: Global Migration, Capitalism, and the Rise of Racist
Nationalism*. Chicago: Haymarket Books, 2021.

Williams, Liza Keānuenueokalani. "Currencies of U.S. Empire in Hawai'i's Tourism
and Prison Industries." In *Gendering the Trans-Pacific World: Diaspora, Empire, and Race*, edited by Catherine Ceniza Choy and Judy Tzu-Chun Wu,
140–61. Leiden: Brill, 2017.

Yukich, Grace. *One Family under God: Immigration Politics and Progressive Religion
in America*. Oxford: Oxford University Press, 2013.

Zambreno, Kate. *Drifts*. New York: Riverhead, 2020.

Zamora, Javier. "Poems." In *Somewhere We Are Human: Authentic Voices on Migration, Survival, and New Beginnings,* edited by Reyna Grande and Sonia
Guiñansaca, 31–37. New York: HarperCollins, 2022.

Zamora, Javier. *Solito*. New York: Hogarth, 2022.

Index

Panchito. *See* Olachea, Francisco

Panchito y Su Cristina, 94–96, 98–99, 121

Panteón Nacional graveyard, Nogales, 96, 115, 126

Papadopoulos, Dimitris, 12

Pelaez, Lopez, Alán, 14

Peña, Elaine, 121

Pérez, Elizabeth, 6, 172n10

Petro, Gustavo, 152–53

photographs, 111, 121–22, 125; violence and, 101

plants, of Sonoran Desert, 41, 43, 56–57. *See also* saguaros

police, 1–2; immigration and, 62–63; Indigenous peoples and, 64–65; protests and, 89, 91

policies: deportation and, 10–11; of detention centers, 78, 81; of ICE, 2–3, 62–63, 171n2; immigration, 27, 121, 158–59; of Obama, 2, 23–24, 98, 171n1; of Reagan, 15–16; of Trump, 98, 110, 119

polleros, 38–39

positive sacred, 34, 40–41, 64, 152; desert as, 29, 42, 57–58; land as, 36, 45; meandering as, 46

Povinelli, Elizabeth, 118

prayer, 82, 96, 144, 155–56; collectivism and, 83; migrant dead and, 139–40; surveillance and, 167

presente ritual, 89–90, 159–65

Prevention through Deterrence (PTD), 5, 105, 132; death and, 35–36; militarization and, 176n19; mobility and, 93

prison, 67, 179n19; border and, 180n22; family and, 68, 84; La Palma Correctional Center, 66, 83–86

profane, 21, 29, 75, 109; Bataille and, 40, 63–64; disturbance and, 135–36; fugitivity and, 12, 36; prohibitions and, 121; sacred and, 6–11, 59, 63–64, 132, 139; tools as, 36–46, 63–64, 176n29; transgression and, 38, 148; violence and, 172n30

prohibitions: on contact, 29–30; disturbance of, 142; profane and, 121; sacred and, 6–7, 67–68, 167, 170

prosperity churches, 119–20

protests, 10, 20–21; border wall and, 52, 55; humanitarianism and, 36–37; ICE and, 88–89, 166–68; No Pride in Detention, 86–91

PTD (Prevention through Deterrence), 5, 35–36, 93, 105, 132, 176n19

Purnell, Derecka, 16

Quaker coyote (Jim Corbett), 15, 17, 19, 37–39

queerness, 58–59, 87; fugitivity and, 17, 21, 88

quotidian (*cotidiano*), 9–10

raids, immigration, 20, 97, 117

Rand, Erica, 179n9

Reader, Tristan, 36–37

Reagan, Ronald, 46; policies of, 15–16

reciprocity, 50, 86, 178n68; care and, 34

Reineke, Robin, 132, 136, 157

relations, with Sonoran Desert, 39–40, 176n29

religion, 11, 21, 49–50, 96, 140; errantry and, 38; fugitivity and, 103

reposo, the dead and, 131–33, 140, 146, 157, 159, 169

resistance, Indigenous, 27, 42–43, 53

resurrection, 96, 136, 158–59

revolutionary movements, 173n52

rhizome, transformation and, 108–9

right hand sacred, 36, 40–41

Río Bravo, 71–72; meandering and, 42, 45–46, 61

ritual, 48, 139, 140–41, 155; criminalization and, 68–69, 171n5; devotional acts as, 6–7, 34, 59, 96, 121, 172n10; fugitive, 149; for migrant dead, 158–65; *presente*, 89–90, 159–65; sacred and, 137–38; transformation and, 120

Robinson, Cedric J., 16

La Roca Albergue Cristiano, 100–104, 116–17

surveillance, 35–36, 48, 141; border and, 47, 138; church sanctuary and, 4; criminalization and, 54–55; prayer and, 167

taboo, 145–46, 148, 152, 167; borderlands and, 142, 169; fugitivity and, 13–14; profane and, 21, 29, 59; touch and, 80, 93; transgression and, 6–9, 11, 65, 138
Taussig, Michael, 137–38, 145, 147–48
testimonios, 15, 20–21, 103, 173n52, 181n10
time: disarticulation and, 133; land and, 46, 53, 57–59, 61; vanishing, 58–59, 61, 141
Tohono O'odham Nation, 33–34, 153; Border Patrol and, 50–52, 54, 178n67
tools, profanity of, 36–46, 63–64, 176n29
too-muchness, 7, 14; of Sonoran Desert, 29, 44–45, 59, 61, 169
Torres, Justin, 11
touch, 92; coercive, 64–65, 67, 81, 179n9; contraband, 30, 65–66, 90, 93; the dead and, 132–33, 139; in detention centers, 64–67, 79–85, 90; the smuggled and, 73–74, 90, 93; taboo and, 80, 93
TQLM (Familia: Trans Queer Liberation Movement), 87–88
trails, of migrants, 51, 96, 128, 143–45, 175n9
transformation, 11, 60, 118–19, 122; borderlands and, 104; death and, 130; migrants and, 9–10, 100; rhizome and, 108–9; sacred and, 120–21, 126
transgender migrants, 87–89
transgression, 14, 22, 74, 121, 173n34; deportation and, 105; haunting and, 156–57; profane and, 38, 148; sacred and, 63–64; taboo and, 6–9, 11, 65, 138
translation, ethnography and, 31
Truett, Samuel, 12
Trump, Donald, 2, 4–5, 22, 25, 50, 72, 179n2; citizenship and, 74–76; policies of, 98, 110, 119
Tsianos, Vassilis, 12
Tucker, Tanisha, 34

Tucson, AZ, 62–63, 91, 158–59; Southside Presbyterian Church, 15, 17–18, 22, 67
Tucson Samaritans, 33, 36, 67, 175n9

undocumented migrants, 3–5, 10, 22–25, 100, 169, 176n29
United States (US): belonging and, 10–11, 172n31; citizenship and, 74–78. *See also* Border Patrol
Unzueta Carrasco, Tania, 23–24, 174n76
Uribe, Sara, 146
Urrea, Luis Alberto, 41; *The Devil's Highway*, 54
US. *See* United States

vanishing time, 58–59, 61, 141
Vega Magallón, César Miguel R., 99
Venezuela, 69–70
Vicuña, Cecilia, 126
Villareal, Aimee, 16
violence, 28, 116, 180n27; Border Patrol and, 55; deportation and, 170; immigration and, 102–3; photographs and, 101; profane and, 172n30
Vogt, Wendy, 26

waitlist, for asylum, 72, 116
wake work, 30, 154, 156
Walia, Harsha, 26–27
water, 37–39, 45–46, 49–50, 59–61, 159; death and, 128, 140, 150, 155
water stations, 39, 48, 52, 175n9; migrant dead and, 51, 56
weaponization, of desert, 36, 38, 43–44, 176n29
Williams, Lisa Keānuenueokalani, 179n19
Wilson, Mike, 51–52

Yukich, Grace, 103–4

Zambreno, Kate, 26
Zamora, Javier, 12, 38–39